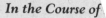
continued . . .

"The *Batfish* story is representative of a 'genetic code,' submariner pride, that transfers from the Greatest Generation to those that followed. What a great book."
　　　　　　　　　　　　　　　—Gene Whitney, auxiliaryman, USS *Diodon* SS349

"To sink one enemy sub is quite something, but to sink three in a single patrol, while coping with one of your own torpedoes jammed part way out of the launch tube with the potential of arming itself and blowing your own boat to bits with the next big wave—now that's the Super Bowl of submarine warfare for sure. Well told. A fascinating and inspiring true adventure."
　　—Captain William R. Anderson, veteran of eleven WWII submarine combat patrols
　　　　and commander of *Nautilus* in the historic 1958 under-ice Arctic crossing

Final Bearing
cowritten with Cdr. George Wallace (Ret.)

"Not since Ned Beach have readers been treated to such a marvelous blend of authentic submarining and great storytelling. Readers will gladly lose sleep reading this one . . . a magnificent achievement."
　　　　　—John G. Gobbell, author of *When Duty Whispers Low* and *The Last Lieutenant*

"A rip-snorting submarine adventure as up-to-date as tomorrow's headlines."
　　　　　　　—Stephen Coonts, *New York Times* bestselling author of *Liars and Thieves*

"Don Keith and George Wallace take you to the heart of the action as America fights a secret battle in a brilliantly portrayed South American setting. This team spins a great tale."
　　　　　—W.E.B. Griffin, *New York Times* bestselling author of *By Order of the President*

IN THE
COURSE
OF DUTY

THE HEROIC
MISSION OF THE
USS *BATFISH*

DON KEITH

NAL
CALIBER

NAL Caliber
Published by New American Library, a division of
Penguin Group (USA) Inc., 375 Hudson Street,
New York, New York 10014, USA
Penguin Group (Canada), 90 Eglinton Avenue East, Suite 700, Toronto,
Ontario M4P 2Y3, Canada (a division of Pearson Penguin Canada Inc.)
Penguin Books Ltd., 80 Strand, London WC2R 0RL, England
Penguin Ireland, 25 St. Stephen's Green, Dublin 2,
Ireland (a division of Penguin Books Ltd.)
Penguin Group (Australia), 250 Camberwell Road, Camberwell, Victoria 3124,
Australia (a division of Pearson Australia Group Pty. Ltd.)
Penguin Books India Pvt. Ltd., 11 Community Centre, Panchsheel Park,
New Delhi - 110 017, India
Penguin Group (NZ), cnr Airborne and Rosedale Roads, Albany,
Auckland 1310, New Zealand (a division of Pearson New Zealand Ltd.)
Penguin Books (South Africa) (Pty.) Ltd., 24 Sturdee Avenue,
Rosebank, Johannesburg 2196, South Africa

Penguin Books Ltd., Registered Offices:
80 Strand, London WC2R 0RL, England

First published by NAL Caliber, an imprint of New American Library,
a division of Penguin Group (USA) Inc.

First Printing, October 2005
10 9 8 7 6 5 4 3 2 1

NAL CALIBER and the "C" logo are trademarks of Penguin Group (USA) Inc.

LIBRARY OF CONGRESS CATALOGING-IN-PUBLICATION DATA:
Keith, Don, 1947–
    In the course of duty : the heroic mission of the USS Batfish / Don Keith.
        p.   cm.
    ISBN 0-451-21659-8
    1. Batfish (Submarine)   2. United States.   Navy—Submarine forces—History—20th century.
3. World War, 1939–1945—Naval operations—Submarine.   4. World War, 1939–1945—Naval operations,
American.   5. World War, 1939–1945—Campaigns—Pacific Ocean.   I. Title.

VA65.B38K45   2005
940.54'51'0973—dc22   2005011060

Set in Eldorado Text
Designed by Ginger Legato

Printed in the United States of America

CONTENTS

"So shall they fear the name of the Lord from the west, and his glory from the rising of the sun. When the enemy shall come in like a flood, the Spirit of the Lord shall lift up a standard against him."

—Isaiah 59:19

"Hence that general is skillful in attack whose opponent does not know what to defend; and he is skillful in defense whose opponent does not know what to attack."

—Sun-tzu, *The Art of War*

"I fear I could not live if there were no war."

—Cherokee Indian warrior in 1834 when asked his attitude toward battle

A Bean
Field in Muskogee

"Within three days, we sank three enemy submarines. There were no survivors. Those men aboard the Japanese subs who died as a result of our actions were combatant enemies. They knowingly risked their lives in war, just as we do. We attacked and sank them in the course of our duty. Within our good fortune that we did not lose our boat or our lives, there is of course some sadness that these submariners have died, and by our hand. But the only way that could have been otherwise in this war would have been for us to die by theirs. Thank you for your excellence, and congratulations on your success."

—Announcement read over USS *Batfish*'s intercom system by Captain John K. "Jake" Fyfe shortly after the sub sank the third of three Japanese submarines within seventy-seven hours

As you leave Tulsa, Oklahoma, toward the southeast, Highway 51 joins up with the Muskogee Turnpike in a peaceful suburb called Broken Arrow. The broad toll road then flows past Coweta before meandering toward the territory of the Cherokee Nation, a land once called the "American Desert" because it was considered so remote and desolate.

A broken arrow, in Indian lore, means peace: an end to tribal war. Broken Arrow, Oklahoma's, name came from a stream in Alabama, by the banks of which many of the Muskogee Creek Indians—cousins of the Cherokee—lived for centuries before they were "relocated" to Oklahoma in the first half of the 1800s. Coweta was named for a village back in Alabama, too, and the name reminded the displaced Native Americans of home. Home, before the government forced them to come to this place. Many of the towns in this part of the world are named for faraway Native American villages, back in North Carolina, Alabama, Tennessee, Mississippi, and Georgia.

As you continue down the ramrod-straight turnpike, entering Muskogee County, and travel a short distance past the bridge that sweeps over the Arkansas River, a quick glance to the left reveals a startlingly odd sight.

There, in a grassy field behind a low cinder-block building, apparently not near any sizable body of water at all, is a submarine.

That's right. A submarine.

If the leaves on the water oaks alongside the road allow a clear enough view, the vessel's profile is distinctive, almost shocking in its incongruity.

It's a dull-gray diesel boat, a thick-hulled *Balao*-class World War II—era submarine, propped up right there in the middle of the wavelike, rolling hills of Oklahoma.

But most passersby don't know what kind of submarine it is. They only know that that thing over there, sitting in a green field beside the highway, looks like a submarine is supposed to look. They've seen them in the movies. In *Run Silent, Run Deep*, the defining World War II sub flick. In *Operation Petticoat*, the silly feature that starred Cary Grant and a former submarine sailor named Tony Curtis (who wanted to be a submariner in the first place because he had first seen them in the movies). The film remains one of the biggest moneymaking military comedies of all time, and features several of the real-life sisters of this very same roadside submarine that gives motorists such a start.

This specter in the Oklahoma plains looks like a submarine to them, more so than the spaceshiplike nuclear vessels they've seen in *The Hunt for Red October* and other more recent movies. But what in Sam Hill is a submarine doing over there in what used to be a bean field?

Continuing on to the next exit after the river, if you look quickly enough, you can spot a fading billboard, next to one for an Indian casino and another for a fast-food joint, urging you to exit now and tour "the submarine-killer submarine." And if you accept the seemingly redundant invitation and steer for the off-ramp, you soon find yourself following faded signs directing you toward War Memorial Park, past several industrial structures, riding on a rough but paved street that heads off to the left just before the entrance to the Port of Muskogee.

"Port" of Muskogee? That sounds odd, too. A port in the middle of landlocked eastern Oklahoma? That's almost as odd as seeing a submarine floating out there on dirt that was once a part of the notorious Dust Bowl.

But then, up ahead, you see it again. The submarine, her bridge and sail towering above her rounded hull, a metal walkway extending from the ground to her stern. Surrounded by memorial plaques dedicated to the fifty-two American submarines that were lost in World War II, and to the more than 3,500 men who are now on what submariners term "eternal patrol."

From the parking lot, through the chain-link fence surrounding the park, other military hardware can be seen strewn around the area like afterthoughts. Cannon. Torpedoes. Several faded army vehicles. Flags snap in the brisk prairie breeze.

But the gray-painted submarine is what draws your attention. The vessel's bulk rests in a shallow indentation in the earth, the silt and grass claiming its underbelly. It seems odd to be up close and see such a thing sitting there, on solid earth, surrounded by grass and memorials and a busload of schoolkids who are noisily attacking the grounds like a whooping war party.

How did a U.S. Navy submarine end up getting herself parked in a grassy field in Muskogee, Oklahoma? Why this particular submarine?

What's the story? What's *her* story?

And what's this "submarine-killer submarine" noise the sign back there on the turnpike was bragging about?

To find out, it would be better if you happen to take this curiosity detour on the correct weekend in the spring. Then, you might also take notice of a crew of gray-haired men milling about the park, many dressed in blue vests splotched with colorful patches that represent submarines on which these former sailors once served. One particular patch is uniform on every vest. It shows a cartoon replication of an ugly, spiked fish and bears the number "310" and the name "USS *Batfish*."

Those older gentlemen would be there for the annual reunion of shipmates, men who served aboard this very submarine from the time she was commissioned in May of 1943 until she was stricken from the U.S. Navy's list of active vessels in 1969. These are proud men. Proud of their old boat's nine battle stars; of her Presidential Unit Citation in World War II. Proud of her service in the Korean War and in the Cold War after that. Proud that *Batfish* and her crew, in February of 1945, in the span of a bit more than three days, accomplished a near-impossible feat that helped speed the end of one of our country's costliest conflicts.

And they are especially proud that they, unlike so many other submarine service veterans, can actually come back and visit their old boat. They can show wives and children and other visitors the very spot where they once bunked among the torpedoes. Or the compartment next to the galley where they neglected to close the valves in the correct order one day and got a foul and unwanted shower when they "blew the head" (flushed the toilet). Or where old so-and-so used to do this or that just to aggravate old what's-his-name. Or where they once skinned a shin dropping from the lookout perch in the shears and down the hatch at the scream of "Dive! Dive!" and the urgent "Ah-oooga!" of the klaxon when a Japanese patrol plane popped up on the SD radar.

Many of the *Batfish*'s sister boats are gone. Fifty-two of them to Japanese dive-bombers and depth charges and, in some cases, friendly fire or tragic malfunction. Other boats ended up in foreign navies. Still more were scrapped, cut up, melted down, sunk for target practice, or simply victimized by the inevitability of the chemical interaction of salt water and air as they rusted away. The men who rode those boats have no place to which to return, no "very spot" to which they can point.

A precious few have been saved, some remarkably well restored and opened to visitors, giving them some sense of what it must have been like to be aboard one of those huge but cramped vessels, a boat actually designed to sink (and, as the submariners always point out, also designed to surface the same number of times). The *Bowfin* (SS 287) in Hawaii, the *Cod* (SS 224) in Cleveland, the *Cavalla* (SS 244) in Galveston, the *Drum* (SS 228) in Mobile, Alabama, the *Pampanito* (SS 383) at Pier 45, Fisherman's Wharf, in San Francisco, and the *Cobia* (SS 245) in Manitowoc on Lake Michigan are among those so preserved.

The *Razorback* (SS 394) is the most recent "smoke boat"—as this class of subs was known, thanks to their diesel platform—to be saved, brought upriver to Little Rock, Arkansas, in 2004, where she will be moored in remembrance and as a memorial to those boats that are gone forever. There's even a German U-boat—the U-505—preserved inside the Museum of Science and Industry in Chicago. It's one of the institution's most popular attractions, with more than 24 million people having examined her since 1954.

It's important to note that the group of men milling about their old boat in Muskogee on that specific spring weekend each year is not nearly as big now as it once was. Attendance at the annual *Batfish* reunion is dwindling. Not from lack of interest, mind you. But if you look in succession at group photographs of the World War II vets who attended, you are immediately struck by how the picture appears less crowded with each year's meeting.

The attendance at the national World War II sub vets reunion bears similar sad witness. Ring binders are set on tables in the main meeting area. Attendees flip through the pages to look up their boats by hull number, and then sign in and write down their hotel room or cell phone numbers so shipmates can easily locate them. Nowadays, even at the end of the reunion week's events, many of the pages remain empty. There are few left anymore who rode those boats. Plus many of those who are still around are no longer able to travel, or their wives aren't up to the trip. Beginning in 2006, the group will no longer hold its own separate convention. They will merge with the other big national group, the United States Submarine Veterans organization—with members from all eras of submarining, not just WWII—for their annual convention.

There aren't enough of the World War II veterans left to go it alone.

With each sub sailor who passes, stories disappear, too. Human stories, personal experiences that die with them. History goes to the grave, and there will soon be no way to gather it once the last one of them is gone.

These are the men who can describe how it felt to hear the ominous click of a depth charge arming near the hull of their submerged boat, then count the seconds until the inevitable explosion. How it felt when a deadly torpedo, dropped from a plane or spat out by an enemy ship, hummed through the water in their direction, aimed to send them to the bottom in a fiery wreck. How it was to stay down so long that the air inside the boat became so foul that a match wouldn't strike, and simply rolling off a bunk and standing up left a man breathless. How life was when it was shared with seven dozen other men, crammed together in a home where precious distilled water had to be used for far more important things than bathing or brushing teeth.

And until you climb down one of those hatches yourself and squeeze through the passageways, feeling the claustrophobia as bulkheads squeeze in on you, as you touch the valves in the pump room and grasp the levers in the maneuvering room and gawk at the torpedo tubes and smell the diesel fuel that lingers even after all these years—until you have done that on one of those lovingly restored boats—there is no way you can fully begin to imagine what it must have been like for those men to voluntarily climb down into one of the subs and ride her off to war.

So there she is, a short ride off the Muskogee Turnpike, in a park several hundred feet away from the Arkansas River. The USS *Batfish*. Resting on dry land over a thousand miles from the nearest salt water that's deep enough to float the 311-foot steel cylinder that displaced over two thousand tons of seawater.

Once you stray from your trip to the Indian casinos or to the Cherokee Heritage Center in Tahlequah or to the Five Civilized Tribes Museum in Muskogee or from the shortcut from Tulsa to eastbound I-40, once you tarry long enough to look her over, once her story is known to you, you are glad you took the time and spent the few bucks it took to gain admission to the park and to its main attraction.

And once you've heard her story, you're glad, too, that those once-young men had the guts to volunteer to take her to war and avenge the deaths of those who were killed on a sunny Sunday morning in Hawaii. Glad that they possessed the skill and bravery required to do remarkable things with her and her complement of weapons, all in the name of freedom.

You're damn grateful that we had her and boats like her when we needed them most.

You're glad that someone had the foresight and will to see that she was propped up out there in that bean field so she would be waiting for you when you got around to taking the detour and spending some time with her.

You're glad that, out of a passionate sense of duty, they brought her to this place and fixed her up so you could get to know her. So you could hear her remarkable story before she, too, was gone, just like so many of those sub sailors who loved her.

Who were they? Who were those boys who rode *Batfish* and the other boats like her?

And who were those strong-willed folks who vowed to bring her to this place, to the heartland, and then did whatever they had to do to make it happen?

What's her story?

What's *their* story?

ONE

The Nature of a Man

According to Cherokee law, the only reason for war was to avenge the death of another member of the tribe. Under the "Blood Law," the clan of the murdered Cherokee was responsible for revenge. The men of the war party prepared themselves for several days before going on the war trail by fasting and "going to water," bathing themselves in a stream or lake.

The Cherokees believed water had purifying powers that made them stronger against their enemies.

December 1941

You'll get a wide range of answers if you ask them why they did it.

Sure, some were overcome by patriotism, ready to fight for their country. They figured they could do more damage to the enemy from a submarine than they could from some cold, muddy foxhole. If you press them, most of them eventually mention love of country—doing their jobs, protecting their nation from the enemy—as a motive for volunteering for the submarine service.

But there were plenty of other reasons.

It's hard for most of us to figure the nature of a man who would knowingly and of his own free will climb down the ladder into an immense steel cylinder, close the hatch behind him, and ride the boat down beneath the surface of the sea, into the cold, blind darkness. Someone who would spend months on such a confined vessel with six or seven dozen other like-minded men. A craft aboard which they would have to sleep on cots dangling among deadly torpedoes, use the toilet in an open closet, and forsake a decent bath for weeks at a time to save precious water for the thirsty electrical storage batteries that were bubbling away below where they lived. A vessel that could just as easily be crushed by the relentless weight of tons of seawater as by the ferocious depth charges catapulted from the deck of an enemy destroyer.

Bill Isbell was one man who chose such a life, willingly and wide-eyed. He can tell you straight up why he enlisted in the service, but he isn't sure exactly what it was that drew him to submarines. The son of a railroad telegraph operator, Isbell grew up in Burnwell, an aptly named coal-mining town in North Alabama. He was convinced of one thing early on: He wasn't going to ride a coal car down into those mines to earn a living. Not if there was something better out there. He enlisted in the Navy at the age of sixteen, before the mines could drag him down like they did most other young men with whom he grew up.

Isbell lied and told the recruiter that he was seventeen years old. He would become the youngest crewman on *Batfish*. Even now, six decades later, Isbell's military records are skewed by a year because of the fib.

Though he had never seen a submersible vessel, much less ridden in one, Billy decided submarine training might serve him well later in life. If he survived it all, of course. Regardless, it would be far better beneath the sea than choking slowly to death on coal dust inside the bowels of the earth.

Virgil "Blackie" Lawrence really was seventeen when he signed up for the Navy in 1940, before the U.S. was officially at war. Speared on by the siren lure of excitement, he gave up his paper route in Greenville, South Carolina, one fine day and, with a lifelong buddy, marched down to the recruitment office to enlist. When it came time to report for duty, his buddy was nowhere to be found. Blackie was on his own at an age when most young men are thinking of little more than raising the down payment for their first car, or trying to determine who their dates might be for Saturday night.

The Navy promptly put Lawrence on a destroyer, the recently recommissioned *Dallas* (OD 199). Before he could get his sea legs under him, he was a part of a fierce, undeclared war in the North Atlantic Ocean. His vessel escorted convoys from Canada to Great Britain, dropping depth charges and running screens against relentless attacks by the German U-boats that patrolled the shipping lanes, trying to cut off supplies and ordnance from the Americas to Europe.

It was tough, dangerous duty. Lawrence was more than ready to get off that old "four-piper" after a year of rough seas and ice-cold salt water. Subs made a lot of sense to him. Someone had told him that they were nice and warm inside and that most of the seawater stayed outside of them. He had also heard that the food was good aboard those "sewer pipes." Better food was certainly a motivating force. The North Atlantic was so violent most of the time that the cooks aboard *Dallas* didn't dare light fires to prepare hot meals. Blackie Lawrence was tired of cold cuts and stale bread.

He didn't find out that the pay was also better in the submarine service until he was already a part of it. Submariners got hazardous-duty pay all the time, regardless of the nature of their mission or duty. They had done so ever since Secretary of War Teddy Roosevelt took his first ride in a submersible, was impressed by the mettle of the men who bravely manned the vessels, and promptly ordained that they be paid extra for their service.

Stanley Javorski grew up in Pittsburgh, near the smoke and belching fire of the steel mills. He read in the papers about the accident aboard USS *Squalus* (SS 192) in May of 1939. She was a newly built submarine conducting a routine diving test out of Portsmouth when she suffered a valve failure and sank 240 feet to the bottom of the Atlantic, a depth that would have previously made rescue of her survivors nearly impossible.

That doesn't sound like the kind of story that would inspire a young Pennsylvanian to want to join the Navy or pursue duty as a submariner, but Javorski was impressed with the amazing effort that was mounted to save the men who made it through the initial incident that caused the sinking. While the accident claimed the lives of twenty-four crewmen and two civilians, the papers all over the country carried stories of the heroic rescue that ultimately saved thirty-two sailors and one civilian.

Stan Javorski wanted to be a part of a service that could work miracles like that.

At boot camp at Great Lakes Naval Training Station, when it became known that he could type, Javorski was hustled off to radio school, and after that, to his delight, he was assigned to submarine training. He would be able to serve in the same branch of the service as those brave men of the *Squalus*.

Of course, young Javorski had no way of knowing that he would one day serve alongside one of the survivors of the *Squalus* disaster. He and Danny Persico, who was one of the last sailors to be plucked from the sunken boat, were both aboard *Batfish* for her seventh and last war patrol.

Though he was a native of New York, Donato "Danny" Persico embodied the cowboy mentality of many sub sailors. He was more than willing to climb right back up on the horse that threw him. In addition to his near-fatal experience on *Squalus*, Danny Persico also survived a near-catastrophic fire on USS *Archerfish* (SS 311), on which he served as chief of the boat (COB). Such brushes with death didn't faze him, though. Persico continued to steam away on the smoke boats. His hometown of Amsterdam, New York, named a city street Persico Square in the old sub sailor's honor after he passed away in January 2001.

Jim Callanan was a young apprentice machinist when the war started. His trade was a valuable one to the war effort. He would have been granted a deferment if he had requested it, and he could have stayed home from the war completely.

He enlisted anyway.

"I guess I had a fatalistic attitude," he says with a laugh. "I chose submarines."

Another *Batfish* crew member, New Yorker Robert "Steamboat" Fulton, was in no particular hurry to leave home. He seemed to have the world by the tail. At nineteen he was already working as the doorman to the back entrance at the Plaza Hotel in Manhattan, a legendary establishment in one of the world's most exciting cities. He saw his share of celebrities and rich folks, most of whom preferred slipping in and out the back way to avoid being bothered. Fulton quickly learned, though, that the rich and famous were often the worst tippers.

When the war started, Robert began catching flak from his friends because he had not yet enlisted or been drafted. He yearned for adventure, too. Lots of potential sub sailors did.

There was one tie that drew young Fulton to the Navy, and it wasn't his nautical namesake (the original Robert Fulton was an early experimenter with submarines and torpedoes before he turned to making steam-powered vessels possible). It was his father. Robert didn't really remember much about his dad. The man died when Robert was only two years old, but he had been in the Navy during World War I. That cinched it.

When he enlisted in the Navy and completed boot camp, Robert had three choices for what he wanted to do. Among his selections were torpedoes and diesel engines. To the Navy, that combination spelled submarines.

Dick Hosler came to submarines because a young naval officer couldn't pay his hotel bill. Dick was born and raised in Hershey, Pennsylvania, where his sister was assistant manager of the Hotel Hershey. A young naval officer had brought his wife down from Portsmouth, New Hampshire, to the Chocolate City for a few days of vacation to celebrate a promotion. When he got ready to check out, he realized that he didn't have enough money to pay his room bill. He pleaded his case to Hosler's sister, and pledged to mail a check to pay the balance as soon as he returned to Portsmouth. The assistant manager was willing to trust the officer, and even invited him and his wife to come home with her for dinner.

That was where young Hosler met his first submarine sailor, Commander Eric Lloyd Barr, who was at that time the skipper of an O-boat. Hosler was so impressed with the man that he vowed someday he would become a submariner as well.

Barr went on to command the USS *Bluegill* (SS 242) on all six of her patrols in World War II. That boat would sink seventeen ships and survive 369 depth charges. She and her crew even captured an island—Pratas Island, in the South China Sea—in May of 1945, and promptly renamed the plot of land Bluegill Island.

Dick Hosler did become a submariner and was a torpedoman aboard *Batfish* on four of her war patrols.

Jim Butterworth's story is typical, not just of *Batfish* sailors, but of other submariners as well. Like Billy Isbell, he was looking for a trade he could learn, a skill that would stand him in good stead once the war was over and he left the service, should he be fortunate enough to survive the experience. He took a test shortly after boot camp in Newport, Rhode Island, and, in a huge room packed with other like-minded young men, Butterworth was one of only a handful to make a good enough score to be assigned to subs. Before he knew it, he was headed for New York City on the train, through Grand Central Station to Penn Station "by way of a bar," as Butterworth puts it, and then off cross-country toward Oakland, California, to ride the "pig boats," as submarines were sometimes known, thanks to the pig iron used to fashion their structures.

Robert Thompson grew up a long way from the sea, in the bluegrass region of Kentucky. He decided early on that tobacco farming wasn't for him, and that led him to enlist in the Navy in 1937. His first duty was aboard a new destroyer, USS *Maury* (DD 401), and he made an around-the-world shakedown cruise aboard that vessel. That tour was heady stuff for a farm boy from Kentucky. But he longed for more. That led him to submarine school in New London, then on to the R-boats in Panama, Key West, and Bermuda, and eventually to five war patrols as a motorman aboard *Batfish*.

Hughston Lowder's timing was notable. Like Blackie Lawrence, he was a South Carolinian. Born in Alcolu, he grew up near Sumter. Like most boys his age, he was tired of school, and, by the fall of 1941, the maps in the daily newspaper were becoming far more interesting to him than the dry history in his textbooks. Besides, as one of ten children in a close farm family, he figured it would be far less crowded on a ship. Or, for that matter, a submarine. He talked his mother into signing the papers that allowed him to enlist in the Navy, even though he, too, was a month shy of his seventeenth birthday.

Their ages would not be a novelty. Most submariners at the beginning of World War II were little more than youngsters.

Hugh Lowder received a train ticket in the mail from the Navy on the first day of December. His train chugged away on the sixth, headed for his swearing-in point in Raleigh, North Carolina. He heard disturbing news while he was still en route.

It was December 7. Pearl Harbor had happened half a world away, but it might as well have been right down the road as far as Hughston Lowder was concerned.

Though tensions between the United States and Japan had been high for several years, few in the States really anticipated war with the Empire. Certainly, if and when the U.S. entered the fray in Europe, it would technically also be at war with Japan because of the Tripartite Alliance of 1940 that allied the Japanese with Germany and Italy.

Still, Japan was too far away, their homeland too small, to offer any serious threat to such a powerful nation as America, even if they seemed doggedly determined to expand their empire throughout the Pacific Rim, from the Aleutians to Micronesia and Australia.

That was one of the reasons the dawn attack on the U.S. Navy's Pacific Fleet in Pearl Harbor, Hawaii, was such a shock. The vicious thoroughness of it was most certainly another.

Ninety naval vessels were at harbor that quiet, peaceful Hawaiian morning, most undergoing repairs or refitting, many resting sleepily in dry dock. They were utterly vulnerable. The attack came from the north, east and south—ironically not from the west, the direction of the Japanese homeland.

The airplanes strategically concentrated first on the Army and Navy airfields near Pearl Harbor and put most of the planes out of commission before anyone had time to scramble and get airborne for a counterattack. Next, they turned their attention toward Battleship Row, where the big warships were lined up like a roll call of the states. Among the boats were *Oklahoma, Nevada, California, West Virgina, Tennessee, Arizona,* and *Utah,* all sitting placidly in their berths.

Before their crews were aware of what was happening, many of the proud ships were ablaze and sinking: the men aboard them dying. *Nevada* was able to get under way, but she was a big fish in a small barrel. Her captain finally managed to steer the wounded ship aground so she wouldn't pose the threat of sinking and blocking the entrance to the harbor.

A perfectly placed bomb hit the *Arizona*'s forward magazine. The ammunition stored there erupted in an awful explosion. Over a thousand sailors died before the thunder of the blast echoed off Diamond Head.

Some vessels were not hit directly but capsized instead with the concussion of the explosions. The water's surface was covered with burning gasoline and diesel fuel. Many men who were thrown into the water drowned because they couldn't surface into such a hellish, blazing sea.

Of the few planes that did manage to get in the sky and try to defend the base, targets were few, and some of the defenders were shot down in the wild cross fire from below. Several Flying Fortresses, returning blindly to base and unaware of what was happening, were also blown from the sky by friendly fire, men desperately shooting at anything that passed overhead.

The scene was chaotic. Those who were there will never forget it. They hope we won't, either.

Over two thousand people died that morning. A thousand more were wounded. Most of the U.S. Pacific Fleet was destroyed or heavily damaged, left sunk or burning at their moorings.

Thousands of miles to the west, in Manila, the Philippines, an almost simultaneous but lesser-known Japanese attack on General Douglas MacArthur's airfield wiped out his defenses there. In one unforeseen blitz, the primary means to defend the island nation had gone up in black, billowing smoke. Within days, the Japanese began their successful invasion of the country. MacArthur was forced to retreat hastily to Australia, but not before his famous "I shall return" admonition.

Other Japanese fighters attacked the remote Navy outpost at Wake Island the day after Pearl Harbor. It took them until Christmas Eve to finally claim the island in the name of Emperor Hirohito.

Guam, another strategic dot of land in the Pacific Ocean, fell to the Empire on December 10.

Back at Pearl Harbor, as stock was taken of the awful toll exacted, the Navy brass realized the destruction of the sneak attack was not nearly as complete as it might have been. Clearly by design but unexplainably so, the Japanese bombers had concentrated on the battleships while ignoring the Navy's extensive repair facilities and fuel tank farms nearby. The base would have been useless for years to come if they, too, had been destroyed.

There was something else left intact: Four submarines that were in the harbor that morning were untouched by bomb or shell.

That was baffling. Japan obviously recognized the value of submersible vessels. They were known to have plenty of them in their fleet and had even used several in the attack on Pearl Harbor. The only explanation was that Japan underestimated the number and range of submarines now held by the United States and felt that these vessels were of little or no danger to them.

Since the development of submarines for military use, the consensus opinion had always been that such craft were good only for defensive work, guarding harbors and shoreline. The Germans knew better. After watching the success of their long-range U-boats in World War I, brighter admirals in the U.S. Navy eventually won out over those who would put more money and effort into battleships and aircraft carriers at the expense of the so-called pig boats.

Quickly, anticipating war in the Atlantic, the Navy began constructing bigger, faster underwater boats, vessels that were capable of patrolling wider stretches of ocean, carrying more ordnance, and possessing much greater sting than their smaller, cramped O- and R-boat predecessors.

With the ominous events in Europe and Asia in the 1930s, the Navy even herded up some of the older boats and converted ballast tanks to fuel tanks so they could range wider around the globe.

Twenty-two submarines were assigned to Pearl Harbor in late 1941. Eighteen of them were spread out all over the Pacific the morning of the attack. The four boats at the piers were left unscathed. That meant the entire submarine fleet survived the Japanese assault.

Within hours of the first bomb that fell at Pearl Harbor, the other boats in the Pacific were told to fire at will at any Japanese ship, military or merchant. The U.S. Navy had never in its history waged unrestricted warfare. Rules of war practiced by the commander of any Navy vessel declared that a merchant ship's crew, passengers, and papers had to be placed in a safe place before any attack could be made on the vessel.

But how could a submarine surface and approach a Japanese ship while politely asking its crew to surrender? Odds are, the sub would be blown out of the water before the request could be completed. It was no longer feasible to fight in a restricted manner against an unrestricted enemy.

Now, for the first time, submarines were allowed to wage the type of war for which they were designed. And it was a good thing for all of us that they were.

The submarines were the primary defense remaining in the Pacific after December 7. And with Japan's anticlimactic declaration of war hours after the attack on Pearl Harbor, and with the similar declaration from Germany and Italy a few days later, the United States found itself in a full-blown global war on multiple fronts. The Navy's foresight in developing the longer-ranging and more aggressive fleet boats paid handsome dividends. In the end, submarines would account for more tonnage destroyed per vessel than any other naval weapon used in the conflict.

The price would be heavy, though. One of every five men—over 3,500 sailors—who served aboard submarines in the Pacific during World War II was killed, the highest casualty rate of any branch of the service.

With the fires still smoldering and the smoke hanging heavily over the tropical paradise, work was sped up on the overhaul of the four submarines that were moored at Pearl Harbor that morning, the *Tautog*, the *Cachalot*, the *Dolphin*, and the *Narwhal*. However, only *Tautog* was immediately seaworthy, and even that was a stretch. A half dozen or so other submarines were rushed to the Pacific—*Pollock, Pompano, Tambor, Trout,* and *Plunger,* among others. They were in place, ready to proceed on to their first war patrols within a week of the attack. However, the men who rode them weren't quite ready for a new kind of submarine warfare.

These new vessels were known as fleet boats, designed to patrol in packs and as members of convoys. Standard operating procedure was to travel at one-half speed on the surface during the day and stop and drop anchor once the sun fell. Now the skippers and crews of these vessels were being told to hunt alone if need be, to prowl at night when they were least likely to be seen, and to do whatever was necessary in order to get results.

Neither the skippers nor the crews were trained for such operations. A boat making half speed on the surface in daylight was a luscious target for a Japanese dive-bomber. Night was prime hunting time for a submarine, not a time to drop anchor and bob benignly.

All these submariners knew one thing for certain: how risky these first war patrols would be. They were pursuing a rabid enemy, a nation who considered this war to be a holy mission, essential to the survival of their homeland and culture. The enemy was out there in numbers, too. From the beginning, Japan virtually owned the Pacific. It would be hard, even for a submarine, to hide.

The men knew that their odds weren't good but they had no choice. They were the best hope the United States had to blunt the Japanese spear until a true war effort could be mounted.

That effort was already under way back home. New enlistees (volunteers all . . . sub sailors are always volunteers) who scored high enough on tests or showed the proper mechanical inclination and aptitude were being shuttled off to submarine school at New London, Connecticut. Others were sent to specialty schools in other parts of the country to learn how to maintain the powerful diesel engines, the generators, and the electrical motors that propelled these odd hybrid vessels; how to keep the extensive pipes and valves and ballast tanks and air compressors in a sub working properly so the boats could dive and surface, hopefully accomplishing each operation the same number of times; how to maintain and fire torpedoes; how to decipher radio code and run and repair the new sonar and radar systems that were just coming on line; and how to use the new torpedo data computer (TDC), an amazing but completely mechanical computing device used to accurately calculate target bearing and range so that the deadly torpedoes ran true to their intended victims.

Something else was going on just up the coast from New London. At the Portsmouth Naval Shipyard, on a stretch of river that separated New Hampshire from Maine, construction was just beginning on a new class of submarine. Keels were being laid for a complex, technically advanced, submersible warship, designed to fight in precisely the kind of war in which the country now found itself.

If the old fleet boats could just hold their own, if the few aircraft carriers in the Pacific could manage to slow the onrush of the Japanese long enough, if the Marines could only somehow seize back and dig in and hang on to some of those lost crags in the middle of the ocean, then maybe, God willing, more help would soon be on the way.

If they couldn't, then God help them all.

TWO

Different
Reasons—
One Job

December 1942–August 1943

Like Stan Javorski, Hugh Lowder could type. As soon as the skipper on his first submarine found out about Lowder's skill on a keyboard, off he went to Radio-Sound School at Groton, Connecticut. Never mind that he had been trained as a torpedoman. The sophisticated new equipment that was being installed on submarines at that time meant that the Navy needed radiomen more than it needed guys to lug those big fish into their tubes and push the "fire" button.

Lowder had been working toward qualification, looking to earn the twin silver dolphins pin that signified that he was a full-blown and duly qualified submarine sailor. He was serving aboard O-8, one of the older short-range submarines that were primarily being used for training now that the U.S. had entered the war. Most sailors called them pig boats, and for good reason other than the iron in their hulls. They were dirty, smelly, cramped, and primitive, and would never have been of any use in the Pacific, even if they had been faster and bigger and had greater range. They lacked air-conditioning, so even when staying down for short periods of time in the chilly waters of New England or Long Island Sound, the crew compartments of the O-boats quickly became unbearably hot.

Fresh out of radio school, Lowder returned to O-8 and resumed hauling would-be submariners on training exercises out of New London, past Fishers Island and Block Island, and into Long Island Sound. It was on one of those trips, just before returning to the sanctuary of the mouth of the Thames River, that he and some of his shipmates watched wide-eyed as the unmistakable trail of a U-boat torpedo whispered by them, exploding on the beach beyond.

The *O-8* crash-dived and lay on the sound's floor for a bit, the crew listening hard for any sound of screws or more torpedoes. There was nothing. They hurried home.

That particular training exercise had become too real. Of course, *O-8* carried only exercise torpedoes, which were not armed. And even if they had live fish in her tubes, the slow, bulky O-boat would have been no match for the Germans and their beautifully maneuverable U-boat.

While Lowder was dodging enemy torpedoes in sight of the U.S. shoreline, a relatively new class of undersea warship was being riveted and welded together at shipyards around the country. One of those yards was just up the coast—Portsmouth Naval Shipyard, on Seavey Island in the Piscataqua River, between Maine and New Hampshire. The *Gato/Balao* class of submarines were first commissioned in 1941, and then rushed through production in anticipation of the need for such a vessel and the strategic role it would likely play in the eventual world war. Shipbuilders and the Navy continued to refine and improve the design as each vessel slid off its blocks into the Piscataqua—a name that comes from a Native American word meaning "a good place to hunt deer"—as well as at the other yards around the country.

These boats were being sent on their way at increasingly rapid launch ceremonies. By 1942, there were several launchings a month at Portsmouth. The yard officials quickly proclaimed to the world that a new boat was ready to float, then rushed to get her final equipment installed, put her through sea trials while collecting together a crew, and then sent her off to war to sink ships and kill men.

On December 27, 1942, just a bit over a year after the attack on Pearl Harbor, the keel was laid for the latest in this series of long-range fleet submarines. She and the others being built at the same time would be the most complex and formidable naval war machines ever produced by man. During this particular boat's design phase, she was named *Acoupa*, after a fish that is better known as the gray sea trout. Later, though, for reasons that are not clear, the name was changed to *Batfish*.

The boat's namesake is, admittedly, one of the ugliest fish in the ocean.

It does vaguely resemble a bat, broad and flat with rough, bony skin. It has large fins on each side that it uses, along with spiny appendages that look like tiny legs, to "walk" along the sandy sea bottom. The long-nosed and polka-dotted batfish range from North Carolina, around the Florida peninsula to the panhandle, in the Caribbean, and across the Gulf of Mexico to the Yucatán. Other species are found in the Indian Ocean and around Australia. Ugly or not, at least one description of the batfish's hunting methods makes it an apt moniker for a submarine. That sketch says the creature "sits on the bottom, supported by its fins, waiting for its prey, which consists of almost anything that comes within its reach."

Batfish wasn't the only boat under construction in Portsmouth at the time, of course. Riveters and welders, many of them female, worked around the clock, turning out the submarines as fast as they could manage. These workers took pride in the news that the submersibles they cobbled together were helping make a difference in the war, especially in the Pacific theater. The Portsmouth facility churned out a total of seventy submarines during World War II, once launching three boats on the same day.

Despite the speed with which these subs were manufactured, there was a constant demand for even more of the vessels the yards created in order to replace those lost in battle. By the time of the surrender in Tokyo Bay in September of 1945, fifty-two American submarines had gone to the bottom forever.

At the end of 1942 and into 1943, five sister ships were in various stages of construction at the Portsmouth shipyard. In addition to *Batfish*, the *Apogon* (SS 308), *Aspro* (SS 309), *Archerfish* (SS 311), and *Burrfish* (SS 312) were either already undergoing shakedown cruises or were well on their way to completion. Scheduling was often problematic. When the torpedo tubes ordered for *Archerfish* showed up, workers were not yet ready to install them in that boat. *Batfish* was farther along toward completion, and she got the 311's equipment. Even now, if you crawl around inside the restored *Batfish* in Muskogee, you'll see ss 311 stenciled on her tubes, even though her hull number is 310.

Batfish was launched on May 5, 1943, in a typical ceremony. These launchings had been toned down by then, not necessarily because of security concerns, but because the work area in which they were held was too small for a sizable gathering and the event inevitably got in the way of the other yard employees, who had plenty of work to keep them busy. Ceremony would just have to take a backseat to practicality. Besides, by that time, sending another submarine out to its fate was relatively commonplace.

Mrs. Nellie Fortier was *Batfish*'s sponsor. She was the one who got to break the ceremonial bottle of champagne across the boat's bow. Though not as famous as some of the others who got the honor of sponsoring the launch of vessels, she had a claim to the privilege that was hard to argue against: Mrs. Fortier was the mother of six New Hampshire sons who were then serving in the war.

Like her sisters, *Batfish* stretched 311 feet from stem to stern and stood just over forty-seven feet from her keel to the top of her periscope shears. Each of the *Balao*-class vessels cost about $7 million to build. Depending on speed, they had a range of about ten thousand miles and could carry enough provisions for a typical crew and enough fuel for its engines so they could be gone on patrol from their home port for about seventy-five days.

The boats were marvels of the efficient use of space. They typically had eight watertight compartments and were two-storied inside, with two decks that ran most of her length. The lower deck held pumps, heavy machinery, and stowage, along with the crucial storage batteries that silently powered the vessels when they were submerged. The upper deck contained living quarters and the operational areas for the subs, including the engine room, the maneuvering room, and the control room. And at each end of the vessels, where the hulls narrowed, were the torpedo rooms—the business ends of the vessel.

Each boat typically carried twenty-four torpedoes. The rest were stored so they could quickly be slipped into the tubes and made ready for attack. Each compartment was separated by a thick steel wall and accessed through narrow (one and a half feet by four feet) passageways that could be sealed in an emergency by bulkhead doors that weighed in excess of five hundred pounds each.

If one compartment flooded or fell victim to fire, that area could be shut off in an effort to save the rest of the boat. Submarine sailors were trained to shut those doors, even if they could not rescue everyone in the compartment beforehand. It was more important to save the boat and the rest of the crew, even if it cost the lives of those few men.

As you might imagine, the purpose of the torpedo rooms was to store and fire the submarine's primary weapon, the torpedo. The front of the forward torpedo room was taken up with six torpedo tubes, their loading doors, and all the apparatus necessary to move the heavy weapons into place so they could be loaded and fired. There were a total of sixteen torpedoes in the forward room—six loaded in the forward tubes anytime the boat was in waters where an encounter with the enemy might occur.

The forward torpedo room had heavy storage racks built into both sides, stacked two high, designed to hold eight of the torpedoes. The forward room was equipped with removable deck plates so that the other two torpedoes could be stored out of the way. Some of the crew's bunks were fitted in above and below the stacked torpedoes. Other bunks hung from the overhead, and the remainder were on the starboard side, in the torpedo-loading pit. It was clearly difficult to sleep anytime the torpedoes were being moved about.

There were other torpedoes way back in the aft firing room. In addition to the four fish loaded into the aft tubes, four others were stored along the walls of the room. But there was no way to get them up front if they ran out of them there. Any other torpedoing would have to be done from the aft room if the complement up front was exhausted. Skippers avoided that if at all possible, since it was usually tactically better to shoot from the bow tubes, facing a target, instead of from the stern.

There was one other important feature of the torpedo room. It had an escape hatch and a supply of Momsen lungs, devices designed to be used by the crew to escape from the boat if an emergency should occur while she was submerged. The Momsen lung was a relatively new innovation, a "rebreathing" device that used a chemical compound to scrub bad exhaled air for a limited amount of time. A man could strap it on and breathe almost normally for the time it took him to emerge from the escape hatch and float to the surface. Even so, the lung was usable only in relatively shallow waters. There was also an emergency escape hatch and a supply of Momsen lungs in the aft room.

If the torpedo rooms were the business ends of the boat, the control room was its nerve center. All the controls that were used during submerged operations—including the submergence "ready light" display, typically called the "Christmas tree"—the controls for the bow and stern planes, the inclinometer that showed the angle of a dive, and the depth gauges, were all located in this room. The Christmas tree indicated whether all systems had been properly set anytime the boat got ready to dive. A red light on the indicator panel meant something was not as it should be, and that a dive would be dangerous to continue. A green light meant all was well and the dive could proceed.

Also in this area were the ship's master and auxiliary gyrocompasses, an auxiliary steering position, the controls and scope for the SD radar, and the radio room. Just below the deck plates of the control room was the pump room, which contained pumps, blowers, refrigeration equipment, compressors, and motor generators—all designed for the operation of the boat's many livability, diving, and surfacing systems.

Farther back, just ahead of the after torpedo room, was a cramped compartment called the maneuvering room, with the motor room (not to be confused with the engine room) directly below. Much of the boat's speed and direction was controlled from the maneuvering room. It was also the area most susceptible to fire because of the mass of electrical equipment housed in the big cabinet called the cubicle.

Above the main deck, roughly in the middle of the boat above the control room and directly below the bridge, there was another watertight compartment called the conning tower. About the size of an average suburban home's master bathroom, this area was where the periscopes were located. The torpedo data computer (or TDC) was also mounted in a rack in the conning tower.

This was the compartment where the officer of the deck (OOD) ran the submarine anytime she was submerged. In addition to the periscopes and TDC, the conning tower held the controls for steering, the motor speed enunciator (the device that sent signals to the maneuvering room to let the controllermen know how fast they needed to go), and the torpedo firing console. The SJ radarscope and sonar equipment were also in the conning tower.

A watertight hatch led down into the control room by a vertical ladder. Another watertight hatch led upward by way of another vertical ladder to the bridge above. In case of emergency, the conning tower could be sealed off and the boat operated from the control room below, but she would have to be driven blindly, without the use of the periscopes.

These submarines carried four noisy but powerful Fairbanks Morse diesel engines that filled the forward and after engine rooms on *Batfish*, two engines in each room. Veterans of the diesel boats claim they never forgot the unique smell of their vessels. Even today, visitors to the several diesel submarines that have been restored can smell the lingering aroma of their fuel when they drop below decks.

Also located in the forward engine room were two distilling plants, used to make freshwater from seawater for cooking, drinking, and bathing, and, most important, for the storage cells. Battery water had to be extremely pure, so it was usually distilled first. If it wasn't clean enough for the batteries, it was used for drinking.

In the aft engine room, below deck level, there was a small auxiliary diesel engine called the dinky. It was used as a relatively low-power replacement for any of the main engines should there be a problem. The forward engine room was an almost exact copy of the one aft, except that it had a small machine shop in place of the dinky.

This model boat had a unique method of propulsion. The diesel engines did not directly drive *Batfish*'s screws unless she was on the surface. For several reasons—including avoiding noise that could be detected by surface vessels and because the engines needed air to run and a place to vent the smoke—the diesel engines could not be operated when the boat was submerged. Later, some of the boats would be equipped with a snorkel-like setup that would allow them to hover beneath the surface while running the diesel engines. These specially modified boats were nicknamed "guppies."

There were generators connected to the main engines. They produced electrical power that could charge the boat's batteries. That electricity was routed through the big switchboxes that made up the main propulsion cubicle in the maneuvering room. Below, electric motors were connected to the two main shafts, which passed through the pressure hull to the twin propellers, or screws, at the stern. The two large electric motors in the motor room below the maneuvering room propelled the submarine both on the surface and when submerged. Each motor drove a separate screw through a rotary speed-reduction gear.

Huge electrical switches, needed for the changeover from generator to battery power and for charging the batteries, were located in the "cubicle," the eight-by-ten-foot wire cage in the middle of the maneuvering room. The cubicle was shock-mounted on springs to isolate the fragile switches from the concussion of depth charges and torpedoes, and from the pounding of rough seas.

One of the more interesting jobs aboard the submarine was that of controllerman. Anytime the boat was under way, two controllermen were on duty in the maneuvering room, working the switches from the "maneuvering panel" at the back of the cubicle. The controllermen had the ability to change the speed of each individual motor as they received commands from whoever was running the boat at the time. They did so by employing a complicated set of levers and rheostats. The men assigned to this task tended to do their jobs with considerable flair.

Underneath the engine rooms were the two battery wells, each filled with 126 tons of potentially explosive but essential storage battery cells. These storage batteries were what provided the electricity to propel the boat when she was submerged. For that reason, this brand of submarine is also sometimes called an electric boat. The submarines could typically run on battery power for up to eight hours, depending on their speed and other strains that might be placed on the electrical cells.

Behind the control room was the after battery compartment, the location of more of the crew's berthing space, the mess and galley. *Batfish* carried a large chill box, a cold room for frozen foods, and an ammunition storage locker, all located below the crew's mess and galley.

Cooks prepared food in the galley. Immediately behind the galley was the crew's mess hall. Four tables were bolted to the decking there, along with benches that ran along each side of the tables. Twenty-four men at a time could dine in that tiny space. The officers had their own dining area forward.

The crew's quarters, just behind the mess hall, were filled with thirty-six stainless-steel-framed bunks that ran in four rows up and down the length of the compartment. Since duty assignments while at sea were typically four hours on watch and eight hours off (except when "battle stations" were called, when everyone was on watch), someone was always asleep there. There were not enough bunks for every member of the crew on most World War II patrols, so some of the bunks were designated as "hot bunks" by the COB. This meant that more than one sailor used that particular bunk. A metal door at the back of the quarters was the entry into the crew's head area. Seventy-five men shared two stalls with toilets, a couple of shower stalls, and two washbasins. The head also contained an automatic laundry machine.

Moving forward from the control room, and above the forward battery compartment, was the living space for the boat's officers. The officers' quarters, above the deck plates that hid the storage batteries, included cabins for both the commissioned officers and the chief petty officers. The forward end of the compartment offered working space for the two steward's mates and included a coffee urn, storage space, and food warmers. The captain was the only officer who had his own private cabin. The rest of them shared sleeping rooms, and all the officers took turns using the single head. The wardroom, the tiny gathering area where the commissioned officers ate and held meetings, had a small table, bunks, and chairs. The ship's yeoman, who acted as a secretary and kept up with all the ship's records, had a tiny office located in this area as well.

Some say one of the main reasons for the closeness of the submariner brotherhood was the communal lifestyle they had in the chummy confines of their boats. It would be difficult for a group of men to live any closer, to share any tighter space, so that analysis makes pretty good sense.

Topside, the fleet submarine's unique profile was defined by its dramatic bridge structure, which, along with the conning tower structure, was typically referred to as the boat's sail. The bridge was accessed through a hatch from the conning tower and not only provided a platform for the captain to stand on while the boat executed an attack, but it also gave support for the two periscopes, the lookout perches, the radar mast, and radio antennas. Everything above the bridge is typically referred to as the shears.

The scope toward the rear of the conning tower was called the attack scope. It had an optical range finder so the sub could easily determine how far away a target was. The forward scope was used for general observation.

Radar developed quickly after the war began. The older SD unit, designed for detecting aircraft, was nondirectional and had limited use, unable to determine a threat's bearing or distance. The newer SJ radar was functionally directional and was used to sweep the surrounding sea for both airborne and surface targets. The radar's range was determined partly by how high the retractable mast was set, since, by the nature of its design, radar is limited to line of sight. The radar on boats like *Batfish* was designed for search and ranging, as well for normal day-to-day navigation. Because the mast could be telescoped, it was possible to extend it above the surface of the ocean while the boat was otherwise submerged, allowing them to scan the area for enemy warships and aircraft before committing to a full-blown surface. That factor alone gave the submarine a big advantage. She only had to pop her nose above water after she knew with relative certainty that the coast was clear.

Batfish also carried a pair of target bearing transmitters, a device that was used to manually find the bearing of another surface vessel or the flying angle of an aircraft. The TBT would then relay the information to the torpedo data computer in the conning tower. The 310-boat had two TBTs, one mounted to the bridge and one on a stand next to the 40mm gun on the after gun deck.

Speaking of guns, these subs typically carried at least one and usually two deck guns that allowed them to mount a surface attack without using torpedoes or to fire at aircraft that might suddenly attack them before they could dive. The type and location of deck guns varied from one boat to another. They could be placed either forward or aft of the bridge. The Navy was kind enough to usually allow the boat's commanding officer to decide. At the beginning of her life, *Batfish* was outfitted with a four-inch gun forward of the bridge. Later in the war, that gun was replaced with a five-inch gun that was mounted aft of the bridge.

The smallest weapon used by the U.S. Navy that fired an explosive shell was the 20mm cannon. Primarily used for antiaircraft fire, its shells were loaded in a drum magazine, and a single gunner aimed and fired it. This weapon was common on fleet subs of *Batfish*'s type, and they were usually mounted on the after part of the conning tower. The sub captains usually used their influence to replace the 20mm weapons with 40mm cannon. These offered significantly more range and boom for the buck.

Most of the boats had mounting points for machine guns at various locations around the bridge. The guns and ammunition were stored in pressure-proof containers near the mounts so crewmen could quickly retrieve them, get them set up, and begin firing as soon as possible after the boat surfaced. Most skippers preferred a .50-caliber Browning.

Another feature of the boat's topside was the "cigarette deck," a small area on top of the conning tower and aft of the bridge with a short railing around it. This was one of the places where guns or the TBT might be mounted on the submarine. It was also a good place to sit during those limited times when anyone besides the men on the bridge and the lookouts were allowed topside. In wartime, that was not very often. The fewer men who were topside, the quicker they could get the boat under if threatened.

The boat's rudder, located at her stern, gave her lateral control. Up-and-down motion was accomplished with the bow and stern planes, which worked almost like wings in the water. They were actually horizontal "rudders," and were attached in pairs to either side of the hull, at the boat's bow and stern. Changing the angle of these planes up or down caused the boat to rise or sink when she was moving, and they helped determine how steep the angle at which either operation happened. The boat itself was normally kept as close as practical to neutral buoyancy—the point at which she neither rose nor sank. For the most part, the stern planes were used to control the angle of the boat in the water while the bow planes were employed to make her rise or sink. Marine propellers are always called screws because that's basically what they do—"screw" through the water. Backward-and-forward motion of the boat was the job of the screws.

Up on the ship's bow was the hydrophone for the JP sonar, a system that allowed the submarines to listen to the sounds of surface vessels. The boat's anchor was housed at the forward end of the boat, too. It weighed 2,200 pounds and was attached to 105 fathoms of one-inch, die-lock steel chain.

People are always curious about how deep these submarines could go if they had to. *Balao*-class subs like *Batfish* were called "thick-skinned boats" and were designed to dive to a test depth of 412 feet, as opposed to the previous *Gato*-class boats that were otherwise very similar in design layout but limited to three hundred feet. This was because the later boats had a much thicker hull. They could, of course, go considerably deeper than that—even twice as deep as their test depth—and sometimes did, primarily to escape the deadly depth charges, but sometimes they went deep quite by accident. Regardless of the reason, such a dive was not recommended, and, once experienced, not soon forgotten by those along for the ride.

Water pressure increases by one atmosphere for every thirty-two feet of depth. The pressure at four or five hundred feet deep is profound—over fifteen times as much as at the surface—and is applied to every square inch of the submarine's hull.

During the war, the Navy attempted to crew its submarines with a mixed group—a fourth made up of qualified men with combat time or at least some prior sub experience, and the rest made up of new recruits. Early on in the war, that was difficult to accomplish. Officers who had any background in underwater warfare were few and hard to find, and a lot of new boats were being built that needed crewmen.

Matching a commanding officer with the rest of the wardroom and the boat's crew was something of a shotgun marriage, too. While officers and even some COBs sometimes had the clout to refuse a man they didn't want aboard, a sailor assigned to a particular sub was generally stuck with whatever skipper he ended up with. It was luck of the draw, and something the sailor had to live with for a while.

"What's the old man like?" was usually the first question a sailor asked of his new shipmates. And as soon as word got around about a new captain coming over to assume command, the research into his background instantly began. As did the scuttlebutt.

As close-knit and self-contained as the submarine service has always been, it shouldn't be surprising that it was typically no time at all before the intelligence on a new captain or executive officer was gathered and disseminated. Everybody knew somebody who had served with him, or who had heard something about him, good or bad. A skipper's history, embellished or not, was common knowledge among his crew before the new "old man" crossed the bow the first time, whether he was coming over from running another boat or promoted into the new commission. Was he aggressive or did he sit back and wait for a target to swim right up his intakes before he shot? Was he a sailor's skipper, taking the part of his men in any dispute with the brass, or did he kiss ass? Was he by-the-book or did he recognize the unusual nature of riding the diesel boats and allow the latitude necessary for them to do their jobs without all the spit-and-polish crap?

Did he know what the hell he was doing?

The first skipper of *Batfish* was a Missourian named Wayne R. Merrill, a 1934 graduate of the U.S. Naval Academy at Annapolis and an experienced submariner. Lieutenant Commander Merrill was a short, stocky man with wide-set eyes. His dark eyebrows and firmly set mouth gave him a rather stern appearance, and there was a sadness in his eyes that may well have come from his two years of hardened experience at sea previous to his taking the helm of *Batfish*. He had a reputation for being able to make quick decisions, and had a keen mind for anything mathematical or mechanical. Crew members soon discovered, with some relief, that he had a ready smile and a pragmatic view on how things should work in the submarine Navy. The enlisted men on the boat got a good dose of it on the August afternoon *Batfish* was formally commissioned.

From the launch in May until August of 1943, work was completed on the boat and training continued, making certain the sub and everyone aboard was ready for the task that lay ahead. At times the crew wondered if they would even get into the war before it was over.

Then, on August 21, the officers, crew, and Navy brass lined up on the deck, and Captain Merrill accepted the keys to his brand-new submarine. The flag was hoisted above her stern and the skipper read his crew their orders. Merrill's first official act after the ceremony was to invite all enlisted men—no officers, please—to accompany him to a nearby barge for a heartfelt lecture.

He spoke bluntly to his crew, telling them that he was willing to cut them some slack, that this was the submarine service, not the surface Navy, but that they had a job to do and they would do it his way. He began the lecture with the subject of gambling.

"You boys can gamble all you want, but I have a few rules of my own. Every game will be cash-on-the-mahogany. If I hear of anyone going in debt or putting out an IOU, he'll be barred from any other gambling. I don't want anybody hurt. Nobody gets broke so he can't make liberty. Where we're going and what we'll be doing, you will need your liberty. I don't want anybody to lose it in a dice game."

Then Merrill's face grew sterner. There was no doubt among any of the sailors on the barge that warm summer day that their skipper meant what he was saying.

"There will be no drinking on this boat, not in port or at sea. Get as wild-assed drunk as you want ashore. In fact, I expect you to relax when you're off duty and on liberty. Believe me, I fully intend to do the same. But come across that brow with brew and you'll be off *Batfish* in a minute."

Then he followed with a caution about the new torpedo alcohol they were now using. Previous recipes for the fuel that ran some varieties of torpedoes consisted mostly of ethyl alcohol. Some sailors had discovered that they could filter it through a chunk of bread, mix it with orange juice to make a horrible-tasting cocktail, and drink enough of the stuff to get tipsy. The fuel mixture for the newer-type torpedoes, though, contained methyl alcohol and was deadly poisonous. The skipper just wanted to make sure nobody got thirsty enough to try that stuff.

The captain also pledged to do all he could to help his crew if they found themselves in a personal crisis, including emergency leave, provided they didn't abuse his good nature.

Merrill finally grew quiet and gazed out across the river, toward Kittery on the Maine side, and down toward where the channel opened out into the broad Atlantic. That was the way to the Pacific Ocean and to the war.

The sailors were quiet, too, as they watched a dark cloud cross their skipper's face. They had heard the scuttlebutt. They knew that Merrill had served on several war patrols in the Pacific already. That some of his boats had been lost with all hands shortly after he had left them. That the last sub on which he had served, the *Grampus* (SS 207), had disappeared without a trace near the Solomon Islands, only days after Merrill left her in Brisbane, Australia.

There had already been arguments among the crew about whether this portended good or bad for *Batfish*. Was Merrill blessed? Was he bulletproof? Or had he cheated the grim reaper one too many times and it was about to catch up with him on this shiny new boat?

"We're all here for different reasons, but to do one job," he continued, looking into the faces of each of his crew. Most of them were so very young. Now they were his responsibility. He couldn't help but think of their mothers and fathers, the rest of their families, and what an awful responsibility it was for him to try to do what he had to do and still deliver these boys back to their farms and city streets when this damned war was finally over.

The sailors had to strain to hear his next words.

"We're being sent out there to kill Japs. That's our job. You may have noticed that Medals of Honor are usually awarded posthumously." He grinned then, and it was as if the sun had suddenly broken through the clouds. "Well, I don't necessarily want one of the damn things on those terms. I've served under some great skippers—several of them bona fide heroes—and I've survived them, every one. What I want to do is the maximum damage we can against a ruthless enemy and still be able to bring you boys back home alive when we're finished. And return this fine submarine intact to the taxpayers, too. That's what I'm getting paid to do. Understood?"

A couple of the sailors looked at each other. What had their skipper just said? That he was more interested in surviving the war and bringing the boat back than he was in killing those murderous Japs?

Both men shrugged and joined in the hearty cheers for their new skipper's rousing speech. They'd know soon enough what kind of man they were indentured to.

In the distance, the rest of *Batfish*'s officers stood together on the new boat's bridge and cigarette deck. They could hear the energetic round of cheers and whoops from the enlisted men on the barge in response to Merrill's pep talk. The boys—and indeed, many of them were little more than boys—seemed to appreciate their skipper's direct words.

No doubt about it: Every one of those guys over there on that barge seemed to be ready to take *Batfish* to war, to follow their new skipper wherever he might lead them. Ready to point their bow toward the Panama Canal and get about their duty of winning this damn war once and for all.

From the civilized, peaceful lives they led prior to joining the Navy, they were about to become vicious warriors, perfectly prepared to kill those who had threatened the things they held most dear.

A Submarine
on Pikes Peak

September 1967

Albert "Ace" Kelly was determined to have his submarine brought to Oklahoma and he was damned tired of people coming up with all the reasons why it was impossible.

Okay, so the boat they picked out first was a tub of rust. And the waterway was too shallow and crooked to float it all the way to Muskogee at the time. And the shipyard workers went on strike the day they were to move the vessel they ended up with. And, all the while, the patience of the state legislature and the banks was fast running out.

Albert C. Kelly was not used to having his ideas sunk before they were ever properly launched. Neither were his fellow former submariners.

Kelly was state commander of the Oklahoma Submarine Veterans of World War II organization. He was also an Ivy League–educated banker who came to the Navy via the ROTC at Harvard University. He served as an officer during the war, including patrols aboard the legendary USS *Wahoo* (SS 238) under her near-mythical skipper, Captain Dudley "Mush" Morton. *Wahoo* was one of the most successful boats of the war before she was lost with all hands during a daring and destructive run through the Sea of Japan in October 1943. Kelly, of course, had left her by then, but he could still see the faces and hear the voices of the men who were serving aboard her when she went down. Men he had slept next to, shared meals in the mess with, went on liberty with, risked life and limb beside. So many of them, and so young to be dispatched to eternal patrol.

Ace Kelly saw it as his duty to provide a way to honor their memory. He also recognized all the advantages—even if many others didn't quite yet—of parking a real-life diesel submarine right there on the banks of the newly navigable Arkansas River, somewhere in the greater Tulsa area. He envisioned schoolchildren filing through one of those classic fleet boats, learning about the sacrifices their fathers and grandfathers made for the cause of freedom. He imagined proud submarine veterans holding reunions there for years to come, keeping alive the memories of their former shipmates with a real, live boat, something solid and authentic that took them back the quarter century since they had served their country and lost their brother sub sailors.

For years, he and the other vets had talked about it over coffee at their regular meetings. Ace Kelly had been thinking about it for a long while before he ever mentioned it to them. Now was the time to get the project under way and set the course.

As he wrote in a letter to his fellow sub vet group members in September 1967, "Our chief project and our intended primary accomplishment for this year will be the acquisition [of] a World War II fleet-type submarine to be brought up the new Arkansas channel and moored at a prominent memorial site near the turning basin at the head of navigation. This will be Oklahoma's sub vets memorial and will be of tremendous educational value to all the citizens of Oklahoma."

The idea would remain in dry dock for a while, though.

By the middle of 1969, there was a strong precedent established for such a wild scheme. The folks down in Mobile, Alabama, had proved it could be done. They berthed the USS *Drum* (SS 228) in the shadow of the restored battleship USS *Alabama* (BB 60) in May of that year. She would see 300,000 admission-paying visitors ratchet through their turnstiles the first year. That was more than enough revenue to make a submarine memorial self-sustaining, Kelly and his group pointed out to the doubters. And it also proved there were plenty of people interested enough in the gallant old ladies to make the project more than worthwhile.

Of course, Mobile was right there on the bay with a deep ship channel and a straight shot to the Gulf of Mexico. Tulsa was thirteen hundred miles up the Mississippi and Arkansas rivers from New Orleans, the place where the initial boat they were considering acquiring was resting in dry dock.

Shoot, the Arkansas was so shallow by the time it flowed through eastern Oklahoma that it was not even deep enough for the flatboats that brought the Cherokees, forced along the Trail of Tears, all the way from the Great Smoky Mountains of the Carolinas and Tennessee to their new home in what was then called the American Desert.

That didn't stop Ace Kelly and the rest of the sub vets, though. Let the doubters take potshots at the whole idea if they wanted to. Besides, as Dr. Glen Berkenbile, a Muskogee, Oklahoma, surgeon and one of the early proponents of the idea, quipped, "If you spent enough money, you could put a submarine on Pikes Peak."

It took a while but the heavy lifting got done. The Navy agreed to let them have one of the fine old diesel boats gratis, so long as they promised respectful upkeep and maintenance, and that they would use the submarine to promote interest in U.S. Navy history.

Well, that was precisely the idea! That, and to have a place where former crew members of this and other vessels could assemble and relive their days on the plunging boats. Where they could stand and touch the diving planes and climb onto the bridge and tell how they helped win the war single-handedly.

An Oklahoma congressman, Page Belcher, put them in touch with the director of naval history, who promised to put a "sold" tag on the USS *Seadog* (SS 401), a moderately successful World War II boat due to soon be decommissioned. But she was all the way up in New London, Connecticut, and the cost to float her from New England all the way down the East Coast, around Florida, through the Gulf of Mexico, and then upriver would be prohibitive.

They passed on *Seadog*. There would be plenty of others from which to choose.

A committee went down to New Orleans and picked out the USS *Piranha* (SS 389) as the boat they wanted. She was a worthy choice, the recipient of five battle stars for her service in the Pacific during the war. Her crew had even pulled off one of the classic ruses, rigging up and flying a Japanese flag from her shears one day so they could chase targets through a convoy of Chinese junks.

Ace Kelly brought to bear some of his political clout. He was friends with the governor, Dewey Bartlett, and easily won his backing for the plan. State Senator James Inhofe, who hailed from Muskogee, shepherded through the legislature a bill establishing the Oklahoma Maritime Advisory Board for the express purpose of bringing *Piranha* up the river and parking her at a new location: the newly donated five acres of prime waterfront land on the Arkansas near Muskogee, compliments of the Muskogee City-County Trust Port Authority.

Never mind that the legislation didn't really provide funding for the board or the project. Nor did it give the panel the authority to borrow money or enter into any legally binding contracts.

That didn't deter Kelly and the sub vets from their plotted course. They'd get the *Piranha*, bring her home, and then work out little details, such as getting the money to pay for the venture, at some later time.

The advisory board's chairman was another old sub sailor, Captain Karl R. Wheland, the former skipper of USS *Gabilan* (SS 252) for three war patrols in 1944. Submariners like Wheland and Kelly weren't used to being told something couldn't be done. And though both men were powerfully connected politically, they had little use for government red tape, political carryings-on, or following proper protocol that didn't directly benefit their plan for parking their fleet boat in Oklahoma.

Hell, they had done more than their part to whip the Japanese, hadn't they? Floating one of those fleet boat beauties up the river a little ways without the fear of depth charges or dive-bombers couldn't be much of a problem, could it?

Especially since the Army Corps of Engineers was nearing completion of the Arkansas River Navigable Waterway system, designed to make reliable river transportation possible from the Mississippi all the way across the state of Arkansas to northeast Oklahoma. It would still be way too shallow in some spots, and there were some turns so twisting that nobody was quite sure yet how they would manage with a 311-foot-long submarine. But Wheland and Kelly figured if they could navigate the reefs and shoals off Honshu, and steam through the Celebes or the Java Sea, they could, by God, make a simple little "patrol" up the Arkansas River.

They apparently had a boat waiting for them down in New Orleans. They had a state-sanctioned commission set up, as well as operating and holding meetings. They had a place to dock the sub once they got her there. And as soon as they could get the pretty lady in place and open to the public, they'd have a long line of folks queued up to pay to get inside her, providing the funding to keep her rouged and powdered and pretty for many future generations.

But when the committee went back to New Orleans in the fall of 1970 to arrange for the transfer of *Piranha* from the U.S. Navy to the good people of Oklahoma, the whole project ran aground. The Navy informed them that they would have to take possession of the vessel immediately after agreeing to do so. They would also have to begin paying the bill for her considerable docking charges as soon as the paperwork was signed.

That was a problem. The new waterway would not be open for another year, and the committee still needed time to raise money for refurbishing the boat to get her into good enough shape so she could be moved. They simply weren't ready to adopt a submarine at that moment.

On follow-up visits to New Orleans, they noticed that *Piranha* was definitely looking even more ragged than the first time they saw her. She had been sorely neglected, and now lay completely gutted in her dry dock. The board would have to spend more money and time than they had anticipated tracking down and purchasing equipment to make her truly representative of what the fleet boats looked like and the kind of gear they carried during the war. She had to be properly equipped and as authentic as possible or she wouldn't portray the true picture of the submarine service in the Pacific. The sub vets agreed that was a crucial part of the project.

Wheland, Kelly, Berkenbile, and the rest of the committee were not discouraged, though. They decided to be patient, to wait until the river channel was wide and deep enough, and until the funding was more in line with what the move would require logistically, and then they could reapply for *Piranha* at that time. They'd gamble she would still be available—that some other city fathers wouldn't get their hands on her first, or that the Navy wouldn't take her and use her for target practice, as they had done with several of the other diesel boats. Even if that happened, maybe another boat would be available when they got ready for one.

As it turned out, *Piranha* would still be there waiting for them when the time came. But a prettier, more desirable boat had shown up at the dance, and she quickly caught the eye of the Oklahomans.

When they were ready to take possession of the boat, *Piranha* still sat forlornly at the New Orleans Naval Yard, showing still more signs of neglect than during the group's previous visit. But berthed right next to her was another boat, also in rough shape and likely headed for the scrap heap as well. But this sub was in marginally better condition, and she was much better equipped.

There was another consideration for the board, as well. *Piranha*'s war record was sound, but the sister boat's was more impressive. She was something of a World War II legend, known in the service as the "submarine-killer submarine of World War II," the boat that pulled off an amazing hat trick back in 1945, sinking three enemy submarines in three days in deadly enemy waters just north of the Philippines.

The committee made a course correction without even bothering to request permission from anyone else, either in government or on the Maritime Advisory Board. They never attempted to modify the language in the bill that allowed the board to acquire *Piranha* in the first place. They submitted a formal application to the Navy for a boat named *Batfish* instead of the one they were given permission to claim by the state legislature and by their charter. To this day, the legislation in Oklahoma City specifies that the board was authorized to bring *Piranha* upriver to Muskogee. It says nothing at all about any submarine named *Batfish*.

After being jilted by the Oklahomans, *Piranha* was eventually scrapped—all except for her conning tower. That was donated to the Fleet Admiral Chester W. Nimitz Memorial Naval Museum at Fredericksburg, Texas, the admiral's hometown.

Effective with Karl Wheland's signature on the donation contract on November 22, 1971, *Batfish* became the first and only submarine in the state of Oklahoma's "navy." They had the title to the old girl free and clear.

Now, all Wheland had to do was figure out how they were going to get her to her new home without leaving her stranded on some river sandbar in the middle of Arkansas.

Little did they know that getting their beautiful submarine home would be the least of their problems, and that the whole "patrol" would be almost as harrowing as anything they had ever endured in the war-raked Pacific.

FOUR

Through the
Prowling Grounds

"Five Civilized Tribes" is the name given to the five major tribes of Native Americans who lived in the southeastern part of the United States, many of who were eventually "re-settled" in eastern Oklahoma. They were the Cherokees, Chickasaws, Choctaws, Muskogee Confederation (Creeks), and Seminoles. These five tribes adapted quickly to the ways of the white men and sought peaceful coexistence with the newcomers. The tribes were primarily a peace-loving people.

However, when attacked or threatened, they were quickly transformed into ferocious warriors, and their resistance to those who threatened them became more and more bloody.

October 1943

A few days before the newly commissioned *Batfish* left for the Pacific, one of her sisters met an awful and controversial fate. That ominous incident ultimately changed the plans for *Batfish*'s own transit to the war and led indirectly to some rather unsettling occurrences before the boat ever got to the Pacific Ocean.

That sister boat, the USS *Dorado* (SS 248), seemed jinxed from the get-go.

The submarine's crew, headed by Lieutenant Commander Earl C. Schneider, proved themselves solidly seaworthy during trials in the summer of '43. The boat, however, didn't even come close. *Dorado* suffered a potentially catastrophic fire, got stuck in the mud underwater for half a day, and continually balked whenever Schneider and his men tried to coax her to submerge.

Some of *Dorado*'s problems were almost comical. She had been built by a mixed construction crew made up of women and men who were, for whatever reasons, not taken in the military draft. Both sexes worked side by side in the cramped compartments of the new boat, usually around the clock. Still, for the most part, such crews did amazing work and turned out submarines at an astounding clip. Over 200 submarines were constructed during World War II, and about 180 were actively patrolling the seas at a peak in 1945. The construction crews' contribution to the winning war effort is one that should be respectfully remembered and honored. But it appears that at least some of the folks who constructed *Dorado* were, shall we say, distracted.

When the boat was launched from the Electric Boat Company in Groton, Connecticut, May 23, 1943, a Navy band played patriotic favorites, politicians gave speeches, and invited guests waved red-white-and-blue banners. That was typical at such ceremonies. There was also the usual launch platform full of dignitaries, including the boat's sponsor, Mrs. Ezra G. Allen, the wife of a U.S. Navy rear admiral. Then the newly christened submarine slid proudly down the skids and into the water for the very first time as everyone in the sizable crowd watched and cheered.

The skeleton crew aboard *Dorado* decided to get into the spirit, adding to the tumult by blowing the vents. When they did, a snowstorm of used condoms blew out the pipes and filled the sky like a blizzard of oversized confetti. The workers who put her together obviously had more than welding and riveting on their minds. Maybe, as some of the crew aboard during her shakedown speculated, that was one reason the boat wasn't as well constructed as she should have been.

Still, the new submarine was desperately needed halfway around the world to help win the war. She dutifully left New London, Connecticut, on October 6, 1943, headed down the Atlantic seaboard and through the Windward Passage between Haiti and Cuba toward the Panama Canal.

But *Dorado* never made it to the canal. In fact, she was never heard from again after she steamed down the Thames River into Long Island Sound, and left Groton and New London behind.

U-boat activity in the Caribbean, up and down the East Coast of the United States, and even in the Gulf of Mexico, was far more extensive and costly to the Allies than most Americans knew at the time, and much of the information about Nazi operations in the Atlantic is just now becoming known. *U-507* sank the first ship in the Gulf of Mexico, northwest of Key West, in May 1942, and averaged dispatching a vessel to the bottom every day for the next month. About the same time, U-boats began destroying an alarming number of Allied ships in the Caribbean as they preyed on traffic heading to and exiting from the Panama Canal. The Roosevelt administration did a good job of keeping the extent of this activity a secret from the American public, ostensibly to avoid panic. But those who patrolled these waters—at sea or in the air—were certainly aware of the threat and were more than willing to pounce anytime they felt they had a worthy target in their sights.

The crew of a Martin PBM Mariner, a two-prop "flying boat" aircraft used for patrolling over enemy water—this one a part of Squadron 210 operating out of Guantánamo Bay, Cuba—later testified to the board of investigation and the court of inquiry that they spotted a German U-boat in the Caribbean near the Windward Passage at about 8:45 local time the night of October 12. The men aboard the Mariner didn't hesitate. They dropped Mark 47 depth charges and a hundred-pound bomb on the "enemy target" and reported that they had inflicted heavy damage on it, and had most probably sunk the enemy sub.

The patrol plane's crew later that evening spotted another submarine. They assumed it to be the *Dorado*, over which they were supposed to be flying cover, and they flashed recognition signals in its direction. The signals were not returned. The sub instead began shooting at the PBM, and then quickly slipped underneath the surface of the sea before the patrol plane had a chance to circle back around and return fire.

Later, a court of inquiry was unable to determine exactly what happened to *Dorado* that warm autumn night. The members of the panel speculated that she had been lost with all hands after an attack by a German U-boat. Such an enemy vessel was known to be operating in the area, based on intelligence reports. And the U-boat's presence was all but confirmed by the PBM crew's contact with the boat that ultimately fired at them in a most unfriendly manner.

Or there was the possibility of operational error. Something could have gone wrong with the boat. She certainly had a history of such mishaps. Her shakedown cruise had been nothing if not shaky. She might even have been unable to dive to avoid an encounter with the Germans.

It was standard practice while an unescorted submarine was in transit in "friendly waters" to impose bombing or attack restrictions within a 4,500-square-mile-radius area—fifteen miles on each side of the course, and fifty miles ahead and one hundred miles astern of wherever the boat was supposed to be at any given time. It could be that *Dorado* was off course or off schedule, maybe due to her nagging mechanical problems. Or the PBM aircraft may have received incorrect coordinates.

Whatever the reason, and despite the court of inquiry's official findings, it was almost certain that the patrol plane attacked and mortally damaged the *Dorado* that night.

In the patrol report of the German submarine *U-214*, declassified long after the end of the war, her skipper, Rupprecht Stock, wrote of being in the area east of Jamaica that evening, and of witnessing the aerial attack on the American sub. The U-boat skipper also logged his own encounter with the PBM two hours later.

It's amazing such friendly-fire incidents didn't happen more often. Some say they did and the government whitewashed the details.

The one factor that makes submarines such effective war machines also makes them vulnerable to attack from "friendlies." Because of their stealthy nature, submarines are often targets for friend or foe. It's a testament to those who planned such operations and devised the friend-or-foe codes that it didn't occur more regularly. Amazingly, so far as we can confirm, only one other submarine, the *Seawolf* (SS 197), appears to have been lost to friendly fire during the war. She was apparently attacked mistakenly by an Allied aircraft and depth-charged by USS *Rowell* (DE 403) between New Guinea and the Philippines. Seventy-nine men were sent on eternal patrol. That tragedy came in October 1944, about a year after *Dorado* was lost.

Such dangers were certainly on the mind of Captain Wayne Rucker Merrill as he prepared to steer the brand-new *Batfish* down the same path as *Dorado*, along the Thames River and out into the open ocean, that dark, foggy October morning in 1943. The *Dorado* tragedy was fresh on everyone's mind. Her disappearance had happened just ahead of them. That had everyone aboard in a somber mood.

Since her commissioning, the *Batfish* crew had been rushing through sea trials, torpedo trials, training, and qualifying. A seemingly endless army of inspectors had traipsed through the new boat, diligently studying every rivet, pipe, and valve. She was ultimately sent from Portsmouth down to New London for still more repairs, and again the crew, from the wardroom to the torpedo rooms, openly questioned whether they would ever get to the war before the rising sun had set for good.

But finally, in mid-October, she was ready to depart. The crew had said their good-byes to New London in the way sailors traditionally did. Hangovers or not, they were ready to go, to finally get to the war where they could do some damage to something besides test targets in Narragansett Bay around Newport, Rhode Island.

Orders said they were to leave at dawn, but Merrill knew they were free to cast off at will. He declared that they would sail as soon as the crew was all accounted for. Just after midnight, everyone was back aboard and reasonably able to man his station.

They were more than ready to go.

But now it was the weather, not bureaucracy or supplies or seemingly endless training, that delayed them. The fog was so thick on that early morning that Captain Merrill couldn't see the snout of his new boat from where he stood on her bridge. Even so, he overruled his XO (one of the few non-Missourians among his officer contingent—a factor that led to other conflicts later), and pulled away into the thick of the murkiness. The skipper guided them blindly down the Thames as far as the highway/railway drawbridge, which would have to be opened if they were to pass through. That was a tight squeeze on the best of days. They decided it was too soupy to try to go farther, so they anchored at the edge of the channel and waited for first light.

At long last, the sun began punching holes in the fog and they pointed due south, running at flank speed, as if the war would be lost if *Batfish* and her crew didn't get there right away. The four big Fairbanks Morse engines pounded like Thoroughbreds, relentlessly pushing them toward their fate.

These waters—even within sight of Long Island, the Statue of Liberty, the Jersey shore, and the Outer Banks of North Carolina—were hazardous prowling grounds for German U-boats. *Batfish* took no chances. From the time they left port, lookouts manned the tiny platforms in the boat's shears anytime they were at the surface, and radar constantly scanned the ocean for any hint of a periscope or the distinctive shape of a German sub loitering on the surface, or the screw signature of one lurking beneath the surface, lining up a torpedo shot at them.

The crew knew about *Dorado* by now, too. And there was scuttlebutt already that she may well have gone down from friendly fire.

"Now's the safest time there ever was for us to be making this run," one of the young lookouts observed as he squinted into the quickly warming sun.

"What do you mean?" The other teenage lookout didn't even drop the binoculars from his eyes to sneer at his shipmate as he responded. Skippers liked to have their youngest crew members in the shears. The kids had better eyes.

"Lightning don't strike twice in the same spot," the first lookout observed. "You know the friendlies are gonna be extra careful about shootin' something they don't know after what happened to the 248."

The other fresh-faced lookout checked the wind first and then spat forcefully over the side for emphasis.

"Yeah, maybe so, but you reckon them kraut U-boat skippers give a damn about whether we're friendly or not?"

The first youngster didn't reply. He just kept his glasses moving, intently sweeping the green expanse of seawater between them and the horizon.

They knew already that their course was to be altered. They would be the first new boat constructed during the war and bound for the canal that would go through the Mona Passage, between the Dominican Republic and Puerto Rico, instead of passing through the Windward Passage, as *Dorado* had done.

Maybe it would be safer. Maybe it would help avoid the hungry U-boats that prowled the previously used standard cut-through, even if it did add miles and time and extended exposure to their trip. Maybe it would be less likely that a friendly craft would mistake her for something enemy and proceed to send her to the bottom.

Merrill and the crew had also gotten word to be careful about getting too close to Allied convoys. Everyone was skittish, nervous on the triggers, doubly anxious to exchange ID information to make sure any vessel encountered was who he said he was. Any mistake could be fatal. No matter who shot, the poor son of a bitch on the other end would be just as dead, enemy or not.

It turned out that the trip through the Canal de la Mona was uneventful. But *Batfish* did receive a powerful scare not long after, and it came, appropriately enough, on Halloween.

As they neared the Panama Canal Zone, Merrill swung the submarine wide to the south, avoiding getting too close to a huge convoy that was exiting the canal and heading eastward. The skipper also had the boat perform choppy zigzagging maneuvers, as much to foil the guys guarding the convoy as to confuse any U-boat that might have its eyes on his submarine. And the boat's sound operator never removed his headphones. If there was anything out there—friendly or not—he wanted to make sure he heard it or got a sonar ping on it in time to react.

But it was the officer of the deck, standing watch on the bridge, who spotted something that sent the crew to immediate battle stations.

A periscope, its eye thrust six feet out of the water, and less than three hundred yards off the port bow.

"Left full rudder! All ahead flank," the OOD sang out. *Batfish* was turning her tail toward the assumed enemy boat, presenting her slimmest profile. Basically, they were running away, but the OOD also ordered that the stern torpedo tubes be made ready to fire. And he requested that Captain Merrill hurry to the bridge.

But the skipper was already climbing the ladder from the control room when the call came, hurrying through the conning tower and up to the bridge.

"Periscope, three hundred yards that way," the OOD told Merrill when he stepped to the bridge rail. He pointed to starboard, in the direction of where he had seen the telltale evidence that they weren't alone in this part of the Caribbean Sea. But there was nothing there now. The scope had already dropped back beneath the surface. The U-boat could have been stalking them for a while. She could have a solid bearing on *Batfish*. Her torpedo tubes could already be flooded, their fish beginning their spin, ready to rocket off toward their target at killer speed.

Merrill sounded the general alarm.

"Rudder amidships. Steady!" the OOD said into the communicator.

Suddenly, one of the sharp-eyed youngsters clinging to the shears above them piped up.

"Scope! Off the starboard side, forty-five degrees."

Sure enough, there was the evil eye winking at them again, maybe six hundred yards away, riding four feet out of the Caribbean, blatantly staring at them. And the captain on the other end of that scope might, at that very instant, be giving the order to fire a cluster of torpedoes.

"Left full rudder!" Merrill barked.

The boat yawed hard and the men on the bridge and in the shears held on tightly to keep from falling. Throughout the boat, men grabbed whatever they could in order to keep on their feet.

"He's still coming at us," the OOD said, his voice cracking with tension. And it was true. Even as they made the turn to try to put more distance between them and the German submarine, they could tell that the bastard seemed like he wanted to give chase.

"Meet and steady her," the skipper called down to the helmsman in the control room. He was trying to get the boat's stern lined up at a zero-degree angle on their stalker. Then they'd be in a position to let her have a fist to the nose.

Below decks, every man was working hard, doing exactly as he had been trained to do, but praying that all this was nothing more than just another drill.

"Nine and ten armed and ready," came the report from the firing officer in the conning tower. Two fish were loaded in tubes in the after torpedo room, awaiting the command to go.

But just as the rear end of *Batfish* swung around to line up with the German sub, the foe's scope slipped down again and disappeared into the salt water. It seemed the U-boat skipper was reading their minds.

"Fire nine!" Merrill yelled into the bridge speaker.

It was a shot in the dark, Merrill knew. They had not really had time to line up on the target, to set the run depth or an accurate lead angle, and the son of a bitch had likely moved by now anyway. It didn't matter. The fish was away and running already. Maybe they'd get lucky and bag a kill before their first official war patrol. Or maybe, just by shooting at the German boat, they'd shake him off their tail long enough to get away.

The sound operator reported in frustration that he couldn't track the torpedo because of the sound of their own engines, rumbling deeply as they propelled the boat farther away from the last spot where they had seen the contact.

The men on the bridge and in the shears weren't any better off in trying to follow the torpedo visually. They couldn't even see its wake through the diesel smoke from *Batfish*'s engines.

Nor, Merrill was thinking, *could we see one of their fish heading our way if they've shot at us.*

"Captain, I think I see . . ." one of the lookouts started.

"What, son?"

"Looks like a bubble, just to the left of our wake, about two thousand yards out. Maybe an impulse bubble, like they've . . . uh . . . fired a torpedo."

The lookout's report had not even been completed before Merrill ordered the boat to begin a quick set of zigzags, and to remain at flank speed. If a German torpedo were headed their way, it would have to hit an erratically dancing target.

A little less than five minutes after launching their weapon, *Batfish*'s sound operator and the men topside clearly heard a distant explosion. Their weapon had reached the end of its run and detonated without harming anything more than some particularly unlucky shoal.

Merrill brought the boat back to its base course, back toward the mouth of the Panama Canal, and slowed to standard speed. If he ever considered diving to further avoid the U-boat, no one knew it. Or if he ever thought about trying to chase the target and try to get a better shot, he never mentioned it to anyone either.

The XO—the officer who was not from Missouri—considered asking but thought better of it. Executive officers didn't question their skippers' decisions unless they absolutely had to.

Everyone aboard the boat was quiet, listening intently, some holding their breath as they tried to hear the tinny hum of an approaching torpedo, or any sound that would tell them if the shadowing submarine was still close by. And if it was, where it might be.

They heard nothing but the throbbing of their own engines and the splash of water against their bow.

Merrill had sent only one torpedo out of its tube because he knew it was a low-odds shot at best. It was difficult for one submarine to shoot another under the best of conditions, even when time allowed for careful sighting, because both vessels were designed to dive and duck, feint and hide, speed up and slow down, and do it all with a minimum of noise, unlike a raucously loud, poorly maneuvering surface vessel that could only dance left or right. The whole concept of a target being able to move vertically as well as horizontally really complicated the geometry of aiming and shooting.

As darkness fell and the topside lookouts were relieved, the men aboard *Batfish* gathered in the after battery mess. Most of them sat quietly, nursing cups of dark, hot coffee as they considered what had happened.

Suddenly, this war was more real than ever to them. Too real.

That was an actual enemy out there trailing them, and the Germans could have just as easily come at them full bore, chasing and shooting at them all the way to Panamanian waters. But for some reason, there had been no pursuit. Maybe *Batfish*'s lone torpedo had scared the Germans off. Maybe it was just one of the U-boats that supposedly swam these waters only to lay mines, without even a single torpedo aboard to fire. Or maybe the Germans were saving their fish for something bigger and more sink-able, like the convoy steaming by the area.

The sailors' sober mood lasted only a short while. Before long, the sea stories began and the tension broke and they had convinced themselves that they had spit right in the Führer's eye.

When *Batfish* and her crew were thirty miles northeast of Cristobal at the Caribbean side of the canal, the radioman called in their position and requested an escort. The return message promised that an escort vessel was on the way to lead them safely in.

Before it could get there, somebody else showed up. A U.S. Navy patrol plane met them and immediately began buzzing about ominously, a mad wasp bumping its head on the ceiling.

On the submarine's deck, crewmen used the spotlight to flash in the di-rection of the aircraft the very latest friendly recognition code. The plane signaled back, but, to the consternation of everyone on *Batfish*'s bridge, it was the wrong code. An old sequence, at least half a day old.

Damn! Somehow the Navy patrol plane had not gotten the latest identi-fiers and thus would assume that *Batfish* didn't know the correct code. That could be a very dangerous assumption for the eighty or so men aboard SS 310.

Wayne Merrill had come back up to the bridge to await the rendezvous with the escort vessel. He snorted and gritted his teeth. He knew this little snafu could be fatal. Somehow he had to convince the patrol plane that the *Batfish* was as American as apple pie.

"Run the Stars and Stripes up the attack scope as fast as you can," he quickly commanded.

"Damn!" one of the lookouts yelped. "He's opening his bomb bay doors, Skipper! He's acting like he's gonna—"

"Launch the recognition flares!" Merrill called out. "And make it snappy!"

They could only hope that the pilot had the latest color combination for the flares. The damned guy was already banking and then flattening out, clearly preparing to move in for a bombing run on Wayne Merrill's brand-new submarine.

"Should we dive, Captain?" the OOD asked hopefully from Merrill's right elbow.

"Not enough water here," the captain said. "And even if there were, that might convince him we aren't supposed to be here. He'd drop everything he had on us then. We're a sittin' duck if he doesn't buy those flares."

The flares looked for all the world like a late Fourth of July fireworks show as they burst high overhead in the clear, tropical sky. But the attacking plane didn't seem to be enjoying the show at all. He was coming their way, ready to send them to the bottom.

"Gun crew! To the conn!" Merrill finally said.

It appeared their last resort would be to try to shoot the Navy plane down before he had a chance to bomb them to smithereens. Or, if he miraculously missed them somehow on his first pass, to make sure he didn't get a chance at a second run. Not a happy proposition, but perhaps the only way to save *Batfish* and her crew.

But just then, in the distance, another set of multicolored flares exploded in the sky. The patrol plane suddenly broke off his dive, veered to the left, pulled up, and climbed to begin circling benignly, as if he were only out for a nice sightseeing flight. It was their escort ship, showing up just in the nick of time, and she had apparently been able to call off the plane by radio.

Merrill dropped his head and studied the rivets in the deck at his feet for a bit. He took a long, slow draw of the warm, salty air.

Not even into the Pacific Ocean yet and they had already been stalked by a U-boat and almost blown out of the water by one of their own patrol planes. Now all they had to do before the day was done was navigate through a likely minefield laid by the Germans near the entrance to the canal, while minesweepers ran ahead of them to hopefully clear the way.

It might be safer to be in the Sea of Japan! Merrill mused.

They finally approached the bay that formed the mouth of the canal, a minesweeper in front of them and another behind. The German mines, in an effort to defeat the minesweepers, were designed to count vessels they encountered, and to explode on a preset click. On the bridge of *Batfish*, the captain and his lookouts kept a wary eye on the sweeper ahead of them as well as the water around them. Below, the crew couldn't help but listen carefully as they worked at their stations, fearing the scrape of something heavy and metal and deadly against the hull of their boat.

That night, tied up to the pier at Coco Solo, safely inside the canal, Wayne Merrill went to headquarters and made his feelings known about their rather unfriendly greeting party. He also managed to locate the aviator who had given them all such a scare earlier in the day. Without explaining who was issuing the invitation, Merrill asked the pilot to come have dinner aboard *Batfish*, to sample some of the famous submarine food, and get a tour of a boat that was actually designed to sink. The young flyboy unsuspectingly accepted.

Before the evening was over, the airman got a complete lesson in updating friend-or-foe signals and an up close and personal demonstration of submarine recognition flares.

That wasn't all, though.

The next morning, as *Batfish* was preparing to get under way for her passage through the canal, the base operations officer unexpectedly showed up at the brow, bearing the boat's orders. Captain Merrill, still a bit unsteady from a full night's celebration of their escape from two close calls, met him at the sub side of the walkway from the pier to the deck.

"I appreciate your kind service, but don't you think it's a bit unusual for you guys to be personally delivering orders to a boat?" he asked.

It was unusual. Merrill wondered what was up.

"Hey, I just wanted to meet the luckiest son of a bitch in the Navy," the ops officer said, and pounded Merrill on the shoulder.

The skipper gazed at him, a puzzled look on his face.

"You've had . . . what? . . . half a hundred boats like ours through here in the last year. What makes us any luckier than the rest of 'em?"

The officer winked, as if he knew something Merrill didn't know.

"Well, first you got away from that U-boat." Merrill vaguely remembered sharing that story with several groups of officers during the previous evening's unwinding. "Then you almost got bombed by one of our own, and would have, the way I heard it, if the escort hadn't shown up at the right moment. I'd say that's pretty damned lucky."

The story of the patrol plane and Merrill's rather pointed instruction to its young pilot might have been the topic of conversation at a few Coco Solo establishments the night before as well.

"Okay, so I'm a lucky son of a bitch!" Merrill said. It was hot and sultry, and his head seemed to be expanding by the second, his pulse pounding painfully in his temples. He was well aware that many already considered him exceptionally fortunate to have left several boats just before they were lost shortly afterward. Frankly, he was growing tired of the unasked questions he saw in the eyes of fellow wardroom types and the whispered comments of the enlisted men behind his back.

"Luckier than you know, Skipper," the ops officer finally said with a sly grin. "The minesweeper that tailed you into the canal yesterday brought up a mine." He waved an arm vaguely back toward the Caribbean. "If that baby had been set for a single click less, you and whatever was left of your pretty new boat would be out there blocking our channel right about now."

FIVE

Not Died in Vain

November 1943

It took most of a day for the U.S. Navy's newest submarine, the *Batfish,* to work her way through the fifty-mile-long Panama Canal. Crew members who weren't on watch were allowed to come up on deck in manageable groups long enough to take in the sights as they slowly progressed through the engineering marvel, her man-made canals, locks, and series of natural lakes. Those on watch below had to use their imaginations. The "Big Ditch" had been open about thirty years, but it was still a novelty, even for veteran sailors, to make the passage across the isthmus from one vast ocean to the other.

Captain Merrill had mentioned only to his officers the close call with the mine as they approached Coco Solo. The crew would have limited time to enjoy themselves before they made the long haul across the Pacific into the heart of the war. He felt it best that they didn't have to consider how near to disaster they had been. Once they tied up at the naval station at Balboa on the Pacific side, they were officially under the aegis of Commander Submarines Pacific (ComSubPac), headquartered at Pearl Harbor. They could relax for a few days here because this side of Panama was a much safer location than the U-boat-ridden Caribbean side.

Batfish and her crew would have a week to wait before they steamed on toward Hawaii. The boat would receive routine maintenance, and the one torpedo they had fired at what they believed to have been a German boat would be replaced, all while the crew had a chance to recharge their own batteries in the bars and brothels of Balboa.

Merrill knew the eleven-day trip to Pearl would be a long and, for the most part, boring voyage, with nothing but empty emerald water and the occasional flying fish to break the monotony. There were no U-boats on this side of the canal, and it would be at least five thousand miles before they entered waters frequented by the Imperial Japanese Navy (IJN). They would use the trip to continue training, and for as many of the crew as possible to become "certified in submarines" and be eligible to wear the twin dolphins. Those who were not yet qualified bore the name of "nonqualified personnel" or NQPs. The slang for NQP was "nonqualified puke," and those who had not yet passed the stiff examination toward qualification were often the objects of derision. It was partly in good fun, but there was a serious aspect to their mockery. A man who couldn't jump in at any station and adequately perform the duties of that job could quite possibly cost them the boat. And their lives.

As soon as *Batfish* was tied up in Balboa, Wayne Merrill sent his crew off to liberty with the command that they have a good time. Only those on watch remained aboard. They would be relieved later as other men rotated back to the submarine to sleep and take their places on watch.

Then, his crew gone, Captain Merrill headed off on his own liberty, not far behind his shipmates.

Two weeks later, *Batfish* was almost within sight of her next stop: Pearl Harbor, Hawaii. It was November 19, 1943. That was a few weeks shy of the second anniversary of the "day that will live in infamy," as an angry President Franklin Roosevelt characterized the brutal attack on the United States.

It was also eighty years to the day after another President, a solemn and subdued Abraham Lincoln, said, while dedicating a cemetery at Gettysburg, Pennsylvania, "that we here highly resolve that these dead shall not have died in vain." It might just as well have been spoken about the naval base that was coming up on the bow of *Batfish*.

As they drew within sight of Diamond Head, somebody put the boat's Victrola in front of the microphone for the PA system and played Hawaiian records. A couple of the enginemen danced a rather risqué hula up and down the narrow passage that ran alongside the engines. Everyone was in good spirits.

Those men who were topside admired the beauty of the island as it grew closer, exchanging recognition signals with a PBY circling overhead that had come out to greet them. PBY stands for "Patrol Boat," with the "Y" designating that the plane's manufacturer was Consolidated Aircraft Company. A minesweeper, YMS 286, steamed out of the mouth of the harbor to lead them in, flashing a friendly "Follow me" with its signal lights.

Then, before they knew it, they were inside Pearl Harbor.

Those who had not been there before looked about, expecting to see some signs of the vicious attack. They looked for the smoking hulks and twisted metal and canted battleships that they had seen in photos on the cover of *Life* magazine and in newsreels just before the Bugs Bunny cartoons at theaters. There were none. The *California*, the *Nevada*, the *Maryland*, and other battleships that had been so heavily damaged had been salvaged, repaired, and already sent out to fight the enemy that had inflicted the pain on them in the first place.

It was hard to believe such destruction had been erased in such a short passage of time.

But then, as they passed near where the *Arizona* still lay on the bottom of the harbor, where the once-proud vessel still expelled trickles of oil and air bubbles to mark the spot where she went down, there was a silent moment. The sunken wreck of the great battleship still held many of her dead. It was a tomb, a memorial, a makeshift cemetery down there beneath the calm waters of Pearl Harbor.

Every sailor aboard *Batfish* likely held the same thought—they had not died in vain.

Submarine pay. Good food. Escape from the prospect of working in the coal mines. Adventure. To learn a trade. Whatever had brought these men to this service, to this boat, to this green-shrouded spot in the middle of a cobalt-blue ocean, it was secondary to that single grave promise.

That those men had not died in vain.

Batfish tied up at the submarine docks, near the tender USS *Griffin* (AS 13), a special ship that contained the offices of the division commanders and a supply of food, clothing, medicine, and the tools and spare parts necessary to repair just about anything that broke on a submarine. This particular ship had been a cargo vessel before the war, but she was acquired by the Navy and converted into a submarine tender in July 1941, before anyone knew for certain how valuable she would turn out to be. *Griffin* was in Newfoundland when the Japanese bombed Pearl Harbor and served in Australia, the Fiji Islands, and Bora-Bora before coming to Pearl. She would crisscross the Pacific many times over the next few years, playing nanny to a fleet of diesel smoke boats.

"I don't believe it!" yelped a young torpedoman as he helped tie off the lines that secured the *Batfish* to the pier.

"What?" his buddy asked, not even bothering to look at what had raised his buddy's curiosity.

"Who is that coming down the dock?"

The other sailor finished securing his line, straightened, and wiped the sweat from his forehead before he looked in the direction that his shipmate was pointing.

"Some big muckety-muck, judging from all that stuff on his cover . . . and the number of dogs sniffing along behind him."

"As I live and breathe, I think that is Admiral Charles A. Lockwood, in the flesh. And it looks like he's coming this way."

"You're loony, Billy. The big boss ain't got no truck with our little, bitty old boat. He's got a whole fleet to worry about."

"No, Eddie, that's him. I saw his picture in the *Saturday Evening Post*. And he's requesting permission to come aboard."

It was true. Lockwood had already achieved legendary status among submariners for the evenhanded, practical way he ran the submarine service during the war in the Pacific. He was next in command to Admiral Chester Nimitz and had been promoted to vice admiral only a month before *Batfish* got into town. Lockwood could be depended on always to back his skippers if he believed they had tried their best. He never castigated a boat's captain for returning from patrol without a kill. A former sub skipper himself, he knew as well as anyone how difficult a job it was out there. And it was clear to each of them that Lockwood deeply appreciated the men who fought and died under his command.

In his later book *Sink 'Em All,* Lockwood wrote: "They were no supermen, nor were they endowed with any supernatural qualities of heroism. They were merely top-notch American lads, well trained, well treated, well armed and provided with superb ships. May God grant there will be no World War III; but, if there is, whether it be fought with the weapons we know or with weapons at whose type we can only guess, submarines and submariners will be in the thick of the combat, fighting with skill, determination and matchless daring for all of us and for our United States of America."

So it shouldn't have been a surprise that the big boss showed up at the pier that morning to greet his newest submarine and her crew. That was the kind of commander he was.

Lockwood brought more than greetings to Captain Merrill. As an early Christmas present, *Batfish* was about to be refitted with a new, more powerful type of SJ radar that would be much more effective in night radar surface attacks than her existing set was.

"Wayne, this gear will give you capabilities we've never had out there before," he told Captain Merrill over coffee in the wardroom. "And as far as I know, you're the only one in the Pacific who will have it for a while. Use it well, Skipper."

Since radar was first used on submarines, it had been the SD type, which searched the airspace in all directions at once while the sub was on the surface or just below it, deep enough to be hidden but shallow enough so the radar antenna stuck up above the sea's surface. SD radar was mostly nondirectional. It gave a reflection that confirmed something was out there, just not much about what it was, how big it was, or—most crucial—from which direction it was coming.

The new SJ radar used a rotating antenna, and that allowed the unit to report very accurately the bearing for anything they might encounter out there, whether it was on the surface of the ocean or in the sky.

Shortly after Lockwood finished his cup of coffee and said his goodbyes, a platoon of technicians climbed aboard *Batfish* and began ripping out cables and tearing into boxes that contained the old radar. It would stay, but they would also have the benefit of the new gear that would be installed on top of it. At the same time, the radio crew learned that their stay in Hawaii would mostly consist of classes, training them on how to operate and get the most use out of the new equipment.

The rest of the crew wasn't much better off insofar as liberty was concerned. There was more training for them to complete as well. Soon they would be in enemy waters, facing a skilled adversary motivated not only by his quasi-religious beliefs in the sanctity of preserving their Emperor's glory but by desperation as well. The Allies were wreaking havoc, and the Japanese were fighting back with all they had.

It was dangerous out there. Men were dying. Submarines were being lost with all hands much too often.

But all it took to remind them of the righteousness of what they were doing was their daily comings and goings past that spot in the harbor, the sacred patch of water where all those fellow sailors met their demise—many of them as they slept in their bunks—the morning of Sunday, December 7, 1941.

There was little grousing about all the work they had to do to get ready for their first patrol. They knew what was coming. They would soon be out there, beyond the hump of Diamond Head, doing their duty to make sure their shipmates had not died in vain.

SIX

Midway on
the Scope

November 1943

The *Batfish* crew had noticed right away that Wayne Merrill could be two different people. It depended on whether they were at sea or ashore on liberty. When they were running their boat or training the crew, their skipper was the consummate by-the-book captain, a hard-core perfectionist. There was no nonsense tolerated, and his stern demeanor appeared to be even more pronounced than usual when they were conducting an exercise or in the midst of a training mission.

But when they were ashore and on leave, he was as social as any enlisted man and seemed to leave rank behind when he crossed from the deck of the submarine to the pier. It was not unusual at all to have him invite his crew members, regardless of rank, to come over and join him at a bar or nightclub, even when he had female accompaniment or was at a table filled with fellow officers. The enlisted sailors usually took him up on the invitation, too, since it was his custom to buy several rounds of drinks for everyone at the table. No sailor could turn down free booze!

Crew members also noticed that their skipper was able to get by perfectly well with very little sleep. He actually seemed to thrive on it. The man was indefatigable.

Despite the pleasures of the Royal Hawaiian Hotel and the other establishments in Honolulu that catered to sailors, the *Batfish* crew was anxious to get going on their first war patrol. As hard as they partied, they worked even harder at completing their final sea drills before they would steam away and encounter the enemy at sea. Other than the continuing friction between Merrill and a member or two of his wardroom staff, the crew seemed to be jelling, working well together and about as proficient as they would ever be at the various stations and equipment on the boat, including the newly installed SJ radar.

Toward the end of November 1943, Captain Merrill wrote in his deck log, "Under way conducting radar rehearsals, radar tracking, and night radar rehearsals. Received two indoctrinational depth charges."

"Indoctrinational" indeed. *Batfish* was operating out of Pearl that morning of November 28, 1943, sitting at periscope depth within sight of a friendly destroyer that was playing the part of an enemy vessel while the submarine practiced using the new radar and honed her stalking technique. The "enemy" destroyer had no trouble keeping track of *Batfish* because she wore a big bright red flag tied to the highest point of her shears—the top of the attack periscope. The flag was lashed to the boat in order to avoid any sudden moves that might result in a collision that could be detrimental to both vessels.

"You boys ready to see what it feels like getting depth-charged?" Captain Merrill asked the crew members who were working around him in the conning tower. They must have missed the mischievous twinkle in the skipper's eyes.

"Sure!"

"Yes, sir!"

He allowed a small smile to play at his lips as he gave the order to close on the destroyer. And he proceeded to take the submarine much closer than the operational orders specified for this particular drill.

The sailors on the destroyer did their part. They dropped their practice depth charges almost directly on top of the submarine. While their explosive power wasn't enough to do mortal damage to *Batfish*, they certainly packed enough oomph to rattle the fillings in the teeth of the fresh-faced young crew members who had never experienced combat before. To these rookies, it sounded like the destroyer had dropped the damn things right down the hatch into the conning tower. Even some of the old hands got wide-eyed and turned pale when far more than the usual amount of seawater began raining down on them from around the number two periscope.

Later, they found that the packing around the scope had been knocked loose, and it had to be repaired before they could leave on their initial war patrol. But of more concern, they discovered that the beautiful new SJ radar antenna had not been properly installed and its shock mounts had failed. If that had happened in the heat of battle, leaving them virtually blind in the middle of an attack, far out in enemy-controlled waters, it could have placed the crew in desperate peril.

But, as Merrill reminded them, that was why they did such testing in the first place. If the new sub couldn't take indoctrinational depth charges, rolled off the deck of a friendly destroyer, they needed to know it now and not weeks later in the South China Sea or amid the Celebes, when the explosives would be for real and much more potent, and those delivering the charges inclined to put the boat and its crew on the ocean's floor.

Finally, after test-firing torpedoes and deck guns, rehearsing endlessly with the new radar, diving and surfacing over and over again until each crewman could perform all of their procedures from any station on the boat and in their sleep, practicing surface and submerged attacks, and running through every scenario they could ever imagine, the boat and her crew were declared ready for sea on December 11, 1943.

Just over seven months after her launch, the *Batfish* was declared fit to go out there and kick the Japanese in the teeth.

When a submarine left port to go on patrol, she was stuffed to the gills with enough supplies to support the boat and six or seven dozen hungry men. There was hardly room for crew members after she was loaded with her complement of torpedoes and ammunition, and enough stores to last for the length of the patrol. The showers were piled full of sacks of potatoes and flour. Cans of foodstuffs were stacked several rows high along all the boat's walkways. Crew members literally walked around on their groceries.

The boat would get hungry, too. Her fuel tanks were filled to the brim with diesel fuel, giving a *Balao*-class boat like *Batfish* a range of about ten thousand miles at nominal speeds.

Every man aboard on the day they steamed away, headed for their first war patrol, was aware that he was leaving Pearl Harbor just a few days past the second anniversary of the sneak attack by the Japanese. They had come aboard as patriotic, thrill-seeking kids, aiming for revenge and a generous dose of excitement and to learn a trade they could use later in life. They were now highly trained submariners, honed at their tasks and ready to do their duty.

They left Pearl just after noon with one additional passenger aboard for the trip. He was a priest, Lieutenant W. S. Brown, to whom they were giving a lift to Midway Island. Some aboard saw that as a good omen.

Once they got to Midway, they would top off their fuel tanks, giving them another three thousand miles of range. They would also complete any needed repairs and pick up their operational orders telling them where to go and what to do when they got there.

It had just gotten dark when *Batfish* sent her escort vessel back to Oahu and steamed along all by herself. Those on the bridge noted what a beautiful night it was, with a full tropical moon painting shimmering streaks in the water and the fragrance of the island following them long after they had left the final view of land off their stern. It was as if she were reluctant to let them go.

The guys operating the radar were having fun, seeing what they could pick up with its startlingly increased sensitivity and directional ability. They painted the small island of Kauai with their strong signal and watched its profile glowing on their screen, even though the spike of land was almost twenty-five miles behind them by then. Then, just to impress everyone aboard, they proudly announced that they had picked up the reflection of a box floating on the sea's surface almost a mile away. These new sophisticated toys were just a fraction of the innovations incorporated on U.S. subs, reflecting the vessels' operational task on the ever-changing war front—that of hunter/killer.

There had been considerable debate among the high-end Navy brass between World Wars I and II about the best use of submarines. Some believed the odd hybrid vessels were better suited to protecting harbors and to defensively patrolling the coasts and not really much good for anything else. Destroyers and aircraft carriers could do the heavy lifting, fighting the major sea battles.

Others, like Rear Admiral Thomas Withers, had a different view. Withers is considered to be the father of the long-range submarine and, at the time of the construction of *Batfish*, he was the commandant of the

Portsmouth Naval Shipyard where she was born. He was convinced that the boats could be constructed to carry bigger crews, have a much longer range, and be as offensive a weapon as anything the Navy could put afloat. All the proponents of the more aggressive submarine had to do was point to what the Germans were doing with their U-boats, which spanned half the planet to attack with fearsome results. That was enough to convince those who were charged with making the decision to go ahead with their plans to create the boats like *Batfish* and her sharp-toothed sisters.

As this new class of fleet boats was being designed and built, the Navy's brighter thinkers also made certain that the submarine's inherent strengths were maintained. Subs didn't necessarily have to be able to dive and stay down for days. They just needed to be able to get beneath the surface in a big hurry, be capable of going deep enough to hide, and have the ability to stay down long enough to evade any enemy that came after them.

The designers also had the foresight to make the submarine a fully capable surface attack vessel as well. In fact, the *Gato*- and *Balao*-class boats were faster and more maneuverable on the surface than they were when they were beneath the ocean. They handled better up top than some surface vessels did.

A sub skipper always had the option of a surface assault, attacking while he and his team were on the bridge, or of a submerged attack, using the periscopes in the conning tower and radar to keep tabs on what they were shooting at. At night, or when the target was slow enough to not be able to run away if it sighted its attacker, a surface assault was perfectly acceptable, as it was when the target was likely to be unarmed or unescorted and there didn't appear to be any air cover. The commander would most likely attack without diving, leaving all his options available to him. He could always sound the klaxon, send the boat down, and scat if somebody hostile showed up.

A scope attack was a bit trickier, but took advantage of the submarine's greatest asset: stealth. With nothing sticking up above the surface but the periscope and radar antenna, she could watch a target like a submerged gator, stalking her game until the poor quarry swam right into perfect shooting range. Then, without any warning whatsoever, the sub could fire her torpedoes and skedaddle before destroyer escorts or the target even knew she was there. Submarine victims often had no way to defend themselves from such an attacker, and they didn't know what to strike back at once they were aware that they were being fired upon.

The submarine was a nearly perfect war machine.

The vessels had other jobs besides launching torpedoes at unsuspecting ships. Subs also laid mines in harbors, hauled ammunition into hard-to-reach battle zones, provided forward observer information, transported troops, deployed secret agents, collected intelligence on troop movements and shipping, delivered guerrilla leaders and supplies behind enemy lines, and rescued over five hundred downed aviators during World War II, including one flyboy named George H. W. Bush, who would one day become President of the United States.

Once the war started, and once some problems with the torpedoes were solved, the results of the insight of Admiral Withers and his cohorts were spectacular. The numbers vary slightly depending on the source, but they are quite impressive. Submarines operating in the Pacific war are generally credited with sinking over half a million tons' worth of Japanese warships, numbering just over two hundred vessels. Just as important, they sent to the bottom over a thousand merchant ships—almost five million tons. Between military and merchant targets, U.S. Navy submarines accounted for better than half of all Japanese ships lost during the war. This represents more kills than the surface Navy, the airplanes of the Army Air Corps, and the Navy's carrier-based aircraft *combined*.

One submarine, the USS *Tang*, sank twenty-four enemy ships, for almost 95,000 tons destroyed. That was the highest total for any boat during the war.

Consider, too, that all this was accomplished by a mere 2 percent of the Navy. This 2 percent sank 30 percent of the Imperial Japanese Navy vessels that were lost, and 60 percent of all merchant ships that were sent to the bottom.

That success came at a cost, of course—a cost of over 3,500 lives lost. One in five submarine sailors who served during the war died. Fifty-two submarines were gone forever.

By 1943, American tactics in the Pacific had changed. Before then the primary aim was to chase and destroy military targets in an effort to blunt the Japanese offensive. But in the summer of 1942, the Empire seized a few tactical islands in the vertebrae of the Aleutians. It would be the last of their expansion; the Japanese shifted their strategy to do all they could in order to hold on to the lands over which they had gained control, digging in and hanging on in the face of the Allied effort to root them out, sometimes a few inches at a time.

Nineteen forty-three was also the first year in which the United States was able to build more ships than were being sunk by Japan and Germany. The war had most certainly turned.

At that point, U.S. naval operations in general—and submarine targets in particular—were switched to try to deny the aggressive Japanese the supplies they needed to survive on their expanded empire. Without food and shoes and oil and bullets, it would be impossible for them to sustain their war effort, no matter how tenacious or fanatical the Japanese were. Certainly battleships, cruisers, and aircraft carriers were still prime targets, prizes to be claimed whenever practical. But merchant vessels and tankers moved right on up the list of desired targets to almost equal stature with warships. And even when the supply ships were not sunk, the constant harassment forced merchant ships and convoys into erratic, zigzagging courses to try to avoid attack, delaying delivery of vitally needed goods. Also, expensive air and sea protection burned up valuable fuel and kept Japanese warships away from their usual jobs, running direct defense against the Americans.

Farther north, plans were already being made for an eventual D-Day-like invasion of the Japanese homeland. These plans were, however, being made with great trepidation. Such an assault would, without doubt, be even bloodier than the one when the Allies finally hit the beach at Normandy was expected to be. But the military planners pressed ahead with the strong belief that such a wave-after-wave direct attack would be the only way to end Japan's desire to own the entire Pacific basin and to finally bring peace to the world.

Of course, unbeknownst to most of those making the invasion plans, experimentation on a whole new kind of weapon was under way in Oak Ridge, Tennessee, and on the shifting sands of New Mexico.

"The Gadget," as it was called, would be a weapon that would eventually, and in two short instants, make invasion unnecessary and would change warfare fundamentally and forever. A weapon so awful that the test director at the first experimental blast, Kenneth Bainbridge, watched the mushroom cloud rise skyward and quietly said, "Now we are all sons of bitches."

Seas grew rougher as *Batfish* made her way toward Midway, a six-square-mile dot of land in the middle of the Pacific. Small or not, the islands were a logistic savior for American warships. Reclaiming Midway from the Japanese in 1942 had been a true fulcrum in the war. On this trip, though, most aboard the newly minted submarine were only too anxious to get to any solid piece of land, tiny or not, considering the state of their stomachs. The truth was that the combination of rough swells and well-earned hangovers was enough to have turned many of the crew members a pronounced shade of green.

Many in the crew appreciated their chaplain hitchhiker, Lieutenant Brown, holding services while they were in transit. Even if he was suffering from a bad case of seasickness and had to pause in his sermon a time or two to heave. As the skipper wrote in his patrol log the evening of December 12, "Our passenger to Midway . . . valiantly fought off an attack of nausea long enough to hold the first divine service in a U.S. submarine en route to a patrol area."

As the giddy radar operators aboard *Batfish* watched Midway appear on their scope and gradually move toward its center, they knew little of the high-level planning that was going on in an attempt to hasten the end of the war. Their sights were much narrower. They and their shipmates knew only what they had to do on their watch to shorten the conflict. They knew nothing of invasion plans or a weapon that could annihilate hundreds of thousands of people in a second. They simply had to sink Japanese vessels—military or merchant—anywhere they saw them, and do it without getting their own asses shot off. They didn't doubt for a moment that they would be able to do their part.

There was reason for optimism. Not only did they ride in the most advanced war machine on the planet, but also they had the new radar to give them even more advantage. And forward and aft, in both torpedo rooms, they carried fish that finally had been proven to do what they had been designed to do.

Earlier in the war, submarine skippers were reporting a flabbergasting amount of dud torpedoes. They reported a disturbing number of instances in which they had watched their torpedoes, rigged with detonators that were supposed to explode on contact, ram full force into the sides of targets, only to bounce off harmlessly. Other fish with magnetic detonators, designed to explode when they came into close proximity with anything big and metal, like a Japanese battleship, would simply run innocuously past, boring through the sea right beneath an enemy's hull, and keep running until they ran out of fuel and sank harmlessly to the bottom of the ocean.

The skipper of USS *Tinosa* (SS 283) reported one especially harrowing experience in July of 1943. On her second war patrol, she was operating under the command of Lieutenant Lawrence Daspit, looking for targets near Borneo, when she spied an eighteen thousand–ton tanker. The skipper quickly lined up for the attack. The first Mark 14 torpedo they fired hit amidships and exploded, heavily damaging the vessel and leaving her dead in the water.

Daspit quickly ordered another torpedo fired at the stationary target. She would be hard to miss. He wanted to finish her off quickly so they could hightail it away from the area. The smoke from the burning hulk would be visible for miles to any patrolling enemy aircraft or warships. The second torpedo ran true and hit hard into the metal side of the tanker, but as Daspit watched through his binoculars from *Tinosa*'s bridge, the torpedo bounced out of the water, up into the air, and sank without an explosion.

The skipper ordered another shot, then another, and another.

In all, he fired an additional *thirteen* torpedoes at the stricken vessel, and not one detonated. The whole baker's dozen were duds.

Though he had one more torpedo left and loaded into a tube, ready to fire, Daspit decided to save it for inspection by the Ordnance Department at Pearl Harbor, to see if they could figure out why the weapons simply didn't work. They stayed around long enough to see the tanker eventually sink, then turned and headed for Hawaii.

Sure enough, the fourteenth of *Tinosa*'s torpedoes was a dud, too. Admiral Lockwood personally took responsibility for firing it against an underwater cliff. He had been trying to tell his superiors all along that the torpedoes were not working properly, that his skippers were not as incompetent as the higher-ups insisted they were.

Still, and despite anecdotal evidence galore, it was easier for the brass back in the States to blame the sub commanders for the lousy kill rate. They maintained that the skippers were setting the fish to run too deep or too shallow, or weren't taking the time to properly aim, or were not making sure the detonators were armed properly. The skippers knew better, but there were just enough relatively inexperienced captains who did mess up that they were unable to make a strong enough case to convince the people who counted that it was all the fault of the hardware.

Still, work was being done on a new class of torpedo that everyone hoped would prove to be much more reliable. The primary problem was that the Navy considered torpedoes to be too expensive and too scarce to waste on testing (never mind that $7 million submarines and the sailors to crew them were relatively precious, too). Most of the testing took place in the Pacific, firing at real targets.

Batfish was loaded with this latest class of torpedo, the Mark 18, the Navy's newest weapon. These babies would actually explode when they hit something solid—or at least the crew hoped they would.

There was another reason for optimism as *Batfish* eased into her slip on Midway and began the process of charging her banks of batteries, refueling her big tanks, and taking on still more supplies. Submarine kills in the Pacific Ocean had doubled from 1942 to 1943. With better training, better equipment, and a growing library of successful war patrols and tactics to study, the submarine was becoming a solid player in the war effort.

It was not all good news, though. Twice as many boats had been lost already in 1943 compared to all of 1942—fifteen to seven.

One of those boats was the USS *Corvina* (SS 226), sunk on November 16, 1943, less than a month before *Batfish* arrived in Midway. She was on her very first patrol, under the helm of Commander Roderick Rooney, operating near the Gilbert Islands. Around the first of December, she failed to acknowledge a series of messages. Later, patrol logs from a Japanese submarine would describe spotting what is believed to have been the *Corvina* on the surface. The Japanese sub fired three torpedoes at her. Two hit with what the Japanese skipper described as "a great explosion sound," and the submarine sank immediately. All hands were lost.

Immediately before taking command of *Batfish*, Captain Wayne Merrill had served briefly aboard *Corvina* during her sea trials.

The skipper's amazing streak of near misses was still alive.

SEVEN

Christmas with "Tokyo Rose"

December 1943

The last thing to come off *Batfish* the day she departed the Navy base at Midway for her first war patrol was an innocent-looking envelope. It contained a small stack of classified papers that were not crucial to the mission on which she was about to embark. The secret papers were to be placed for safekeeping aboard the sub tender USS *Bushnell* (AS 15). That way, if the worst happened, and *Batfish* came under fire, the documents would not fall into enemy hands.

As they left the tiny island behind that morning, most of the men aboard had no idea where they were headed. Only Captain Wayne Merrill and his officers knew their destination: They were bound for "patrol area 6-A," a prime, rectangular-shaped hunting ground that stretched southward from one of the southern Japanese home islands, Shikoku. Of course, thanks to the rapid dissemination of information, rumor, and conjecture aboard the confined space of the sub, within hours, most everyone on the boat knew that they would be within spitting distance of the Empire, and not far from the fearsome Bungo and Kii straits. The narrow passes that separate the main Japanese islands were known to be submarine graveyards.

For most of the crew, too, this would be their first taste of combat. Sure, they had been through all the simulations, the endless drills, had heard the horror of the colorful sea stories relayed to them by the few old hands on board. But soon they would face the real thing themselves. Despite the bravado of youth, most every man who had not been through it yet wondered what a sea assault would be like. How the man on either side of him would perform. How he himself would react when faced with a brutal enemy intent on killing him.

No one admitted fear. They rarely even talked about the quickly approaching danger. It simply wasn't something to discuss. Instead they spoke of home, of scuttlebutt, of what silliness or mischief some shipmate had perpetrated while on leave back in Hawaii.

But it wasn't the Imperial Japanese Navy that first rattled the *Batfish* on the patrol. It was a storm that bordered on being a bona fide typhoon, whipping the sea into a frenzy with thirty- and forty-knot gusts. Merrill kept the boat submerged as much as he dared, seeking a smoother ride at depth. But they had to stay up top as much as possible, too, to ensure that batteries were fully powered so they could dive if something far more ominous than a Pacific typhoon charged at them. Too, they could make only minimal speed when submerged, and they needed to get to their assigned patrol box as soon as they could. Other vessels were depending on their being where they were supposed to be, on time and ready for a fight.

Bob Fulton and Robert Thompson were on watch in the control room, doing their jobs as well as they could manage on the roller coaster on which they suddenly found themselves. They held on to anything solid, doing all they could do to keep from getting thrown about the compartment with the boat's violent rocking and rolling. Thompson carried a bucket with him because seasickness was threatening to purge him of his last meal at any moment. Fulton noticed his shipmate's distress and couldn't resist giving him a rough time.

"You know what I'd really like to have right now?" he asked, smacking his lips.

"Aw, Steamboat, don't."

"Yeah, I'd like to have me a big old greasy pork chop, covered with gravy, and . . ."

Fulton couldn't fight it any longer. He buried his head in the bucket and lost his breakfast. But Fulton wasn't finished.

"You know what you need, partner? You need an oyster on a string. That way you could swallow it down and not even have to wait for it to come back up. Just give that string a yank and . . ."

Thompson was already back facedown in his bucket.

When the boat was on the surface, procedure required lookouts to be in the shears, lashed to a structure to keep from getting washed or blown away. Someone would also man the bridge. The wind-driven rain made their binoculars virtually useless and kept them soaked to the skin beneath any amount of foul-weather gear they may have donned.

"I reckon a Nip plane could sneak right up on us if he was a mind to," one of the lookouts said to another, yelling to be heard over the squalling of the wind and the pounding of the sea against their bow.

"I reckon so," was the reply. It was just too hard to talk. And besides, like Thompson, breakfast was hanging heavy in this young sailor's gut as he and his perch swayed continuously from side to side in the towering waves.

That was when radar reported a pip that was obviously an airplane, six miles out and closing rapidly.

"Keep an eye at bearing oh-three-oh," Captain Merrill called up to the lookouts. He already had one hand on the dive klaxon, just in case the aircraft bore the rising-sun logo when it came into view.

"I see him!" one of the sharp-eyed youngsters shouted. "It's one of ours. A B-52."

Merrill still kept the klaxon close at hand as he ordered that the boat identify herself to the bomber by searchlight. Thank goodness for the radar, alerting them to the approaching plane. And for the sharp eyesight of his lookouts.

The bomber signaled back as he circled the sub, bobbing in the roiling seas, then turned and flew away.

Merrill snorted. Odd that something as basic as the exchange of "friend or foe" recognition signals was more reliable out here, this close to their mortal enemies in Japan, than it was within sight of the U. S. coast or in the Caribbean.

The slow going had them way behind schedule but they couldn't hurry without risking foundering the boat. By December 19, *Batfish* was over a hundred miles from where she was scheduled to be. Forward speed had been trimmed to less than ten knots to keep water from spilling down the hatch into the conning tower every time there was a change of watch. Worse still would be if water made it into the main engine air-induction lines—the engines needed air, not ocean water, to run.

It was miserable out in the weather, but submarine life below decks during a storm was no picnic, either. Lookouts coming off watch were drenched and chilled as they peeled off rain gear and wrapped themselves in blankets. Subs like *Batfish* were air-conditioned, but a rain-soaked sailor didn't really appreciate such constant amenities. Anytime the hatch was opened, gallons of frigid Pacific Ocean spilled down into the conning tower, shorting out electrical equipment and lighting fixtures, leaving those on watch in the cramped compartment with water up to their ankles and sparks around their ears. The combination of tropical moisture and air-conditioning had metal bulkheads in most compartments sweating, creating slick and uncertain surfaces. Bedding and clothing were quickly damp and smelly and uncomfortable to sleep on or wear. The boat was rolling sickeningly, too, thirty or forty degrees at a time, and sometimes an especially vicious and totally unexpected wall of water would pound them into a lurching yaw that had anyone who was not lashed down or holding on to something solid rolling around on the deck, bouncing off the walls and jagged equipment corners.

Captain Merrill ordered that the radioman call a weather report back to Pearl so that other boats could be routed around the storm and avoid misery, danger, and delay. But there was nothing he could do for his own vessel but paddle on and try to outrun the storm. Drive on, despite waves that looked to measure thirty or forty feet high.

There could be no hot meals. It was too dangerous to try to cook anything in the galley. One of the cooks had already been burned badly when he tried to catch a flying coffeemaker. Supper was cheese and crackers, tins of sardines, canned peaches, or a ham sandwich. So much for that fine submarine cuisine.

On one especially pronounced tumbling roll, the entire library of 78 rpm records for the boat's Victrola slid out of their storage compartment and broke like glass on the deck. Most disheartening for the crew, it also cost them a half dozen blueberry pies that had been baked before things got so rough. That catastrophe made one sailor mutter about enlisting in the infantry next time.

In all compartments up and down the narrow walkways, items rolled around, garbage was strewn, personal effects scampered free, vomit spilled from overturned buckets. It looked as if the monsoon had been on the inside of the boat. But there was no point in cleaning up the mess until the carnival thrill ride they were on finally ended.

It seemed it never would. For five days the crew steamed on, buffeted by harassing wind and water. Some speculated that Hirohito must have conjured up this storm, just to welcome *Batfish* to his part of the world. They could clutch to the hope that the weather would give them a break if they ever reached their patrol area.

As they drew deeper into enemy waters, Captain Merrill took the boat down more frequently, seeking calm so they could check the condition of their load of torpedoes. The crewmen took advantage of the blessed tranquillity to tie up anything that could be tied, and to do as much housecleaning as they could. The batteries were a mess. Electrolyte had spilled out of the cells and a strong odor of acid reacting with the seawater that had spilled down the hatch from the bridge made everyone's eyes tear and sting. A work party went down and washed as much of the acid away as they could. It wasn't merely a quest for neatness. The gas could cause illness and even death if it was not cleaned up or vented. And that would be difficult to do if an enemy patrol plane or destroyer chased them to the depths.

At about two in the afternoon, they surfaced and were pleasantly surprised to see that the storm had finally broken. The wind had died down noticeably and the seas were comparatively calm. The sun was trying to peek through a thinning overcast.

That was when one of the officers reminded them all that it was Christmas Eve.

With the better weather and the prospects of a special holiday dinner the next day, spirits ran high aboard *Batfish*. The fact that they were almost a thousand miles from the spot south of Japan where they were supposed to be was conveniently forgotten.

As the crew members enjoyed turkey, stuffing, yams, and pumpkin pie for their Christmas Day dinner, they also had the benefit of a pastime that was a guilty pleasure for many soldiers and sailors fighting in the Pacific— listening to the broadcasts by Tokyo Rose, beamed across the region from the Japanese homeland on Radio Tokyo. American servicemen gave the name "Tokyo Rose" to a collective group of females who hosted music shows and spouted Japanese propaganda in English between the songs that were played. There was never actually a single Tokyo Rose and the women never referred to themselves by that name, though the name gained notoriety when one Japanese-American, Iva Ikuko Toguri, was convicted of treason for her alleged participation in the broadcasts.

The music played during the broadcasts was well received by Americans so far from any other source of familiar entertainment, especially now that their Victrola records were shattered. Except for those times when the women broadcast information that was too close to the truth about attacks and sunken ships and lost submarines, their crude party line was often more humorous than demoralizing. And their taunts often did more to fire up the troops than to demoralize them.

As the *Batfish* shipmates enjoyed their delicious and hearty holiday meal, the sounds of the Japanese broadcast were piped throughout the boat. Through the staccato static crashes and whining interference, they could hear some of their favorite Christmas carols, compliments of the enemy. When their mouths weren't full of mashed potatoes or pie topped with whipped cream, some of them sang along with the familiar lyrics.

When the music died out and the female host began talking, she said, "Our Christmas selections today are especially going out to you American submariners out there. You know who you are." The men went suddenly quiet. The host went on. "You are all alone, while your wives and mothers and babies cry themselves to sleep because you are not home with them on Christmas. Draft dodgers back home eat turkey and stuffing and pie, and you are forced to eat cockroaches and mice, and you are happy to get it."

The howls of laughter throughout the boat drowned out the next holiday selection that boomed out from Radio Tokyo.

As they plowed on through the Pacific, trying to get to their patrol area, every man aboard knew it was only a matter of time before they encountered their first enemy contact. It finally came at just after four in the morning, in the cloudy, predawn blackness of December 27, 1943.

"Captain, contact!" The voice of the youngster manning the radar set, still in the throes of puberty, broke in excitement. He cleared his throat and went on. "Contact, Captain! Target is at eighteen thousand yards, tracking west!" The young sailor's timbre climbed higher with each word until "west" came out almost as a screech. Nobody giggled. Each man felt the kid's excitement as surely as he did.

Their first enemy contact!

The familiar chime of the general alarm bells sounded throughout the boat just as they had in so many drills, but they sounded different this time—more insistent, almost strident. They could feel the boat decelerate as the skipper brought their speed back to one-third so they could get a good look at whatever it was out there in the last of the darkness.

There were still rain showers in the area, the clouds masking any other potential light, and it was still several hours before sunup. The lookouts could see nothing but ink.

A minor argument had broken out between the two men studying the radar scope data. One said the pips represented a small vessel being escorted by another. The second man maintained it was two patrol boats.

The XO didn't care which one it turned out to be. He was debating with another officer about the best way to attack and sink whatever they were.

"We could do a surface radar attack. Visibility is no more than a couple thousand yards. If we can't see them, they can't see us. We could kill them before they even knew what hit 'em."

"Maybe," the other officer agreed. "But as slow as they're going, we could do an end run and sneak up on them at first light, submerged. We could see for certain what we were shooting at before we wasted any torpedoes."

But the man who would make the ultimate decision was up on the bridge, staring into the night. When the executive officer climbed the ladder from the con and reviewed the options he and the other officer had been discussing, Wayne Merrill merely stroked his chin and thought some more.

"I don't want to shoot at something I can't actually see," he finally said. As good as the crew was getting with the SJ radar, he had learned his craft from the old-line sub skippers—ones who preferred to watch their torpedoes all the way until impact. They didn't care whether that observation was from the bridge or from the periscope, with their boats nicely hidden from the other guys' lookouts and radar. "Besides, we don't know for sure where we are by now. It's been a while since our last fix."

The XO shrugged. He knew how anxious his boys were to engage the enemy. But the skipper was probably right to be cautious. Best do it by the book than have their maiden voyage be their only one.

"One of 'em is flashing a light, Captain!" came the call from the shears.

"I see it, son."

Sure enough, there was a shimmering light out there on the horizon, blinking at them. Had the Japanese captain detected their radar?

The radar operator chimed in next.

"Captain, the escort—the one we think may be the escort—has turned, and he's coming our way. Fast!"

"Range?"

"Fifteen thousand yards and closing."

Merrill ordered the boat turned as he tried to open some distance between him and the approaching enemy vessel. He had to have detected the SJ. It was too dark. No other way for him to have known *Batfish* was out here. Not even if he was equipped with the junk the IJN were calling "radar" aboard their boats.

"Range twenty thousand yards," came the report. They were opening a gap.

Merrill's executive officer nudged his skipper.

"What are you doing, Wayne?"

"We'll keep them twenty to twenty-five thousand yards away. Then, when it's daylight, we'll take a look at them through the scope. See what they are and if they're worth the taxpayers' weapons."

Admittedly, the first contact for *Batfish* was presenting quite a quandary.

The target didn't seem in any particular hurry to go anywhere. And just when Captain Merrill was convinced the escort was going to chase them all the way to Taiwan, the guy suddenly veered away and headed back to be near the other vessel. If the target had some kind of radar Merrill didn't know about, he may have known only too well that an enemy submarine was out there, stalking him. He may have called in air cover already, set to pounce on them at first light. Or he and his buddy might be getting ready to give chase at that very minute.

"I don't like the way this smells," the captain said. "And I'm not sure we have time to waste sitting here and watching him meander along. We need to get to where we're supposed to be."

The navigator used an old-fashioned sextant and took advantage of a brief break in the cloud cover to determine precisely where in the world they were. Radar kept surveillance on the target and its escort, watching them as they slowly, deliberately made their way between the tiny islands that dotted the sea near the Japanese homeland. Darkness and passing squalls prevented the lookouts from seeing anything at all since spotting the brief flash of the searchlight half an hour before.

Later, Wayne Merrill would detail his decision in his entry into *Batfish*'s deck log for December 27, 1943.

> 5:02 A.M. In consideration of the appearance of the target pips on the radar screen, his apparent destination, his patrolling tactics, etc., decided that he was not worth a chase and I set course for my own area. It was a difficult decision to make, and I didn't feel particularly aggressive in letting him go, although my decision was based upon the following data.
>
> a) Am late for my own area.
> b) *Salmon* close behind me and I want to clear her area.
> c) Want to avoid disclosing my presence further, if practicable.
> d) Estimate target to have been either a small supply vessel running between southern islands and returning northward probably empty, under escort, or else an antisubmarine radar-equipped patrol.
> e) According to my navigational position I would have to run close aboard Sumisu Shima in order to attack, with visibility very low.

The two sailors talking quietly in the maneuvering room didn't have the benefit of seeing their skipper's logic as inscribed in the deck log.

"Okay, smart-ass, you tell me why we turned tail and ran without even getting close to that target?" the younger one asked.

"Listen, you don't know what all was going on. The skipper has his reasons."

"All I know is we had some Nips in our crosshairs and we didn't even try to shoot 'em."

The older sailor looked around, making sure no one could hear the complaints of his younger shipmate.

"You watch what you say, boy. You been in the Navy long enough to know you don't question your captain."

"I just know what I saw. And what I heard about Captain Merrill." The boyish sailor leaned across the board, with its spiky row of levers and handles, put his face close to that of his shipmate, and talked more quietly. "You heard what some of the crew's saying. How he's turned skittish with all them close calls he's had. You heard what he said out there on that barge before we left. That his main job was to get us and his new submarine back in one piece. Nothing about sinking no Japanese ships."

The older sailor gently pushed his shipmate back out of his face.

"I'll say it again. You better watch what you say about the skipper or you'll spend the rest of the war in the brig. Then how you gonna get any of that little girl you were making sparks with at the Royal Hawaiian?"

"Awww!"

The young sailor was still mumbling under his breath as he stepped back through the doorway into the aft torpedo room and headed for where his bunk hung there among the stack of still-unused torpedoes. They had just missed their first opportunity to strike a glorious, vengeful blow against the enemy that had murdered so many shipmates at Pearl Harbor.

What were they waiting for? An engraved invitation from the Emperor, begging them to please shoot their asses off?

The sailor was still muttering to himself as he dozed off.

EIGHT

"A Screwball Idea"

September 1967

The members of the Oklahoma sub vets group got an inkling of how serious Ace Kelly was this time about his big plans for bringing a fleet boat to the middle of the Dust Bowl when they received his letter. Addressed to "Ole Submariner!" it was primarily a dun for dues owed to the group. At that time, it cost four dollars per year to be a member of the Oklahoma Submarine Veterans organization. That also included membership in the national group, the United States Submarine Veterans of World War II, and a subscription to *Polaris*, the big organization's magazine.

Another paragraph in the form letter talked about the success of the Oklahoma group's scholarship fund, with a report about the son of the former chief electrician's mate on the *Wahoo* who had just completed medical school, thanks to help from the state sub vets group.

In the final paragraph, Kelly added, almost as an afterthought, "As you know, navigation on the Arkansas River to the head of navigation at Catoosa will be a reality next fiscal year. Our chief project and our intended primary accomplishment for this year will be the acquisition of a World War II fleet-type submarine."

There was never a question of "if" Kelly would get his submarine. At the time of the letter to his fellow sub veterans, it wasn't even a question of "when." It was going to happen and it was going to happen soon.

It was not a new idea. Kelly had floated the idea as early as 1962, when he brought up the subject at a state veterans' convention. But now it was clear he was finished biding his time. He was going to get his boat, and he was going to have it parked somewhere in the state of Oklahoma by the end of 1968.

As it turned out, Ace Kelly's optimism was just a bit premature.

Things looked good when, only a couple of months after Kelly's announcement, Oklahoma congressman Page Belcher contacted Paul Ignatius, the Secretary of the Navy, on behalf of the sub vets. The congressman made a compelling argument for allowing the group in his state to take possession of a fleet boat, even if theirs was an inland state and otherwise not connected in any way to submarines, sea assaults, or even salt water. In fact, Belcher's help made the project look so promising that Ace Kelly dashed off a note to Nick Guagliardo, another member of the sub vets group. Kelly suggested rather strongly that Guagliardo and sub vet "shipmate" E. E. Hendricks, who made up the land acquisition committee, get cracking on finding them a permanent site at which to moor their new/old boat, as it looked real promising that they were going to need it soon!

Kelly had performed some scouting on his own already. He had his eye on a site on the Verdigris River at Will Rogers Point near the little town of Catoosa. It was a pretty location, east of and not very far from downtown Tulsa, but Guagliardo did some checking of his own. He quickly determined that Kelly's desired mooring spot was out of the question. Land speculators had driven the price way too high already. Suburbs and shopping malls were coming that way, and it would be no place for an old submarine to come for her final mooring.

The Corps of Engineers was helpful—to a degree. They generously offered a spot on the Arkansas River about a hundred miles out of Tulsa. It was cheap, on what would someday be a navigable stream, and made up mostly of gently rolling land. But it was nowhere near a major highway, too far off the beaten path even for the most die-hard and dedicated submarine buff to wander, just so he could crawl around on an old boat. And Guagliardo knew they would have to depend on more paid admissions than just what they could get from old sub sailors.

The Corps of Engineers also casually informed Guagliardo that there was another slight problem with the spot. The land tended to be ten feet underwater anytime they had a wet winter. That wouldn't do. While a subma-

rine was designed to dive if need be, it wouldn't be good for business if their
main attraction was underwater when visitors showed up to take their tour.

Guagliardo politely turned down the Corps of Engineers' kind offer.

In the course of their conversation, when Guagliardo told the Army engineer why they wanted the mooring in the first place, the man laughed in
his face. He also told Guagliardo that he and his bunch of old submariners
had been breathing diesel fumes too long if they thought they'd ever be able
to bring a submarine to the area.

"I was treated very poorly and, in a roundabout way, was told we were
nuts," Guagliardo reported to the board.

Still, the government engineer must have admired Guagliardo's determination, if not his sanity. Or maybe he simply felt sorry for him and his misdirected bunch of pig boat sailors. The engineer discreetly shared a name
and a phone number of someone who might be able to help, but made him
swear he wouldn't tell anybody where he got the information.

Guagliardo didn't want to go back to Ace Kelly and have to explain to
him that, now that they had a line on a fleet boat, they didn't have a place to
park the thing. He quickly followed up with the person the Army engineer
had put him onto. Of course, he got more heckling and ridicule for his trouble, but still managed to get the second gentleman to share the technical information and some other key contacts that they needed in order to
investigate the new potential site. Even then, the man said not to mention
his name to anybody, that he wanted no part of such a wrongheaded idea.

Soon, they had identified a possible place to tie up their submarine—all
fingers were pointing to a spot on the Arkansas River, about fifty miles
southeast of Tulsa, in the little town of Muskogee.

Nick Guagliardo was also charged by the submarine vets group to go
back east and give a good look-see at another possible boat to bring to
Oklahoma. Guagliardo had grown up in Hammond, Louisiana, not far
from New Orleans. His hometown was along the main highway that ran
between Fort Polk, Louisiana, and Camp Shelby, Mississippi, both very
active Army bases during World War II. While in his teens, Guagliardo
took note of how the Army troops passing by his house had to travel
crammed together in the backs of uncomfortable trucks or march in loose

formation along the hot, dusty highway. They sometimes bivouacked along the road and slept on the ground, regardless of the weather or the ferocity of the bayou mosquitoes.

The young man decided he didn't favor the miserable existence of a foot soldier. His dad had been in the Navy, so as soon as he turned seventeen in January 1943 and could do so, he enlisted. At machinist school, he saw a movie about submarines and was immediately hooked. He took the exam with two hundred other sailors and was one of only five men selected for submarine service. He was able to hold his breath for a full minute and had good teeth, so he soon found himself in sub school in New London, Connecticut.

Guagliardo never regretted his decision.

Now here he was, involved in obtaining a boat for his adopted home state as a memorial for his shipmates—those who made it back from the war and the ones who didn't. He was anxious to see the *Seadog*, the boat back east that they had learned about. The Department of the Navy's director of naval history, E. M. Eller, informed the board that they could take charge of *Seadog* as soon as she was struck from the Navy's active list. Eller assured them that she was in tip-top shape, since she was still in service as a training boat, and that most of the equipment the sub vets wanted intact on their boat was still there, still being shined and polished on a regular basis.

All that sounded fine and dandy, but Eller must have been a used-car salesman in a previous life. Guagliardo was disappointed with what he saw when he got to the naval yard in New London. He found *Seadog* to be in rough shape, despite—or maybe because of—her recent service. It was also clearly impractical to bring that boat all the way from Connecticut to Oklahoma, down the East Coast, around Florida, then up the Mississippi and Arkansas.

The Oklahoma submarine veterans group had no money and was operating mostly on enthusiasm and good intentions.

Guagliardo told Eller, "Thanks, but no, thanks."

Besides, by this time Kelly and his gang had a line on a better boat. They had located the USS *Piranha*, about to be put out of commission down in New Orleans, and they were already putting out feelers with the Navy about laying claim to that old gal and bringing her to Oklahoma.

Things really got moving in early 1970. The *Tulsa Tribune* reported the latest development in its February 26, 1970, edition, under the headline, "Up Scope, Muskogee!" It told of state senator James Inhofe's intention to introduce a bill to establish the Oklahoma Maritime Advisory Board, with the express purpose of acquiring the USS *Piranha* and bringing her back to Muskogee to be used as a World War II memorial.

The irony of a submarine being on display in a prairie state was not lost on the *Tribune* reporter. He wrote, "[Inhofe] wants the sub base—which really would only have one sub—not only as a tourist attraction for once land-locked Oklahomans, but also to tell the world that a submarine can be floated to a former dust bowl state." The article went on to say that the submarine could begin its journey as early as December 1971, when the Arkansas River waterway project was scheduled to be finished, and "when the shoofly bridge at Little Rock comes down, the twin diesel sub can chug to its final docking place at Muskogee." No problem!

The plan was backed by an editorial in the *Tribune* a week later, with the headline, "Don't Torpedo It." The opinion piece began, "Sometimes apparently screwball ideas have a lot of sense behind them." It went on to say, "Hauling a submarine to 'dust bowl' Oklahoma should be a smashing way of breaking down damaging old stereotypes about this state and to publicize our new asset of water transportation. The idea is not nutty. We hope the legislature doesn't torpedo it."

Little chance of that. Ace Kelly was politically connected, despite his distaste for bureaucracy and bullshit. He was practical enough to know that it paid to have friends in high places. He had a job in the governor's office at the time and wasn't afraid to throw that political clout around if that was what it took to have his boat bobbing in the Arkansas River current.

To no one's surprise, Inhofe's bill passed. A state that was about as far from the sea as it could be now had its very own Maritime Advisory Board. And it had the approval of the good people of Oklahoma to go get them a World War II submarine, the *Piranha*.

But now there were problems with the boat they wanted. About the time the advisory board measure passed the legislature, the sub vets got word that the *Piranha* had been stripped of her engines. That wouldn't do—they needed a fully equipped vessel so they could show visitors and school groups what life had been like aboard the boats, how they were put together, how they operated when they were stalking enemy targets. It would be hard to explain their unique form of propulsion if the engines weren't even there!

The newly minted board immediately began looking around for another boat that would better serve its purposes. That was when they learned that *Batfish*, a boat with a more distinguished war record, was berthed right alongside *Piranha*, and that she was in much better shape.

At its first meeting in June 1970, the advisory board elected former sub skipper Karl Wheland to be its chairman and Dr. Glen Berkenbile, the surgeon from Muskogee, to be its vice chairman. They also voted to pursue the contacts Nick Guagliardo had made, and to continue talks that had already begun with the Industrial Development and Parks Board in Muskogee. Having Dr. Berkenbile on the board and serving as an officer promised to spur those discussions along, too. The doctor was a good ace to have in the hole.

But there was trouble with acquiring *Batfish*.

Everyone on the board was excited about getting a boat with such a remarkable distinction. The slightly redundant but intriguing title of "submarine-killer submarine" had such a nice ring to it. But when Nick Guagliardo went down to New Orleans in August of 1970 to explore their options with the Navy, he found the boat was about to be hooked up to a tug and towed away, headed to Orange, Texas, hundreds more miles away from Muskogee, Oklahoma, via a water route.

Karl Wheland and Ace Kelly pulled in all the political muscle they could muster for a meeting with the Navy brass, trying to convince them to leave the boat in New Orleans until they could get everything ready to bring her upriver. They hit a brick wall. The Navy flatly refused to delay the move.

They maintained that they could not afford to keep *Batfish* berthed in New Orleans at a cost to the taxpayers of the princely sum of twelve thousand dollars a year. Besides, the pier where she was moored was set to be demolished in October, and the new pier they were going to build to replace it was to have commercial applications, and then it would cost up to a hundred dollars per day for mooring the hulk. Furthermore, the commandant of the Eighth Naval District, which included New Orleans, considered the proud old boat to be a navigational hazard and wanted her out of his jurisdiction as soon as possible.

There was also the problem of the Oklahomans not yet having made formal application to take possession of the boat. That bureaucratically twisting paper trail could take months to steer. Months at a hundred bucks a day. Money that would have to be paid by a board that had no funding mechanism built into it when it was created, and wouldn't have any source of revenue until the submarine was parked in Muskogee and open to the paying public. While there was supposed to be a bond issue to cover costs, nobody knew when that would happen. For the moment, the board had no money at all.

Well, there was no choice. The waterway they would have to use to float and tow the submarine would not be ready for quite some time. The group decided to try to "tag" *Batfish* for future acquisition, and to ask the Navy to do whatever it could to keep the boat from being stripped until they could claim her. Albert Kelly was given the assignment of keeping that issue before the Navy.

So their boat went off to Orange, three hundred miles farther away, and *Batfish*'s proud arrival before the schoolchildren in Muskogee was postponed indefinitely.

That didn't faze Ace Kelly or Karl Wheland or Glen Berkenbile or Nick Guagliardo or the rest of the board. They got busy anyway, drawing up plans for the berthing and memorial site in Muskogee as if the boat were already on her way upriver. A five-acre plot of land at the north end of the Port of Muskogee was selected for the park. The loan process was initiated with the Fourth National Bank of Oklahoma and other Muskogee institutions. The note was to be guaranteed by the signatures of the members of the advisory board, with the debt to be repaid by proceeds from the eventual bond issue, and by paying visitors to the sub, just the way the USS *Alabama* and USS *Drum* had done in half the time allotted by the note issued to find their own conversion to memorials. Kelly announced that it would take only about a hundred thousand dollars to get the *Batfish* from Texas to Oklahoma, and that it was his intent to get the boat tied up and open to visitors in time for Muskogee's Azalea Festival in April.

Engineering plans were developed, including a scheme for a flotation system to be used with thirty-six-foot barges to get the submarine upriver through shallow sections of the Arkansas River. A St. Louis firm was going to bid on doing the actual towing, and several professional firms were working on plans for flotation of the vessel. Lloyds of London agreed to provide $150,000 of hull insurance and $3 million worth of liability coverage. One of the board's committees was working diligently to get the full history of *Batfish*, including all deck and patrol logs, so the adjacent museum would have answers to any questions visitors might ask.

Nick Guagliardo imposed upon the folks who maintained another restored fleet boat, the USS *Cobia* (SS 245), to take some photos of how the stairway they had built for visitors to enter and leave their boat was constructed. He thought *Batfish* might be able to devise something similar, and he liked their method better than that employed at the time by the *Drum*, which used steep steps at the forward and aft loading hatches that visitors had to negotiate as they entered and exited the boat's interior. *Cobia* had been restored and moored at the Wisconsin Naval Museum at Manitowoc, on Lake Michigan, and had also been spectacularly successful in attracting paying visitors.

The arrival of the submarine was to be a gala event. A committee was appointed to locate and invite all submarine veterans in the state to a glorious dedication ceremony, featuring the Navy band, dignitaries that would include the Secretary of the Navy, and a massive fireworks display.

Now all they needed was a submarine to welcome.

The Corps of Engineers finally reported that the waterway construction would be completed to a point upriver from Muskogee in late 1971. They also agreed that they would dredge away 25,000 cubic yards of mud, carving out a nice nesting place for a 311-foot-long submarine at the edge of the river, near the Port of Muskogee and just across from where the Verdigris met up with the Arkansas.

That was all the sub vets needed to hear. As chairman of the Oklahoma Maritime Advisory Board, Karl Wheland was only too happy to sign his name to a contract with the Navy on November 22, 1971. It was witnessed by board treasurer Ned Lockwood. By executing the contract, they agreed to accept possession of and responsibility for *Batfish*. The contract went back to the Navy on December 9.

Because of the requirements of Lloyds of London, and because the old girl was simply too broad to move up the Intracoastal Waterway from Orange to New Orleans, she would have to be inspected and prepared for an ocean tow, through the Gulf of Mexico. That costly work would have to be done in the nearby dry dock at Orange, not far from the navy yard. The high bidder, U.S. Salvage, was the only one who could logistically do the job. Then, one day before she was to come out of the water and begin her makeover, the dry-dock workers at Orange went on strike.

Ace Kelly had no intention of allowing a little labor dispute to keep his submarine from making its date at the Muskogee Azalea Festival in April. He arranged to have her towed upriver to the Bethlehem Steel dry dock in Beaumont, where there was no strike. There her hull was inspected, and the fuel (including 2,200 barrels of diesel fuel that were supposed to have been pumped out by the Navy before she was mothballed), oil, and most of her ballast were removed. Her tanks were flushed clean and all hull openings were sealed to make her ready to be pulled out into the Gulf of Mexico.

With yet another possible delay averted, *Batfish* was towed out of Beaumont on March 1, 1972, and delivered safely to Avondale Shipyard in New Orleans the next day. This little change in plans cost a bit more than thirty-six thousand dollars, a debt guaranteed by the board's good credit and nothing else.

The next day—the same day the boat got back to New Orleans, where the whole thing had started—the board received the estimate for the trip up the river and for preparing the site for *Batfish* in Muskogee. Avondale's work, raising and putting the boat on a cradle of steel lifting straps strung between four barges, would cost about twenty-five thousand dollars. The tow itself would be another eighteen thousand, plus eleven thousand more for barge rental and for returning them to New Orleans. Engineering fees for the whole project, to be done by Williams Brothers of Tulsa, would be about forty-five thousand dollars, assuming there were no snags.

Even though everything seemed to be costing more than estimated and taking much longer than planned, Wheland, Kelly, and the board were not at all worried. They remained confident everything would work out. They proceeded with their plans at flank speed.

The March 3 issue of the *New Orleans Times-Picayune* carried the headline "Submarine Batfish Here, to Become Prairie Sight." The article reported, "The submarine U.S.S. *Batfish* arrived in New Orleans Thursday morning, and is now tied up at the Avondale shipyard in preparation for its conversion into an Oklahoma prairie schooner. It will become both a monument to World War II and a sightseeing attraction for the area, where there have been no reports of submarine sightings in the news lately." The reporter noted the submarine's outstanding war record and called her, in something of an overstatement, "the best known submarine ever built."

But there was no hyperbole involved when the article detailed the formidable task ahead. The sub was only twenty-seven feet across, but with the flotilla of barges and the hammocklike rigging, the whole shebang would be almost a hundred feet wide. Some of the fifteen locks they would have to negotiate along the route north were only a few feet wider than that. For that reason, they would be able to go through the locks only in daylight and couldn't even attempt to negotiate them if there were strong winds. The Corps of Engineers didn't want any damage done to their brand-new locks.

Still, the article quoted those involved as being confident that *Batfish* would be in Muskogee, safely moored and ready for swarms of excited visitors to tour her, by April 15, 1972, the first day of the area's famed Azalea Festival. The old boat's "eighth war patrol" would be just as successful as her previous jaunts, the board members promised.

It didn't take long for the workers at the Avondale yard to determine that four barges wouldn't do the trick. In some places, the channel the boat would follow up the Arkansas was only nine feet deep. Without the sling-and-barge system the engineers had devised, *Batfish* would draw fifteen feet of water. But even with the rigging, she would still drag bottom and possibly get stuck, even with four barges lifting her up. It would take two more barges, all of them heavily ballasted on their outside, to assure that didn't happen.

Two more lifting straps were hastily rigged, with the same stabilizing and breasting cables as the others. A small army of steelworkers, welders, riggers, and dockworkers labored night and day, often at time-and-a-half or double-time wages, as Ace Kelly urged them on. He was bound and determined to make his income tax–day deadline.

Now *Batfish* was almost ready. The Sunday, March 12, 1972, edition of the *Tulsa Daily World* giddily announced that Oklahoma's submarine "has had her last taste of salt water" and predicted that she would be arriving at the Port of Muskogee the following Saturday. The story mentioned how striking the scene would be as she pulled out of New Orleans headed north, with the submarine's shears reaching almost forty feet above the water.

But the very next day, the hero submarine of World War II came as close to getting herself sunk as she ever did in the Pacific.

All six barges had been partially secured to the submarine by way of the custom-built lifting straps, but cables did not yet tie them down. That would be the last step before the trip began. The tugboat that was to push her up the river was parked nearby, ready to get under way, its meter already whirring like that of a Manhattan taxi.

That afternoon, a British tanker, the *Silvermain*, came barreling up the river nearby, making at least eleven knots in an area where five knots was the speed limit, and creating a powerful wake. The huge wall of water hit *Batfish* and her flotilla of barges broadside.

Amazingly, no one was hurt, but two of the barges were heavily damaged, and one immediately sank to the bottom of the Mississippi River. In all, five of the six barges were ripped away from the submarine by the tanker's wake, and the one that somehow stayed lashed to *Batfish* was warped and buckled by the strain.

The only good news was that the submarine seemed not to have been damaged at all.

The Coast Guard immediately began an investigation into the incident, and Avondale started exploring its options in filing a claim against *Silvermain*'s owners. But the fact remained that the submarine was still tied up at the yard and her new owners, the Oklahoma Maritime Advisory Board, were expected to foot the bill for replacement barge rental, repair, salvage and the construction of another harness, and they were going to have to do this until there was a settlement of some kind. They were even obligated by contract to continue paying rent on the barge that was resting at the bottom of the river until the matter was settled.

Karl Wheland didn't bat an eye. He sent a telegram from Tulsa, giving approval to proceed with getting *Batfish* ready to float north and accepting responsibility, on behalf of the board, for an additional forty thousand dollars in costs. The board still didn't have a dime of its own or any source of revenue, but its chairman, like any good smoke boat skipper, didn't hesitate when it came time to attack.

He committed the money as if it actually existed.

The banks back in Muskogee had agreed to loan them some money at some point, but a proposed bond issue by the Industrial Development and Park Board to help fund the memorial park and the submarine site had yet to materialize. The state had talked about issuing bonds as well, but so far nothing had happened on that front either.

Meanwhile, bills continued to mount. It could take years to get a settlement from the tanker's owners. The Maritime Advisory Board was operating on loans personally guaranteed by its members, and it now appeared it would be several months before they could sell the first ticket to a visitor who wanted to ramble around the World War II hero sub.

But if you think the board members were discouraged, you'd be sorely mistaken. Their shipmates on eternal patrol, those who had not come back from the fifty-two boats lost in World War II, deserved their best efforts, and they had no intention of letting down the spirits of those men.

It was, as the submarine veterans saw it, their *duty* to bring a submarine to their state and park her out there so everybody could come take a look at her. And whatever it took in the course of performing that duty, they were bound and determined to do.

At the board's regular meeting on April 10, 1972, at the VFW hall in Muskogee, the minutes indicate that the setbacks down in Texas and in New Orleans did not even come up for discussion. Instead, a committee was formed to work on invitations and a guest list for the eventual dedication celebration. Another was designated to be responsible for welcoming distinguished guests and assuring proper protocol would be followed at the event.

Karl Wheland reported to the group that *Batfish* was now scheduled to begin her journey upriver from New Orleans one week from the date of the meeting, on April 17, two days after she was supposed to have already been berthed and open for visitation by the attendees at the Azalea Festival.

If there was any fear that the boat would never make it to Muskogee, it was not apparent at that meeting. Instead, as usual, optimism prevailed.

The final order of business before adjournment that afternoon was deciding specifics for the convoy of yachts, bearing board members, wives, and special guests, that would soon lead USS *Batfish* up the final stretch of the Arkansas River to her new home.

NINE

The Whites of Their Eyes

Cherokee legend says that in the beginning of the world, there was no fire. Then the Thunders sent lightning and left fire in the bottom of a hollow sycamore tree on an island. The animals could see smoke and knew fire was there, but they were cautious about crossing the broad water to get it.

Finally, Raven, whose feathers were white in those times, said he would go fetch fire. He managed to fly high and far across the water and landed on top of the sycamore. But now that he was there, he was unsure what to do. He perched there, thinking, wondering, trying to make up his mind, until the heat from the fire burned his feathers black.

The frightened bird flew away, back across the waters, without getting fire.

That, the Cherokees say, is why the raven's feathers are black today.

December 1943

Late on the night of December 27, *Batfish* finally arrived at her designated patrol area south of the Japanese home islands, as Captain Merrill had been so determined to do. They had spent most of the day submerged, dodging patrol planes or any hint of patrol planes, coming up only long enough to pump in fresh air, charge the batteries, and run as fast as they could for their designated patrol box. Over the course of the next day or so, they kept picking up radar signals on or about the same frequency and with similar characteristics as their own newly installed SJ system.

There was considerable discussion in the wardroom about whether or not the mysterious signals could be coming from USS *Finback* (SS 230), which was supposed to be operating in the area as well, or from USS *Salmon* (SS 182), which was also supposedly crossing the area, heading homeward, already at the end of her ninth war patrol.

There was another worrisome possibility: Could it be that the Japanese had developed similar technology and were busily painting *Batfish*, readying an attack? In the mind of the one man who really counted—a certain Missourian named Captain Wayne R. Merrill—the way the other vessel seemed to be acting, apparently maneuvering for an end run, made the latter a distinct possibility. He wrote in the deck log:

> 4:45 A.M. Strongly suspected enemy radar, although all characteristics indicated our own forces. I am anxious to check this with other submarines concerned. If it was not them, then the

Japs have radar very similar to our own and apparently fully as efficient.

There was no way to radio his sister boats now and find out if they were close by. And even if the radar signals were from friendly craft, they might assume *Batfish* was an enemy boat and start firing away. So they did the most prudent thing, at least to Merrill's way of thinking. They skedaddled.

The weather turned sour over New Year's, and pickings suddenly seemed slim. When the sun finally came out on the second day of 1944, *Batfish* emerged from the depths and ran on the surface for a while. The men who oozed out onto the deck were cave-eyed, blinded by a rare appearance by the sun. The warm, welcome sunshine and the opportunity to finally get a little fresh air down the conning tower hatch improved everybody's disposition.

Just after the sun had dropped into the sea, radar detected a vessel about three miles away. The sky was clear enough and the moonlight bright enough that the lookouts soon spotted a sampan, a small boat usually used by fishermen. But experience had taught them well that these vessels often had more sinister purposes in this part of the world. Merrill guided his boat around so they could not be spotted in the streak of moonlight reflecting off the water, all the while keeping an eye on the lone white light on the small vessel's mast.

The captain felt it would be better to remain undetected than to try to sink what could be an enemy observation boat. Once again, he documented in his logbook his decision and the reasoning behind it:

> 6:20 P.M. Believe sampan was an observer rather than a fisherman, as this isn't a likely fishing ground. Would like to have sunk sampan, but consider it inadvisable, as I haven't revealed my presence to date. This was our first visual contact during the patrol. Something better should be turning up in his wake.

Most of the crew agreed with his decision this time. Maybe it was better to not advertise their presence by dunking some poor fisherman. Maybe, here in this box, something tastier would indeed come swimming past if they were just patient and kept their eyes open.

They continued to patrol the main shipping lanes that bore traffic from Kobe and Osaka on the Japanese island of Honshu, to and from the Palau Islands, north of New Guinea in the South Pacific. That was a key supply point for the Japanese troops hunkered down in the region, trying to hang on to the far-flung lands they had conquered. Bad weather was back with *Batfish* by the fourth, but the skipper remained positive and optimistic.

"It begins to look like something may be coming along soon on this route," he wrote. "I intend to stay on it until I find out."

But after ten days in one of the most heavily trafficked areas in the Pacific, they had yet to fire a shot.

"It's becoming possible that the enemy is purposely avoiding the normal routing between ports," Merrill reasoned in his deck log entry on January 5, blaming the enemy for their maiden voyage drought.

Then, two days later, he hopefully scribbled, "I have a hunch something is coming through here soon."

Finally, on the ninth, his hunch proved valid.

Batfish was patrolling on the surface, performing a battery charge after passing most of another day hiding beneath the surface. Though it was cloudy and quickly growing dark, the lookouts spotted smoke in the distance. Even with modern radar, wartime patrols still often learned of somebody else being in the area the same way attackers had done since the invention of the steamboat. The telltale black plume of smoke from their stacks gave them away. The smudge was often visible on the horizon well before even the new high-priced radar could spy the ship.

"Range twelve miles, Captain."

"Let's close and see if we can tell what it is," Merrill ordered.

Finally the radar screen below showed a pip, then, a few minutes later, a total of six of them. A convoy! Not a tiny sampan or a piece of driftwood, but something they could actually shoot at!

The word spread throughout the boat. At long last, they could quit being tourists and do what they had steamed halfway around the world to do.

The air in the boat was instantly electric. Every man was poised, more than ready for the call that would send him to his battle station.

Even the elements seemed to be at last cooperating. The clouds parted, allowing a nearly full moon to bathe the oceanscape with a yellowish glow. Up in the shears and on the bridge below, everyone could soon see the targets, swimming along in the moonlight. There appeared to be three cargo vessels, a destroyer, and some kind of smaller escort. The sixth vessel that was showing on the radarscope was nowhere in sight. The craft were following a pronounced zigzagging course, trying to make it more difficult for any submarine who might try to line them up for an attack.

Merrill ordered the crew to battle stations with gusto. There were no slackers. Everyone was ready. The chase was on!

Batfish maneuvered to keep her distance at about nine miles. Captain Merrill had decided he wanted to complete the battery charge before he launched any assault on the convoy.

But by the time the charge was secured, visibility began to come and go. Clouds scudded in to obscure the moon, and rain squalls passed between the submarine and the target vessels. Still, the radar was locked onto the targets, and they could still make occasional visible contact from topside, weather permitting.

It was hard work. Keeping the images on the radar and no longer able to continuously see them from the bridge and shears, they kept up the chase for three hours, until they were approaching a point ahead of where the group of ships would eventually pass. There they could simply wait for the unsuspecting convoy to come along. Then they could drive closer, aim, and shoot.

Captain Merrill's skittishness about shooting at the sampan now seemed like a sound move. Nobody knew they were here. Certainly not those cargo vessels and their escorts.

But suddenly, the moon broke through the tumbling clouds overhead and there, less than four miles away, were the patrol boat they had seen before and another vessel, which must have been the one on radar that had not been discernible to the lookouts. It looked like a "sub chaser," a small, quick vessel specially equipped to seek out and destroy submarines.

Merrill ordered an immediate backing off in speed and steered the boat radically away from the course of his end run at the convoy. If they could see the patrol boats in the moonlight, then the patrol boats could certainly see *Batfish* racing along on the surface, flinging foam and spray everywhere.

Once they were certain they were still undetected, it took almost three more hours for them to catch up again with the string of vessels. Now the weather had turned downright nasty, with visibility varying from almost unlimited when the rain passed and the moon broke through, down to practically nil in the midst of a tropical downpour. The seas, too, had become much rougher, and they found themselves plowing through towering waves.

Merrill gave several indications to the crew that he was going in for a periscope attack. He would order a turn to draw closer to the convoy, but each time he called it off, the bottom dropped out of the sky and the seas built higher and higher. Once, they drew to within nine thousand yards, and again the moon broke through and covered them with near daylight. Luckily the convoy was in the middle of a downpour at the moment and had no chance to spot their stalker.

Three tense hours passed, with everyone at battle stations, straining to do his job as the submarine bounced along in the choppy waters, ready to skewer the tasty targets, but not ever getting close enough or stable enough to try. Water poured down the conning tower hatch in torrents, soaking those on watch there and threatening to knock out vital equipment. Men at their battle stations fought to hold on to anything they could to keep from getting thrown against a bulkhead or protruding piece of gear. That would not be an honorable way to earn a Purple Heart!

Finally, just after one thirty in the morning, Merrill ordered them to break off the chase and pull back to a safer seven miles or so. Maybe the weather and sea state would improve at dawn and they could attack from periscope depth, he explained to those around him. The captain was also afraid that he would have to set the torpedoes to run at a depth of at least fifteen feet because of the rough seas, and with the cargo ships sitting high in the water, they could very well run right underneath them without doing any damage. These were not magnetic torpedoes. They had to smash their noses against something rigid in order to explode.

Nobody complained. They simply did what they had been trained to do.

Besides, it was just a matter of time before they sent their torpedoes away. The convoy wasn't going to shake them that easily.

The sonar gear could easily hear the noisy ships as they made their way southward, and the new radar was performing flawlessly, having no problem keeping the reflections of the vessels locked on its scope. There should be no problem for them to submerge anytime the captain wanted to, pull up closer without fear of detection, use the radar if they could and the scope if they had to, and send the convoy to the bottom.

But the skipper seemed bound and determined to fire the torpedoes only if he could see what they were shooting at with his own eyes. Like Prescott at Bunker Hill, Merrill was hesitant until he could see the whites of his enemy's eyes.

Just before daylight, *Batfish* submerged and then pulled in directly on the track that the convoy would follow. It was so rough it took them over two minutes to get the boat beneath the surface. During the dive, both sound and radar had lost contact with the convoy a while back, but the skipper was sure they were still out there, still coming their way.

They ran along in front of where the ships were last headed, keeping a distance of about a dozen miles, biding time as the sun slowly made its appearance, even if it was mostly blotted out by the stormy sky. Merrill wanted to take a look at first light, to get a good view of the Japanese vessels as they bore down on them.

But just as the captain raised the scope to take a peek, a sudden massive swell grabbed them in its jaws, shook them violently, and, seemingly without effort, tossed them upward and out of the water, breaching the boat. Almost all of her 311 feet were above the water, luridly exposed, hanging there plain as day for anybody looking her way to see.

"Get her under!" Merrill yelled. "Get her down, damn it! Get her down!"

Commands flowed throughout the boat as the diving officer and the rest of the crew quickly fought the power of the sea and took her back down to where she would once again be hidden from her prey by the churning waters. Hopefully it was too dark and dim on the stormy surface for anyone in the convoy to have seen them.

When Merrill next raised the periscope and took a look about, he was confident that was the case. Even with the scope fully extended, he could see only snatches of black sky, sea spray, and fog before another wave splashed over the top of the viewer, obscuring his vision.

Radar had not reacquired the convoy yet. Neither had the sound equipment. There was only the roar of the sea.

The skipper tried to hang on for the rough ride when they moved back near the surface again, bracing himself against the scope support as he worked to spot anything that looked like a ship in the distance. Once again they were grabbed by the force of the waves and thrust upward until most of the boat was totally out of the water. Once again, the diving officer and the rest of the maneuvering crew fought to get her back beneath the surface where she belonged, before the sub chaser or a patrol plane spotted her.

The mood aboard *Batfish* was deteriorating as quickly as the weather. They had been at battle stations for hours, and tension had a grip on every sailor aboard. Frayed nerves were all right, though, so long as they were on the verge of getting their first kill. But now it seemed that they would never get around to firing a shot, that the convoy had steamed right off and left them while they maneuvered for the perfect shot.

"Secure battle stations."

Merrill said the words, and there was a moment's hesitation before the men began winding down.

Just like that, their first real assault was called off.

The XO checked the chronometer: 9:05 in the morning. Over fourteen hours since they had spied the smoke of the ships in the convoy on the horizon. Fourteen hours with nothing to show for it but a wasted crew in a foul mood.

"I decided the enemy had too valuable an ally in the weather so secured from battle stations and gave it up as a bad job," the skipper would write. "I am convinced the convoy made a radical change in its base course at sunrise."

Again, the crew members didn't know what their captain's reasoning had been. All they knew was that they had had a clear view of some luscious targets and they had fooled around and let them get away.

"We could have made a radar attack anytime we wanted to," one member of the attack team said, mostly under his breath.

A shipmate put his finger to his lips.

"Ssssh! Maybe so, but if we had missed, those patrol boats would have been on top of us before we could catch our breath."

"How the hell could we have missed? The damn ocean was full of Jap ships! If we had only fired a couple of fish we would have been just about certain to hit something with a rising sun on it."

"Hey, pipe down. It was rough up there. I saw you rolling all over the deck. Hell, who knows what would have happened?"

"We had our chance, right there at the first. We could have taken them then if the old man hadn't waited to finish the charge."

As if he felt their frustration, Merrill ordered the boat to go deep so the crew could get some rest and recharge their own batteries. Weeks later, when he summed up the aborted assault for the patrol report, it was almost as if he had read the mind of the disgruntled crew member.

> The convoy contacted on 9 January, on which no attack was made because of developments in the weather, might have been effectively attacked had I not waited to recharge the battery. I'm now convinced that it doesn't pay to delay an instant in launching an attack once contact is made. Anything may happen to frustrate an attack if delayed to gain more advantageous conditions.

Batfish was Merrill's first command, but he was an experienced submariner. Two of his officers were green, but the others were veterans. Half the crew was new, but the other half had been qualified before they ever showed up for duty on this new boat. The boat and all her gear had performed flawlessly. It was hard to find a reason why they had not sunk at least one of the targets they had encountered on their first run.

Some of the crew insisted on trying to find someone to blame, carrying on the arguments quietly up and down the length of the boat. There was little else to do. Their decks of cards were worn thin from too much pinochle. Lips moved along with the actors when the same old movies were unspooled over and over again in the forward torpedo room. All the good records for the Victrola had been broken in the rough seas on the way out to the patrol. Scuttlebutt and speculation became the primary pastime.

Batfish dodged more sampans, as the skipper seemed more interested in hiding from any potential observer boats than he did in bagging IJN ships. And anytime they surfaced for any length of time, it seemed to some of the more critical members of the crew that they were too quick to duck. The skipper pulled the plug anytime there was even a hint of a patrol plane on the radar.

Captain Merrill kept pushing them, trying to get every last man qualified, but the drills had long since begun to drag. The men had lost their spark. They were wearing on one another's nerves. They were beginning to tussle and scrap with each other, rather than with the Imperial Japanese Navy.

Just as spirits had hit a new low aboard *Batfish*, along came word of a potential target that quickened the pulse of every sailor aboard. Smiles broke out everywhere on the boat, as if the lights had suddenly been turned on.

Forget that convoy of a couple of freighters, by God! Their holds were probably full of nothing but boots and rice and dried fish anyway.

Something far more inviting was coming. Not just a big target.

The *biggest* target.

TEN

Errors in Judgment

January 1944

News travels through a submarine like shit through a goose. Even busy submariners, attentive to their tasks when at battle stations or on watch, somehow manage to find the opportunity to spread the word to the next man down the line about where they're going or what the lookouts have seen or what's popped up on the radar. Within minutes, it seems, everyone on the boat is updated.

That was what happened the morning of January 13. The radio shack had received a message from Pacific Command, informing them that the ULTRA (short for "ultrasecret") code breakers had picked up and translated a message confirming that *Yamato*, the largest battleship ever constructed, would be passing through *Batfish*'s patrol area.

Yamato was one of two superbattleships built by the Japanese (*Musashi* was the other) and she was a monster—65,000 tons that included the most armor ever floated, and nine eighteen-inch battery guns that fired 3,200-pound armor-piercing shells. Most—certainly the Japanese—considered her unsinkable. But they still made sure that the newest destroyers escorted the behemoth, with the IJN's best marksmen manning their guns.

The giant had been commissioned only a few days after Pearl Harbor and had served as the flagship of Admiral Isoroku Yamamoto, the commander and chief of the Imperial Japanese Navy before he was shot out of the sky while being flown into the Empire's outpost at Bougainville Island in April of 1943. In December 1943, *Yamato* had been torpedoed by one of *Batfish*'s sisters, the USS *Skate* (SS 305), and had most recently been undergoing repairs for that damage. Now, according to the intercepted message, she was out of the barn on sea trials, getting ready to head back south to continue defending Japanese positions in the central Pacific.

In short order, every sailor aboard *Batfish* knew the Japanese monstrosity might soon be sharing a bit of the Pacific Ocean with them. *Batfish* was ready. They still had the twenty-four torpedoes with which they had left Midway, and they could justify using every last one of them on a single target if it meant that they could sink or even damage *Yamato*.

That would certainly be a good antidote for this sick patrol they had had so far.

Then the rumors made the rounds that Captain Merrill had known about this development, that this was the reason he had kept the boat submerged so much of the time and why they had passed up those sitting-duck sampans and avoided air contact and why he had so desperately tried to keep their presence in this area a secret as long as he could. The skipper had known they had bigger fish to fry!

For once the weather would not be a factor if the battleship should happen to swim nearby. "14 January 1944. Sky was clear, sea slightly choppy, and when the moon rose at 2042 visibility was excellent. A perfect night for a submerged periscope attack," Merrill recorded.

There was an expectant excitement among the men on *Batfish*. Bagging *Yamato* would put them in the record books. Even wounding her would keep the awful monstrosity in the barn where she could do no damage, and that would cost the Japanese dearly. But, as some of the more pessimistic among them noted, if just one of the battleship's gigantic shells came anywhere near their boat, they would instantly be "missing, presumed lost" and on eternal patrol.

The captain and his XO were on the bridge, and the usual quartet of lookouts were clinging to their perches above. It was nearly midnight, and so far there had been no sign of anything, especially a battleship the size of a Manhattan apartment building.

"Captain!" came the call up the conning tower hatch. "Radar contact, bearing one-three-zero true, range two-five-eight-five-oh! And, Captain, it's a very large pip!"

Merrill ordered his crew to battle stations, instructed that the boat be turned in the direction of the new target, and then disappeared down the hatch to see this pip for himself. Once he saw it, he ordered the SJ gear shut down to avoid detection. They would have no trouble seeing something that size without the aid of radar.

Soon enough, the XO and a lookout reported sighting the upper works and mast of a vessel that looked like a battleship, even at night and from over a dozen miles away. And there were two escorts, too, visible by eye as well as showing up as relatively small pips next to the one big, bright one on the SD radar.

Word of the sighting had already spread the length of the boat. Pulses quickened. Here came their chance for greatness, their opportunity to inflict some revenge on the bastards.

Radar kept calling out ranges up the hatch, counting the battleship closer and closer. When they were within 21,000 yards—under twelve miles—Merrill ordered them to dive and begin a periscope approach. Once they came steady, the soundmen could easily hear the strong throbbing of *Yamato*'s massive screws, growing louder by the second.

"Captain, if she makes any kind of course correction, we'll lose her if we try to stay submerged," the XO offered. The boat could run only about six knots while submerged. *Yamato* could easily run four times that.

"If we get close enough to shoot without her seeing us, there's no reason for her to change course," Merrill shot back. "If her guns have a range of twenty-one thousand yards, you can be certain she can see that far."

"Yes, but we've got the biggest target most of us will ever encounter, and if we don't chase her on the surface—"

"Here's the deal, XO," the skipper interrupted. "If I thought we had more than a one-in-ten chance of doing real damage to that battleship, I'd risk this submarine and seventy-six lives without batting an eye. But I don't see even that good a chance. Our best hope is to stay down and pray that she keeps coming in our direction instead of turning away. Then we'll be ready. If she turns—and I see no reason why she would—then we'll do all we can to catch her. But I won't put this boat in needless peril on a foolish try."

Those who heard the discussion kept their heads down, their eyes on their duty stations. There was no point in taking sides. Both men had points. As was so often the case, there was no black and white, no certain correct decision. Either move could lead to victory. Either pronouncement could lead to untimely death for *Batfish* and her crew of youngsters. Most of the men within earshot simply felt relief that it wasn't their decision to have to make.

Now the boat's listening gear could make out the sounds of the screws of *Yamato*'s two escorts. In another few minutes, with the battleship's course remaining the same, she would present an almost unmissable target.

Captain Merrill pulled the periscope up to eye level and snapped down the handles. When he turned the scope to the bearing of the battleship, he grunted but said nothing.

Then he quietly ordered an alteration of course.

"She's turned away from us, to the east. We'll assume she's making eighteen knots and we'll try to run north, out to where she'll be if she zigs back toward us."

The executive officer dropped his head but said nothing. Much of the air seemed to have left the conning tower.

"You think she spotted us?" someone asked.

"I doubt it," Merrill said. "She's probably just zigzagging as normal procedure." He cleared his throat. "Set all the torpedoes in all tubes to low power, depth at twenty-two feet."

Low power would give the torpedoes the maximum range. If *Batfish* should get anywhere within ten miles of the battleship, they might try a long shot. But nobody believed for a minute that the skipper would actually waste good weapons on such an unlikely attempt.

Sound tracking later confirmed that *Yamato* did, indeed, zig back in their direction, but by then her speed had taken her well out of range. There was no hope of catching her now, even if they had been on the surface, running all-out.

At 12:48 in the morning, a little over an hour after the brilliant pip popped up on the radar screen, sound reported they could no longer hear the thrashing of the battleship's screws.

"Secured from battle stations and commenced surface patrol to the eastward," the skipper later wrote in his log. "Either we were unlucky enough to get in the middle of a long, looping zig to the eastward or else the target picked us up by radar about the same time we did him and purposely ran out around us. The conditions were perfect to carry out the approach as planed [sic], putting the target between us and the moon, avoiding radar detection, etc., but the breaks just weren't with us. Our principle [sic] weakness was our lack of ranges, as the telemeter scale could not be seen, and at over ten thousand yards the target appeared as just a very large grey mass. I earnestly believe a zig to the left would have put him in a beautiful position for a successful attack."

Once again the crew had been on the verge of their first kill, and this time a major one, only to come up short, not firing a single torpedo. This up-and-down emotional roller coaster was wearing them out. And, right or wrong, they were more apt to blame the skipper for their dry spell than to attribute it to luck, the weather, or the skills of some Japanese battleship captain.

Word of the discussion between the captain and XO in the conning tower had spread throughout the boat, too. The skipper had been dead wrong, some were thinking. They lost *Yamato*. The XO's plan would have worked. They'd have sunk the bastard for sure. They would all have been standing on deck in Pearl after the patrol, getting so many medals and commendations and citations that they'd have trouble crossing the brow wearing them all.

The sailors aboard the *Batfish* would have to wait until the early morning of the twentieth of January, the twenty-fourth day of their initial patrol, before they fired their first torpedoes. And when they did, the results were so spectacular that the onboard grumblings ceased.

Again it was smoke that led them to a convoy of three large passenger freighters and one smaller transport. There appeared to be a couple of escort vessels riding alongside the other ships, and a seaplane circled lazily above the convoy. *Batfish* waited until dark to surface, charge the batteries, and try to track down the ships. They caught up with them again just before midnight on the nineteenth.

At 3,400 yards, with her bow pointed directly at the target vessels, Merrill gave the command "Stand by to fire!" Suddenly, as the captain and escort watched from the bridge, one of the convoy's escorts made a turn and headed straight for *Batfish*.

Had they been spotted? Had they shown up on somebody's radar? Or was the escort just moving around for grins, a maneuver that coincidentally had him bow-on with the stalking submarine?

Merrill glanced at his XO, who kept his glasses aimed at the distant convoy. He would like to be closer to the targets before he fired. But the escort was still headed his way. The skipper made a quick decision.

"Fire four!" he said into the speaker at his side. In quick succession, he ordered the other five fish in the forward tubes released and sent on their way, next from tubes five and six, then from one, two, and three. It was technically two separate attacks, since three of the torpedoes were aimed at one target and the next three at another. As soon as the Mark 18-2 was clear of tube three, Merrill spun the boat around to try to get ready to run away from the escort vessel that was still coming in their direction.

Suddenly a vivid explosion rent the night sky. The power of the blast rattled the submarine, even though she was a good two miles away. Merrill and his executive officer looked back and watched orange flame climbing from the waterline of the first freighter, racing up the side of the ship and then up the stack. The second target was also ablaze, a boiling column of smoke towering above it already. More explosions rocked the sub as those topside tried to see the destruction they had wrought, despite the loss of their night vision from all the flames. At least three of the six torpedoes had scored direct hits.

The escort craft had turned around, called back by the urgent distress signals from the first stricken vessel. As he went, he dropped depth charges at random, all much too far away to do any harm to *Batfish,* who still rode on the surface, watching all the fire and brimstone she had set loose. The men on the sound gear listened with awe to the creaking, groaning, rushing-water noises of the IJN ships breaking up. One ship had sunk immediately. The other was dead in the water, afire, but she was still floating.

Soon, it was hard to hear anything for all the cheers and shouts of elation that rang out below decks.

They had done it! They had struck a blow! Now they wouldn't have to go back to Midway without anything to show for their trip to these prime hunting grounds.

When the moon came up just after one a.m., Merrill positioned the boat so they could take another look at the damaged freighter. Except for one escort that circled the dying vessel, likely to pull in survivors, the other ships had steamed away, trying to make a getaway from what would certainly be a pursuing submarine that had claimed two of their sisters already.

"Captain, aren't we going after the others?" the XO asked.

"No, I want to make sure this one is finished," Merrill said. "We'll radio back so any other boats in the area can chase those guys. Anyway, we have to make sure this one goes down or they'll never give us credit for the kill."

The XO started to argue with his skipper again. Credit or not, he couldn't see allowing two freighters to get away when this one was obviously going nowhere but down. But Merrill was adamant.

He fired two torpedoes at the hulk. One hit.

Batfish sped away in case the escort destroyer came after them, but they heard a very loud explosion and clearly saw the single pip that had been the freighter break into two, and then disappear completely.

"It is believed the target sank," Captain Merrill recorded in the log.

Sinking the two freighters had mitigated the disappointment of the earlier incidents. Still, Wayne Merrill made sure to accept the blame for some of that when he summed up the patrol in the required report: "Viewing the entire patrol as conducted in retrospect, the Commanding Officer feels that he is guilty of several errors in judgment."

He acknowledged he might not have made the best decision in allowing two targets to escape from the convoy.

"After the first attack on the convoy during the morning of 20 January it is now thought that a chase of the two undamaged ships would have been preferable to staying to sink the damaged ship. Which would probably have sunk anyway. At least more opportunities to make later attacks on the damaged ship would have presented themselves whereas two undamaged ships were making port at best speed," he admitted.

After fifty-one days at sea and outlasting more typhoon weather, *Batfish* arrived back at Midway on the last day of January 1944. The U.S. Navy seemed pleased enough with the efforts of Merrill, *Batfish*, and her crew. They pronounced the patrol successful and presented them the Combat Insignia Award.

The skipper thought his guys had done as good a job as they could have done. And merely making it back safely to Midway was enough to call the run a successful one.

In the patrol report, he wrote, "Once a patrol has been successfully completed by a new submarine it is felt that she has won half the battle. All hands are surer of their footing and they have ceased to be 'the BATFISH detail'—they are instead a fighting unit, 'the BATFISH crew.' Admittedly this metamorphosis is largely psychological, but its importance cannot, I believe, be overestimated."

Spirits were high, even if they weren't going to be rerouted back to Pearl Harbor for R & R. Instead, the Navy put them up in quarters that had been designated the Gooney Bird Hotel, named after the goofy-looking birds that inhabited the tiny islands that made up Midway.

There was plenty to celebrate, and they did, with an abundance of beer and a bath anytime they felt like taking one. The officers celebrated their patrol pretty much the same way as the enlisted men did: by getting roaring drunk, then sleeping it off. But once again, their skipper proved to have a much higher tolerance for alcohol and sleeplessness than did the rest of the wardroom crew. When all the other officers had worn down and given up, the captain simply moved over to where the enlisted men were hanging out.

Sailors from other boats kidded the *Batfish* crew about their skipper dropping in on their parties, but they ignored them. If the old man wanted to spend some time with the guys who really made a submarine float, then more power to him.

Several of the crew noticed, though, that their skipper had lost a great deal of weight and looked almost scrawny. Clearly, the pressures of running a fleet boat in enemy waters had been a heavy burden on Merrill.

It had been a testy relationship between Merrill and his XO since sea trials began back in New England. Very late on the final night on Midway before leaving on their second patrol, the captain—obviously well oiled after a night on what passed for "the town" on Midway—showed up at the executive officer's room, vowing to try to patch things up with him. The XO and his roommate, the boat's diving officer, wanted to get some sleep before their early departure the next morning. They tried to talk the skipper into going on to his room and doing likewise. They even summoned two other officers to try to talk Merrill into calling it a night.

The captain refused to leave until they buried the hatchet.

Finally two of the officers lifted their skipper bodily and tossed him out the window. Fortunately the room was on the first floor, and the only damage done was to the gooney bird's nest in which Merrill landed.

That whole ignominious episode perfectly foreshadowed *Batfish*'s second war patrol. The boat departed Midway on George Washington's birthday, February 22, 1944, and fifty-four days later, on April 15, they were moored back at Pearl Harbor with nothing at all to show for their run. An inventory of the torpedoes confirmed what was written in the patrol report: Not a single torpedo was fired.

The reason? According to Captain Merrill, there had been nothing at which to shoot.

Merrill complained that the area was virtually devoid of targets and recommended that no submarines be assigned to that region for the duration of the war. Boats passing through while heading to other patrol boxes could do an adequate job of patrolling that area. Besides the fact that nobody got hurt, the only good thing the ComSubPac commander could find in the report was the notation that twenty *Batfish* crewmen earned their qualifications during the trip.

Issues of the onboard newspaper, the *Agitator*, showed there was little news about the boat's activities to report to the crew. The paper was typed up on carbon paper every day and consisted mostly of Associated Press reports copied from radio broadcasts and inside jokes poking fun at the crew. The issue for April 3, 1944, for example, told of victories in Europe and repeated a heartening report that Allies were sinking about nine out of every ten ships attempting to bring supplies to the over 100,000 Japanese stranded in the Marshalls, Bismarcks, and northern Solomons, all previously captured islands in the South Pacific. There was also a mention of the sordid story of movie star Fatty Arbuckle. Final arguments were scheduled to start the next day in his trial, in which he had been charged with violating the Mann Act, transporting a young woman from Hollywood to New York and back for "immoral purposes."

Of course, a few weeks in Honolulu and at the Royal Hawaiian could make anyone forget this "lost patrol." Some sailors didn't like liberty in Hawaii. It was always crowded with military on leave, so bars restricted the amount of time and number of beers a man could enjoy in each establishment. There was also an abundance of shore patrol and brass around to put a damper on the fun. Still, it was a good time compared to where they had been, and certainly better than Midway.

The crew members couldn't help but notice that their skipper, who had appeared tired and gaunt after the first patrol, was now almost skeletal. One crewman estimated that the old man could not have weighed more than 130 pounds.

When it came time to leave on patrol again, twenty of the sailors who had made the second patrol were gone, most of them shipped back to the States to crew new boats. The XO was gone as well, off to the prospective commanding officers' pool at Midway. So were Joe Adams, Ray Baldes, George Beck, Sherman Burns, John Cleppe, Juan Cosmijo, Leon E. Labrecque, O. A. Morgan, Numeriano Morrill, Art Murphy, Dom Paolo, Walter Rogers, Lyford Smith, and Robert Sweet—all "plank owners," crewmen who had put the boat into her first commission. It was the Navy's policy to gather up as many qualified submariners as they could when a new submarine was launched. And that meant a score of NQPs were coming in to replace these men on the boat.

Batfish had taken on some new equipment, too, during her refit in Pearl. She was ready to go back to war. But apparently, her commander was not.

There was plenty of scuttlebutt when the division commander came down to the boat to talk with Captain Merrill the day before they completed their testing and were scheduled to leave Pearl Harbor for her third run. The new XO, the former diving officer, Jim Hingson, had been conducting the trials because Merrill was too ill.

That afternoon, a new captain unexpectedly showed up to relieve Wayne Merrill. Captain John Kerr Fyfe came aboard *Batfish* before the day was over as her prospective commanding officer. He insisted that his wardroom call him Jake. The sudden appointment of a new skipper fueled rampant rumors when someone heard that the former skipper was to be called up for some kind of investigation.

Indeed, there was an inquiry, which the group commander held in his office. Each of *Batfish*'s senior officers was called in to testify. Captain Merrill was there. So was an impressive array of Navy brass.

The subject of the inquiry was the incident at the Gooney Bird Hotel when two of the officers threw their inebriated skipper out the window. Even though all of them, including the XO who had had his differences with Merrill, testified that the incident had all been in good fun, the group commander saw it as "a terrible thing to have happen." He felt that any submarine captain who had been thrown out a window by his officers had lost his usefulness to the boat, so Wayne Merrill was summarily relieved of his command.

No one aboard then is sure if Merrill's punishment was really because of the silly incident that night in Midway, or if it was the Navy's way of replacing someone they felt was not getting the job done in the simplest, cleanest way. Most who served with Merrill report that he was a fine skipper and a good commander. Others speculate that the pressures of war, the things he witnessed before his command, the narrow misses with all those boats he served aboard and that were promptly lost after he left them—all of that may have been more pressure than he could handle, once the burden of running a submarine was heaped on him.

With a new skipper and XO and a one-quarter new crew, *Batfish* steamed out of Pearl Harbor on May 10, bound for Midway, then off to some patrol area somewhere in the Pacific Ocean.

But headed for what? More boredom and frustration? Glory? Death? Who knew what awaited them this time with a new skipper on the bridge?

It wouldn't take them long to find out.

ELEVEN

An Actual World War II Submarine

May 1972

Muskogee, Oklahoma, is a burg of roughly forty thousand citizens, located in the rolling hills of the eastern part of the state. A quote on the city's official Web site claims that "Muskogee was conceived in the spirit of the Native American and born when steel rails bridged the muddy Arkansas River. As it matured, it was flavored by a mixture of hide and horn, of farmers' unremitting toil, and of pioneer merchants' vision. Muskogee—city and county—has been blessed with extraordinary talent in diverse fields, people who hoped and dreamed, who built and created, and who have been willing to contribute to projects the pessimists said could 'never be done.'"

The chamber of commerce is properly proud of Muskogee's Five Civilized Tribes Museum over on Honor Heights Drive; the annual Azalea Festival, named by a group called the National Bus Association as one of its top one hundred events to attend; and a "unique attraction, an actual World War II submarine," the USS *Batfish*, over near the river.

Still, it's likely if you ask people in other parts of the country about Muskogee, if they know anything about the town at all, it would probably be the song "Okie from Muskogee." Oklahoma native Merle Haggard wrote and recorded the song and took it to number one on the country music charts in 1969, during the Vietnam War. Its lyrics proudly proclaimed that folks in Muskogee didn't smoke marijuana, take LSD, or burn their draft cards like "the hippies out in San Francisco do." To the contrary, they preferred living right and being free.

The citizens of Muskogee don't disclaim Haggard's words. The chamber of commerce even offers for sale merchandise—belt buckles, T-shirts, and key chains—so anyone can advertise how proud he or she is to be an "Okie from Muskogee."

Plenty of others identified with the song, too. The original lyrics are on display in the Smithsonian Institution in Washington, D.C. Haggard gave a command performance of the song in the White House for President Richard Nixon, and a recording of the song is encased in a time capsule on the moon. It was Haggard's biggest-selling record, even though the controversy over the song's political stance cost the country star numerous bookings and kept him off network television for years.

As Haggard pointed out in his song's lyrics, people in Muskogee are patriotic. That was one of the reasons they were so excited when they heard that "their" submarine was finally on its way upriver.

On Monday, May 1, 1972, the Tulsa paper ran a small update article, just below another one that detailed then–FBI director J. Edgar Hoover's secret memos about the sex lives of various government officials. The tiny blurb reported that the *Batfish* had passed through Vicksburg, on the Mississippi River, the previous Saturday. The United Press International story said the tugboats *Billy Harbison* and *Razorback* were towing the sling-and-barge contraption with the submarine lashed between them.

In a bit of overstatement, the UPI writer went on to say, "The *Batfish* was one of the first subs sent out to patrol the Pacific Ocean after the bombing of Pearl Harbor." That statement would likely be disputed by the men who rode the more than one hundred other subs that were built before *Batfish*, as well as those existing boats that were on patrol the same day as the attack. The article did, however, acknowledge that the 310 boat was "a highly decorated World War II submarine."

Another article chronicled the boat's passage near De Witt, on the Arkansas River in the southeastern part of Arkansas, and there was a photo showing the unique multiboat contrivance as it passed through a lock on the river near Little Rock. It was barely able to slide into the lock. In the news photo, several men leaned against a rail on the shore and watched the odd spectacle as it eased into position before floating higher as the lock was flooded, then carefully pulling out and on its way.

She had made it through the narrow Lock and Dam Number Six with no mishap, but when the flotilla got a bit farther upriver, they ran into a snag. There was a bridge just to the north that everyone suddenly realized would be much too low for *Batfish* to pass underneath.

The tow crew was considering how they might remove enough of the submarine's masts, radar towers, and other structures of the shears to try to get her under the bridge, when someone hit upon a much simpler idea. A quick call to the Army Corps of Engineers solved the problem. The Corps agreed to open the gates back down at Dam Number Six and lower the level of the river by about three feet, to literally drain a portion of the river at that point. The old submarine was able to sneak under the bridge with a good inch or two to spare.

Once they were beyond Little Rock, things were going so well that one of the tugs turned back toward New Orleans. The second tug shoved on toward Fort Smith.

Waiting upriver at *Batfish*'s soon-to-be new home there were other problems that would be much more difficult to overcome than a low bridge or a tight squeeze in a lock. The Maritime Advisory Board had been promised a bond issue by the state Industrial and Park Department, the board's nominal boss. But there had been changes in the political landscape of the state since Kelly and Wheland had begun their quest for a pig boat. The governor had been narrowly defeated in the last election, and the new chief executive seemed disinclined to assist the board in their folly.

Through sheer force of will, Ace Kelly convinced the state to finally authorize the bond—now up to three hundred thousand dollars—and to back the two hundred thousand dollar promissory note that he and his band of submariners had already personally guaranteed. The Maritime Advisory Board would finally have a few bucks to work with. And they would need every bit of it. It would be over two years before that bond issue took place, and even then, the bonds would be worthless. Each bond was marked with a notation that it was in default upon its issue, a clever way for the state to meet its obligations by technically issuing a bond without actually incurring any debt. They would never contribute a cent to the *Batfish* project.

Sunday, May 7, was a blustery, cold day, the kind of weather that can happen even in late spring in Oklahoma. A light drizzle fell from a depressing, slate-gray sky.

Despite the gloom, a couple of thousand people braved the elements and lined the riverbank and stood along the pier at the Wills Brothers Port of Muskogee Terminal, near the temporary home of *Batfish*, to welcome their boat after her thirteen-day journey from New Orleans. The crowd ignored the howling wind and light rain and cheered heartily as the unusual convoy made its way around the bend in the muddy Arkansas River at a bit less than four knots.

First, a small fleet of pleasure craft appeared, each boat decorated with streamers and balloons. A yacht named the *Goodwill,* on loan from a local company, led the way. On her deck, Ace Kelly and a group of friends and other submarine veterans waved to the crowd on the bank.

Behind the boats were a river tug, several pushing barges, and, caught in the middle of it all like some kind of captured leviathan, the *Batfish*.

Truth be told, to most the gallant old lady looked downright ugly. Gray, battered, and rust streaked, she rode along reluctantly in the drizzle, high out of the water, her tank sides lewdly exposed.

But if any of the folks on the riverbank were disappointed with the appearance of their prized "submarine-killer submarine" when she came into view, they kept their thoughts to themselves. Even so, that first appearance by the vessel had to be a bit disconcerting. It might even have been anticlimactic after all those years of grand plans and dreaming out loud, then the three-month delay after she finally started the trip, followed by all the starts and stops and rumors of her backers running out of money, mixed with the hopeful promises of the submarine veterans.

Now, sure enough, there she was.

Of course, if Ace Kelly and the other dignitaries were anything less than thrilled with the appearance of their submarine, they didn't show it either. They saw only the proud old boat trailing along behind their armada, riding high, the decorative flags flying from her sail and shears, and the house broom that was now lashed to her mast. Tying a broom to the mast was an old submarine tradition signifying a return from a successful mission.

The rain intensified, and about half the crowd departed before the barges were tied up at the pier. The ones who remained moved over to where the presentation of the colors and a short docking ceremony were planned to formally welcome *Batfish* to Oklahoma. It was not to be an official, full-blown dedication ceremony—there were plans for that later, after the boat was cleaned up, painted, and open to the public.

Charles Williams, the Oklahoma state commander of the World War II submarine veterans group, led the crowd in a moment of silence in honor of the 3,500 submariners on eternal patrol as a result of hostilities during the war.

The pastor of an Eastern Orthodox church in Tulsa gave the invocation, praying to God that America's armed strength would always be greater than that of her enemies.

Mr. Albert C. "Ace" Kelly was the master of ceremonies. He stepped to the podium, surveyed the crowd, and then glanced toward where the submarine towered over the pier. The old girl had made it. After all the naysaying and negative thoughts that had been launched in her direction, there she was, right where he and his shipmates had promised everyone she would eventually be, even if she had shown up to the square dance a few years late.

Never mind that the meter was running on the six barges that still held her captive and would do so until she was finally secured somewhere. One other barge was also technically still under rental, even though it lay in silt on the bottom of the Mississippi River in New Orleans. The bill was adding up already to something north of six grand per month. Never mind that there was no channel dredged out yet to move her over to the War Memorial Park. And never mind that the bond issue money was still months away in the best-case estimate, and that the Maritime Advisory Board's bank account was practically empty of borrowed money.

The hard part was done. The submarine veterans had delivered *Batfish* to Muskogee, just the way they had set out to do. Soon the citizens and schoolchildren of Oklahoma would be able to enjoy her and to truly appreciate the brave things she and her crew—and all the other sailors like them—had done.

"Ladies and gentlemen, let's all welcome *Batfish* to her new home," Kelly said to applause and cheers. He informed the crowd of a bit of historical trivia: At that moment, *Batfish* was at the highest elevation any submarine had ever been in the United States. The water level at the Port of Muskogee is about 490 feet above sea level. It wasn't quite Pikes Peak, but it was something of interest to note.

He went on to speak about the crew members who had served on the vessel, and about the men who had helped in the monumental task of bringing this memorial to Oklahoma.

"Folks, this submarine is immaculate inside. We have plans to have her in fine shape by the middle of June so you can all go aboard and see what life was like aboard one of these boats. It will take us thirty days to have her ready!" he stated emphatically.

The crowd cheered again. Kelly, ever the determined optimist, knew how much work was yet to be done, even as he swore in front of God and a thousand other witnesses that it could be completed in a month.

Batfish would have to be completely ventilated. The odor of diesel fuel below decks was so overpowering that people, workers or visitors, would not have been able to stay inside for more than a minute or two. Even the most confident observer could see that she needed to be sandblasted, repainted, and have her missing and rotten decking replaced. There were ladders to secure, stairways to build, hatches to replace, and much more to be done before the schoolchildren of Oklahoma or old sub sailors who had long since lost their sea legs could safely wander about her.

Karl Wheland then got up and announced to the crowd that five acres of land near the U.S. 69 bridge over the Arkansas River had been obtained for a park that would salute not only the new submarine and others like her, but all veterans in all branches of the service who had given their lives for their country. He also told them that the boat would not only be a tourist attraction but would serve as a training facility for Sea Cadets, boys between the ages of twelve and seventeen who were interested in careers in the Navy.

Then Wheland brought up Navy captain Joe Chambliss, a member of the Maritime Advisory Board who also happened to still be an actual naval officer. Captain Chambliss at that time served as commander of the Naval Depot at McAlester, sixty miles south of Muskogee. He had already promised Wheland and the rest of the sub vets that the depot would cooperate in outfitting *Batfish* and in coming up with other items to be displayed in the War Memorial Park's combat museum. Wheland and Chambliss had already discussed getting a deck gun and some disarmed torpedoes for folks to take a look at.

One of the project's earliest and most influential supporters, state senator James Inhofe, had driven down from Tulsa to help welcome the submarine. He told the crowd that he had hoped *Batfish* would end up at the Port of Tulsa in Catoosa, but the Verdigris River was just too shallow and narrow for something the size of this old girl. Still, he promised, she would be a major tourist attraction for the entire state and region.

In order to tie *Batfish* even tighter to Oklahoma, the sub vets had made certain that W. E. Battenfield was there to welcome her to Muskogee. He was the only Oklahoman they could dig up who had actually served aboard the boat, even though that billet came in 1946, after the war was over. Battenfield was now a member of the Maritime Advisory Board. A Tulsan named Bill Conklin was introduced as well. He had helped install sonar gear on the boat when she was in Key West in 1952.

E. E. Reardon, the engineer for the *Batfish* project from Williams Brothers Engineering, may have gotten the biggest ovation of the day. Those gathered there had followed the boat's progress upriver in the papers and knew what a chore it had been and how unique the method Reardon had come up with was. Kelly made mention that the engineering firm had financed the transportation of the submarine as well. He didn't say anything about the fact that the company had yet to be paid a cent for their efforts, or that their invoices were already past due.

Kelly and Wheland smiled and exchanged handshakes with the rest of the members of the Maritime Advisory Board and other dignitaries gathered there that damp day. If Kelly had any doubts that his thirty-day deadline could be met, he didn't show it.

But then, Ace Kelly had never had any doubts about the project from the very beginning. And now that his submarine was home where she belonged?

What other catastrophe could possibly come along now to blow their bold plan out of the water?

TWELVE

Crush Depth

The Cherokee Indians believed that bodies of water were almost certainly gateways to the underworld, and the underworld was, of course, a place to be avoided as long as
possible. That was one of the reasons many of them resisted
so violently being placed on flatboats to float down the Tennessee River and toward their new forced homeland in
Oklahoma. They were afraid the boats would sink to the bottom, sending them straight to hell.

May 1944

Considering the lack of success on her first two war patrols, it may be surprising to some that *Batfish* became considerably more productive on her next five. Only a few of her crew made all seven patrols, including Bill Crockett, Tex Davis, Joe Farnsworth, Jim Garnet, Bill Gibson, Lew Hammond, Dutch Larch, Wayne McCann, Bob Oswald, Ruben Pepper, George Becker, Vernon Slunaker, Joe Tuma, Ernest Witte, and Charlie Cartmill. But despite the prevalence of fresh, inexperienced faces aboard, the next patrols enjoyed better weather, more fruitful patrol areas, changing tactics that improved the chances of U.S. subs against their enemies, and better equipment. But a part of the thanks should certainly go to her skipper on each of those next four runs, John Kerr "Jake" Fyfe.

And that was partly because his methods were markedly different from Wayne Merrill's. Some might say different *and* riskier. Some might also speculate that his aggressiveness came from an experience he had the Sunday morning that the war began.

On December 7, 1941, Jake Fyfe was aboard the USS *Dolphin* (SS 159), a 1930s-vintage submarine parked at pier number four, berth S-8, at Pearl Harbor. From there, as he and his shipmates used the deck guns on their boat to fire at the attackers and bring down at least one dive-bomber, he could also see across the harbor as the Japanese aircraft dropped their loads of bombs and torpedoes on the ships lined up along Battleship Row. Among those battleships was USS *California* (BB 44). She was one of the first ships struck that morning, and almost one hundred of her crew members would die in the attack, many of them in the hellish flames in the oily water of the harbor. Three crewmen of the *California* would receive the Congressional Medal of Honor for their actions that morning, all posthumously.

Jake Fyfe knew many of those men well. Some of them had been among his best friends, former classmates, and former shipmates. The *California* had been Fyfe's home for over two years after he graduated from Annapolis and before he went to submarine school.

As soon as she could be made shipshape, *Dolphin* steamed out of Pearl shortly after the attack, looking for Japanese submarines. Fyfe went on to serve aboard her for two more years.

He rarely talked about how witnessing the attack might have affected him. He had always had a "pleasant nature" and was "a good conversationalist," according to the Naval Academy yearbook. But those who served with him described him as all business, a skipper who saw sinking an enemy ship as a problem to be solved. And he seemed to take great personal delight in solving that problem effectively. He had mentioned on occasion that, as he stalked and prepared to violently dispatch a shipload of human beings to their graves, he pictured his own former shipmates, floundering in the fiery water of Pearl Harbor or valiantly trying to save their ship and her crew as the sneak attack raged on all about them.

On Fyfe's first patrol as commander of *Batfish*, the boat sank five vessels—almost ten thousand tons—got themselves soundly depth-charged and torpedoed, ran into a volcanic peak at 240 feet deep where charts said they should have had four hundred feet of water, and even got the submarine entangled in a fishnet, from which the crew extracted themselves with penknives. They came through the depth-charging with only some frayed nerves, rattled fillings, and popped gauge covers and lightbulbs.

The first time they sank a ship under Fyfe's command, new radioman Stan Javorski listened to the death rattle of the enemy vessel and said to himself, "May God have mercy on their souls." It was the first time Javorski had participated in an action that directly led to people dying. But he had little chance to consider the situation. They were quickly in the middle of a cluster of depth charges, and Javorski was counting them out loud as they hit the water, as they armed themselves and exploded, bouncing the crew around inside the boat as if they were inside a pinball machine.

"May God have mercy on *my* soul!" the young radioman cried out.

The boat was shadowing a convoy very near the Japanese mainland on the morning of June 28 when Fyfe's refreshing aggressiveness led to some anxious moments for the crew. In his patrol report, the skipper would later describe his attempt to take a look at a convoy of enemy ships through the periscope. The light tone of his words belied the tense few minutes that resulted. It started when the Japanese dropped a bomb on them, and things got worse from there.

"Up periscope for a setup on the new course. Down bomb. This was a light bomb but it landed very close, knocking cork loose, breaking a few gauge glasses, electric light bulbs and doing the usual misalignment job on fans and the like. It was so close to the periscope that the two feet or so that was inside the boat whipped around like a willow rod. It also smashed the bridge repeater and knocked the master gyro follow-up system out of line."

Undaunted by almost having a bomb land on top of them, they were lining up for an attack using the stern tubes when the soundman suddenly yelled over the intercom, "Torpedoes! Coming fast in our direction! Bearing one-six-oh!"

"Take her down!" Fyfe barked. "Right full rudder! Flank speed!"

They had to do some quick ducking and dodging to try to get out of the path of those deadly fish. The skipper motioned for everyone to be quiet. Then, in the near silence, every man on board could clearly hear the whine of the approaching torpedoes, growing ominously louder by the second.

No one breathed.

The propellers on the incoming torpedoes fairly screamed. No one had the time to panic. There was nowhere to hide. Nowhere to duck for cover. They could only hope their sudden dive and course change would get them out of the way of the rapidly approaching missiles.

Then, fortunately, as Fyfe took the *Batfish* through evasive maneuvers, the sound of the torpedoes' screws changed in pitch, weakening as they missed close behind them, and continued harmlessly through the water. A collective sigh of relief was audible throughout the boat.

Captain Fyfe seemed more upset about their losing their setup on the targets than he was about the enemy launching torpedoes at them. He had no idea how the enemy had even had an inkling that they were there.

The next patrol, *Batfish*'s fourth, was not nearly so dramatic or productive. Fyfe would later speculate that the area, near the islands of Palau, had lost the interest of the Japanese. He suggested in his report that, should the Marines decide to make an assault on the enemy garrisons there, he would expect resistance to be light.

Batfish did encounter an unidentified submarine on August 5, and they indulged in a frustrating game of hide-and-seek for almost two hours before ultimately losing contact with the other pig boat. Captain Fyfe put an entry in the log that evening that read: "Unable to regain contact and since it's a big ocean out here, and this is like looking for a needle in a haystack, gave up the search and continued on toward our area. A surfaced submarine or, for that matter, a submerged submarine is not very adaptable for hunting down another submarine which is submerged and which was 7½ miles away when last seen."

A week later, they did another dance with an unidentified submarine with the same results. Fyfe showed not only his wile but his sense of humor when he wrote: "This is the second time this situation has come up, and each time I've closed too much while trying to get ahead of him and on his track in order to dive, identify him undetected, and fire either torpedoes or smoke bombs. Next time we will stay out of sight and use a Ouija board."

They sank only two vessels on the boat's fourth patrol near Palau, but they were both Japanese destroyers—quite worthy targets and well worth the nine torpedoes that were fired on the trip. The first was a *Minekaze*-class destroyer, sunk near Ngaruangl Island amid the treacherous reefs and islets north of Palau. The second destroyer was a *Fubuki*-class destroyer, and while she wasn't technically sunk, *Batfish*'s torpedoes cut her in half where she had run aground in the Ngaruangl Passage.

This time, instead of Midway or Pearl Harbor, *Batfish* went to Fremantle, Australia, and then nearby Perth, for repairs and R & R. Some of the crew, including Captain Fyfe, had been there before, but it was a special treat for most of the men to have a few weeks to spend in a new locale designed almost exclusively as a submarine base, with amenities that were most attractive to submariners.

On *Batfish*'s fifth patrol, taking her to the western approach to the Mindanao Sea, she had a near-fatal encounter with a Japanese sub-hunting Q-ship.

Just after dark on October 19, 1944, the boat began tracking a radar contact at eighteen thousand yards, an apparition that slowly revealed itself to be a large tanker, and two small escort vessels. The tanker was a prime target, considering the Japanese Empire's unquenched thirst at this stage of the war for petroleum.

With an almost perfect setup on a slow-moving bull's-eye, *Batfish* sent six torpedoes in the direction of the tanker, three set to run at a depth of four feet, three at six feet. Then they watched, waiting for the anticipated eruptions of explosions and fire.

They never came. Instead, the dim trail of all six torpedoes disappeared beneath the big target. Every one of them had underrun the ship!

Fyfe and his fire control crew were baffled. How could something that big not draw more than four feet of water?

Fyfe documented his thought process: "Pulled out to 10,000 yards and started pacing him while I mulled over the situation. I was beginning to smell a rat but hadn't quite made up my mind just what we had. Trying to reconcile the large appearing silhouette, and the strong radar signal with the light draft, the high speed screws and the fact that he wasn't zig zagging and took no evasive measures after firing was a little on the vague side; so I decided we would work up ahead, get on his track and look him over from periscope depth in the morning."

But the skipper couldn't wait. The apparent sheer size of what seemed to be a tanker was about the easiest target he had ever seen. Just after midnight, he fired off one more carefully aimed torpedo from the number ten tube, with the fish set to run at only one foot deep.

The damn thing ran true, so near the surface it actually breached a time or two. Then it disappeared right underneath the tanker with no explosion.

The torpedo wasn't a total waste, as it did hit the escort on the far side of the intended target, sinking the smaller vessel immediately. The tanker and second escort vessel acted as if nothing had happened. They merely continued to amble along, as if they had not even noticed that somebody had lobbed seven deadly torpedoes in their direction.

"By this time I was mad enough to chew nails and we started working up ahead so as to be on his track at dawn and I went down to sleep it off for a couple of hours," Fyfe wrote.

The OOD sent someone down to wake him at four a.m. The lumbering target had made a radical course shift. Fyfe went back to the conning tower and watched through the scope until daylight confirmed that the target was still there. He also decided anything that big and deserving of two escorts was more than worth the time and trouble to try to bag.

Since it seemed that they would never be able to sink the thing with a torpedo, Fyfe decided to go up and make a surface attack, using the deck guns. They should have far more firepower than the little escort vessel, and the tanker was most likely unarmed. Maybe they could lob a few shots from the four-incher and do enough damage to send the enemy boat to the bottom. Or at least put enough holes in the tanker that it would be a long time before she hauled any more Philippine oil back to the homeland.

But as they drew to within about three miles, the lookouts noticed something peculiar.

"They're turning our way!" one sailor shouted. "Coming right at us!"

That was peculiar. Tankers would normally try to zig and zag and avoid getting hit until they could get away from a sub attacker. This big, fat sitting duck seemed to be spoiling for a fight. Fyfe looked fore and aft on the deck of his boat. Gun crews were in place. Ammo handlers stood by, ready to pass along more ordnance as needed. His men were ready.

"Captain, they're taking tarpaulins off stuff on the deck of the tanker, uncovering something," the lookout shouted. "Damn! They got guns! Big guns!"

Fyfe could see it for himself now. On the deck of what he thought was a tanker, men were hastily unhinging and dropping plates, removing canvas covers, revealing what looked to be a phalanx of four-inch guns, depth-charge launchers, machine guns, torpedo tubes.

What they thought was a tanker turned out to be a cleverly disguised Q-boat, a special ship designed to flush out and kill enemy subs. Such stealthy methods, born out of desperation, had actually started with the British in World War I and were used against the German U-boats. Then the idea continued in World War II, with the United States employing their own Q-boat decoys off the Atlantic seaboard, again against the Germans and their deadly submarines.

The ruse consisted of camouflaging gunboats to resemble innocent, unarmed merchant vessels, but in reality, they carried heavy armor to repulse torpedo attacks and a full complement of weapons they could use quite effectively to attack an underwater vessel that might be lured too close. And it worked. A submarine, believing the target was benign and easy pickings, would get within range of the ships' guns. And if the guns didn't get him, the torpedoes and depth charges had a good chance to do so if the sub dived to try to get away.

It was quickly obvious to Jake Fyfe that the Japanese had now adopted their own stratagem, and they were about to unleash hell upon *Batfish*.

"Emergency!" he called. "Hard right rudder! Full speed!"

The men on deck scrambled, balancing themselves against the sudden sway of the boat as they scurried back down the fore and aft torpedo room hatches. Just then, giant plumes of water erupted on either side of the submarine, close enough to drench Fyfe, his XO, and the lookouts.

At least a dozen more salvos fell all around the fleeing sub, some so near that the crew could feel the concussion of the blast on their faces as the boat yawed noticeably in response.

Though *Batfish* had a one-knot advantage in speed, it would take time before they could outrun the range of the Q-boat's guns. And just one of those shells could do mortal damage to the boat.

Fyfe sounded the klaxon and ordered them to dive deep. The well-oiled crew was able to get the *Batfish* beneath the surface in half a minute, but they were still hardly safe.

Depth charges, one after the other, began to explode all around them as the boat pierced the depths at a steep angle, diving toward the bottom of the Pacific. The Japanese on the Q-ship knew exactly what they were doing. Each succeeding cluster of ash cans were set to explode deeper and deeper, the depth charges following their prey as it went farther down.

Aboard *Batfish*, the lights flickered out, replaced by red emergency lighting. There was a harried damage report from up front. The word from the forward torpedo room was that the loading hatch had sprung and water was pouring in, threatening to flood the compartment. It would be hard to control a dive as steep as the one they were in the process of if the front of the boat was filling up with seawater. There was a real chance they would sink too fast, unable to level off, and plummet toward the compressing depths of the ocean.

The crew hastily rigged a block-and-tackle apparatus and managed to dog the hatch as best they could to stop the flooding. Meanwhile, the diving officer finally got *Batfish* leveled off, somewhere between the boat's test depth (the deepest she was supposed to ever dive on purpose, about 412 feet) and her crush depth (the depth at which the pressure of the seawater would be expected to buckle her solid-steel superstructure). It was hard to tell how deep they were now because the instruments that measured such things had already broken.

The *click-boom!* of the depth charges was now mixed with the continuous, menacing groan of the submarine's hull and superstructure. No one wanted to think about what might happen if there was a faulty weld somewhere, or a flawed expanse of iron that might not hold up under the tremendous pressure the boat was now forced to endure.

Slowly, deliberately, they were able to bring the submarine up again, but that put them in the middle of the fireworks. Then, at about 390 feet, *Batfish* stumbled into a submarine under siege's best friend: a temperature gradient, an area of seawater whose temperature varies significantly from the water around it. That temperature difference can actually bend or bounce back a surface vessel's sonar waves and effectively hide the submarine. It was the same as floating into a cave to hole up for a while.

Batfish stopped and waited at a depth of nearly four hundred feet, hoping the depth-charging would soon cease. They waited for hours, so long it became hard to breathe if anyone stood or moved around the boat at all. A cigarette wouldn't stay lit in the thin, dirty air, and everyone's breathing had become shallow and raspy.

When the explosions had subsided, they left the cover of the temperature gradient and sped away. They went as far as they could go before the air inside *Batfish* became too polluted to sustain them any longer. Men were dizzy, trying to remain as still as possible to reduce the amount of air they needed. A quick run up to periscope depth confirmed that the Q-ship and her partner were nowhere in sight.

At last, they could surface.

When the hatch popped open, the fresh sea air that poured down into the conning tower was the sweetest anyone could remember smelling. The welcome breeze swirled trash and scraps of paper all about the boat's interior. It also fanned clouds of chemical powder that had been spread about the decks to help scrub unbreathable CO_2 from the fetid air.

"A curse on all 'Q' ships!" Jake Fyfe wrote in the patrol log.

On a patrol in which she experienced several mechanical problems, had limited success with her attacks, and was ambushed by a Q-ship, the main problem experienced on *Batfish*'s fifth run—according to her crew, anyway—was the food. The boat was reprovisioned before she left Fremantle, but it wasn't long before the complaints about the quality of the food were the order of the day. Even the boat's newspaper complained about how lousy the provisions from Australia were. Captain Fyfe made it a point to let his superiors know that such food was detrimental to the success of a patrol.

"On two different occasions 300 pounds of beef had to be thrown overboard, and fowl once. Weevils were encountered in both the rice and the macaroni, cutting the supply of these staple foods almost in half. In many cases canned fruits were found to be green and canned fruit juices, except for apple juice, were so bitter that it was impossible to drink more than a swallow," Captain Fyfe documented in his official report. "In my opinion, morale and patrol results are in a direct ratio to the food served, and while the preparation of it is the responsibility of the boat, no navy cooks are capable of performing miracles. We have two first class men, both with experience above average, and many of their best efforts went to feed the sharks."

It was one thing to face a hail of Japanese depth charges. It was another altogether to have to drink acidic fruit juice and eat rancid beef.

Despite the food, the crew was in good spirits as they headed to Hawaii for refitting that conveniently would have them there over Christmas. Captain Fyfe had gotten them in a few pickles and close scrapes, for certain, but at least he was going after the enemy. That was what they were out there for, right?

Once in Hawaii, the men who had been aboard for the last three runs were only too happy to regale the two dozen or so newcomers to *Batfish* with stories about Captain Jake. That included Clark Sprinkle, her new XO, who had shipped over from *Batfish*'s sister boat *Archerfish*.

"You better get used to getting your ass depth-charged," they warned Sprinkle. "And don't think nothing about it if he runs you right up into a harbor to get a target, neither."

Fyfe had done just that at San Fernando, in the Philippines, during their fifth patrol, torpedoing two Japanese freighters head-on as they sat at their moorings at the wharf in the former tourist town. They didn't get official credit for damaging or destroying anything, since they weren't able to stick around and watch their torpedoes explode. Instead, they found it necessary to turn, dive as deep as they could manage in the shallow bay, and get out of the harbor while a swarm of buzzing planes dropped explosives right on top of them.

"Yeah, and don't be surprised if he pops his head up in the middle of a pack of patrol boats either."

Fyfe had done that, too, almost putting the periscope through the bottom of an IJN vessel.

By the time they were refitted, retrained, reprovisioned, and ready for their sixth war patrol, the crew of *Batfish* was taking bets on what Captain Jake would bag next, what feat he would attempt this time.

It is not known if anyone put money down on "three submarines in three days," but we do know nobody was betting against Captain John Kerr Fyfe.

And nobody was betting against *Batfish*.

THIRTEEN

First Target

February 1945

The radar signal on 158 megacycles was screaming, steady, certain. Then, just a couple of minutes after it first appeared, it abruptly grew even louder and finally hit saturation.

Whatever kind of vessel was out there in the dark night, it was close to where the USS *Batfish* (SS 310) bobbed gently in the soft roll of the Babuyan Channel. Eleven hundred yards away from them was the best estimate, tracking on a course of 310 degrees. The specter was driving off toward the northwest at what appeared to be a rock-steady twelve knots.

The electric thrill of it all ran up and down the length of the interior of the submarine within seconds of the signal coming up on the radar detector.

Once again, the chase was on.

It was a perfect night for stalking. Beyond the lip of the boat's bridge, there was nothing out there but velvet blackness. The sky was still cloudy, with no moon. Not even a sprinkle of starlight to wash away any bit of the night. Even the phosphorescence that usually played in the sea wash at the boat's stern seemed to have given up trying to put on any kind of a show in this stifling gloom.

Ears were sharpened, lookouts alerted, equipment tuned. Every minute or so, as the officer of the deck looked on, the radar operator in the conning tower below the bridge called a series of numbers up the hatch, citing the range and course of this new contact. Each report was an echo of the previous one. The vessel they were trailing was not varying its speed or direction of travel enough to mention, but duty and procedure required that he testify at regular intervals anyway.

Two men stood on the bridge of the submarine, just above the open hatch, staring intently into the darkness. They talked quietly as they rested against the chest-high metal enclosure that surrounded them. Neither their posture nor the tone of their voices hinted that they anticipated any sort of life-or-death struggle in the next few minutes. But that was exactly what the seething radar pip and their sudden chase promised them.

It was the ninth of February 1945, just after ten p.m. local time. The *Batfish* was now in the midst of her sixth patrol since the beginning of World War II. So far, the run had been less productive than most of the five previous ones. Her crew was hungry.

The pair of officers who stood on *Batfish*'s bridge used the railing to steady themselves against the roll of the waves as they gazed through their binoculars, searching the night for any sign of this unidentified vessel that now shared their portion of the sea. The lookouts above them peered off in each direction of the compass, looking for the new contact as well as for other vessels that might be slipping up on them with the sinister idea of making *Batfish* their target.

Captain John K. "Jake" Fyfe stared fiercely into the blackness. The skipper of the *Batfish* was an experienced sub sailor. He was now guiding *Batfish*, his first submarine to command, through hostile waters for his fourth run at the helm.

Fyfe bore some resemblance to the young actor Karl Malden, but now there was a frown on his handsome face as he tried to make out something—anything—out there ahead of their bow. He hoped to catch a glimpse of a form that might give him a clue as to what it was that they were chasing. He needed only a hint of a silhouette on what little horizon there was so he could determine the size of their prey. The quick flare of a carelessly lit cigarette on the deck of a tanker. A sliver of light from some destroyer's porthole, its blackout curtain maybe shaken loose in the previous few days' bad weather.

But there was nothing to see. Nothing but tropical night enveloping them, and only the intercepted radar signal to let them know there was somebody else out there.

Fyfe wasn't complaining about the darkness. These were perfect conditions for a submarine to hunt in. But the captain knew the setup was equally ideal for the Japanese to stalk them if they were of such a mind. If they even suspected he and his boat were here, the enemy would certainly be on the hunt.

Fyfe could hear the voices of the lookouts in the shears above him, talking softly to each other as they continued their own scan of the darkness.

"You think they're really carrying gold?" the starboard lookout whispered to his shipmate.

"Gold. Generals. Collaborators. I don't give a damn. I just want to send their asses to the bottom."

"Hey, what was Captain Jake chewin' your butt about when we surfaced?"

"I had on a white T-shirt. He told me he wouldn't have such a perfect target runnin' around on the deck of his submarine. He sent me back down to put on a blue shirt."

The starboard lookout snickered.

"Hell, 'Ski, don't you even know how to dress up for a torpedo attack yet?"

Fyfe grinned. He liked the hearts of the men with whom he rode on *Batfish*. Truth was, he liked the hearts of most of the submariners he had encountered since he first began riding the plunging boats not long after graduating from Annapolis. They were such a close brotherhood. Not once had he ever heard anyone seriously question the job they had been called upon to do, or the way they went about doing it. Though he could see and feel and smell the fear on them sometimes, he had never heard a whimper or a cry or even so much as a whispered prayer, no matter the ferocity of a depth-charging or the viciousness of an aerial attack.

Now here they were, racing along on this shadowy bit of sea, feeling their way blind-eyed for some of their counterparts. They were also submariners, sailors who rode the "devil boats," or eel boats, as they were sometimes called. But these particular submariners were the enemy. The enemy who were just as sneaky and shifty and hard to pin down as *Batfish* was.

That was why they were out here this black night, running the pass between Fuga and Camiguin islands, two jagged little pissant splotches of land north of the main Philippine island of Luzon.

Intelligence claimed that the Japanese had sent four submarines—

almost half the boats they had left in the entire sixth fleet—down to the Philippines. They were supposed to be on a high-risk mission to evacuate the last of the Japanese brass who were left in the Philippines, and to pick up pilots, air crews, and technicians stranded there. They were said to be taking them all back to Formosa, where they still had planes to fly. And they could possibly be taking along some civilians who were still loyal to the Empire, and picking up essential wartime documents and plans as well. Of course there was plenty of scuttlebutt making the rounds among the boats that made up "Joe's Jugheads," the group of *Batfish*'s sister submarines that was patrolling this area with her. There were rumors about mounds of gold and stacks of money and the Filipino mistresses of the Japanese generals.

Whatever they were hauling, the Japanese were in one hell of a hurry, trying to get out ahead of General Douglas MacArthur, who was fulfilling his promise to return and reclaim the Philippines.

The ULTRA intelligence intercept had been cryptic but intriguing:

BELIEVE SUB RO-46 WILL ATTEMPT TO EVACUATE PERSON-NEL FROM NORTH LUZON 8 FEBRUARY BETWEEN 2030 AND 2130. LOADING POINT 1,000 METERS WEST OF BATULINAO POINT. WILL BE POSTPONED ONE DAY IF DIFFICULTY EN-COUNTERED.

"You think this might be one of the boats we're looking for, Skipper?" the man standing on the bridge next to Fyfe asked. This was Lieutenant Clark Sprinkle, executive officer of the boat. Sprinkle knew that the captain had access to no more information on the new contact than he did. But he also knew already, even though he had served with the skipper only since the beginning of this run, that Fyfe had a sixth sense about these things. Sometimes it appeared that he could smell a destroyer before it topped the horizon or before it had been marked by SJ radar. It seemed that he could hear the screws of a merchant ship or tanker before the guys with the sound gear could even detect the telltale noise signature.

"I'd bet my breakfast pancakes on it," Fyfe replied with certainty. He kept the glasses to his eyes, scanning the thin line where the horizon would most likely be if they could only see it. "And no matter what it is, I intend to ruin his damn day."

Sprinkle grinned. He liked his skipper's sense of humor almost as much as he did the man's aggressiveness once he began an assault. Fyfe believed in attacking first and getting the details later.

The contact wasn't an airplane. They could be certain of that. Their SD radar would have seen it already, even if the old equipment didn't have the ability to tell the direction from which an aircraft was coming.

It couldn't be any kind of sizable surface vessel either, a battleship or freighter, or their relatively new SJ radar would have spiked with at least a pip by now, as close as the contact seemed to be. But so far, the radar operator had reported nothing showing up on his screen.

The sound operator had nothing to report either. Whatever the vessel was, she was running quiet, too. Dangerously quiet.

Still, the radar signal the mysterious bastard was spitting out was strong, potent. It was obviously nearby, and on a channel that left little doubt about the affiliation of its owner. It wasn't a fishing boat. Not unless the fisherman was trying to poach his fish with radio-frequency energy before he caught them.

It had to be a submarine.

There was nothing to do but shadow the contact, keep close enough so as to not lose it in the blackness. At the same time, *Batfish* would have to stay far enough away so it would be less likely that they would be spotted or heard itself. That would give them a chance to line up a higher-odds shot, and keep an eye out for some other adversarial vessel that might want to crash the party. The hunter could become the hunted in this deadly game, and he wouldn't even know it until he was bagged and barbecued.

Almost an hour after first contact, Fyfe got the call up the hatch that he had been eager to hear since the first report that they had company.

"Captain, SJ contact. Bearing two-four-zero true. Range eleven thousand yards."

The target had finally popped on *Batfish*'s radar. The bearing was off the port bow. Now they at least knew the direction in the murkiness in which to look, even if they still couldn't see squat.

Fyfe repeated the bearing loud enough for the men in the shears above him to hear, and then asked, "You boys see anything?"

"No, Skipper."

"No, sir. Not yet. We will."

The contact had not changed course or speed in the entire time they had been tailing him. But the bastard finally made enough of an impression to bounce back a shard of the radar sweep. Still, whoever it was, the craft gave no indication that it suspected *Batfish* was out here on its tail, getting ready to play a deadly game of tag.

No matter. Fyfe and his navigator and the maneuvering room watch and the guys in the engine room and those in the conning tower and control room below made certain that they kept the boat to the east of the contact, shadowing the enemy's run, ready to dive in an instant if need be or get ready to make a surface attack if that method seemed more prudent. On an almost completely dark night, keeping the target to the west made it marginally darker, and there would be less chance of the Japanese catching sight of *Batfish*'s silhouette while they steamed along on the surface, hopefully still unaware of their stalker.

Jake Fyfe concentrated on the reported radar bearing, resisting the urge to look over his shoulder. There were other Japanese submarines in these waters, too. That was why *Batfish* hunted here in the first place. Other warships, too, though not so many as there might have been a few months before. The war had clearly turned already, its end all but inevitable, but everyone aboard *Batfish* knew that a cornered enemy was the most dangerous kind of varmint there was. Especially an enemy who felt that dying for the Emperor was a punched ticket to a blessed afterlife.

Fyfe hoped the radar or his soundman would catch sight or hear the noise of anybody creeping up on their behind. There was little hope the lookouts could see anyone approaching in this gloom, any more than he and Sprinkle and the port lookout could see any sign of the guy who was now boldly painting the Babuyan Channel with his radar energy.

"Sound reports quiet screws, four thousand yards," came the next report.

Fyfe dropped his glasses and looked at Sprinkle, a cocked grin on his face.

"XO, if I were you, I wouldn't take my pancake bet. Looks like we got ourselves an IJN submarine."

"It would have been a sucker bet, Skipper," Sprinkle said with a crooked grin of his own.

IJN. Imperial Japanese Navy. A submarine. One of their own kind.

No one had to mention how difficult it would be for one sub to bag another. They were simply too stealthy, too sneaky. But *Batfish* and her crew were duty-bound to try.

Especially if their skipper was Jake Fyfe. His crew swore that Captain Jake would take the five-inch guns to a bumblebee if the damn thing got in his way.

"Battle stations—surface," Fyfe sang out.

Those three words set the entire boat into an even more intense hum. Every man on watch was quickly at his position, if he hadn't been there already. Those not on watch ran to whatever their assigned stations were, ready to get about the work of sending the enemy to the bottom of the sea. Every man did just as he had been trained and qualified to do.

No telling what kind of anthill they were about to kick over. They were poised to launch hot torpedoes at one of the most elusive targets of the Imperial Japanese Navy. At a vessel that was perfectly capable of shooting deadly fish right back at them.

Indeed, they could very well be lining up to do that very thing even as *Batfish* steamed in fat and happy, stalking them. Fyfe knew from hard-earned experience that the Japanese could be suckering the American sub in with that blatant, blaring radar signal on an unfamiliar frequency. They could be lulling them closer by steaming on a steady, true course, the perfect bait for a mighty dangerous trap. They could be waiting now for *Batfish* to drive close in and then blow them to hell and back.

It didn't matter to Fyfe and his crew, though. This was precisely what they had been sent halfway around the world to do. And they were the kind of men who did their duty when called upon.

Batfish, her skipper, and her crew were about to go shooting.

FOURTEEN

A Second Chance

February 1945

The best estimate from *Batfish*'s radar and sound gear put the newly acquired target's speed at twelve knots. He was still moving toward the pass between Fuga and Camiguin islands, steaming along at a leisurely pace, as if he didn't have a care in the world and was oblivious to the American sub that was tailing him. The speed and course information had been fed into the TDC. Torpedoes were already loaded and ready in tubes fore and aft. Everyone was on station, waiting, hoping, watching the radarscope, and listening to the exchange on the boat's PA and up and down the hatch from the conning tower to the bridge.

"Let's stay up top," Captain Jake Fyfe ordered from the bridge of *Batfish*. If an attack was indeed imminent, it would most likely be on the surface. Unlike previous submersibles, this new breed of sub was built to be more maneuverable on the sea's surface than when they were submerged.

"Aye, Captain."

"They'll never see us in this darkness." Fyfe looked up at the murky sky. "But let's stay east of him just to make sure." Clark Sprinkle nodded his concurrence, though it was both unnecessary and unseen in the thick night. "Bow tubes ready to fire?" the skipper asked, knowing already what the response would be.

The confirmation came immediately. Four torpedoes were loaded, ready to be sent spinning off in the direction of the suspected Imperial Japanese Navy submarine.

Still, a couple of things were bothering Commander Fyfe. The radar signals they were picking up from the target didn't carry the usual Japanese signature, even though it was being beamed out on a known enemy wavelength. It seemed to be from a more sophisticated set, designed to look for air targets, and nearer the equal of the more advanced equipment installed in the American submarines. If it was better radar gear, it further confirmed they were trailing something valuable, not some variety of lesser warship.

But the signal could indicate something else, something that was quite worrisome. Fyfe knew there were at least five American submarines operating in the area, seeking the same set of mysterious vessels he and his crew were. There was the very real possibility that this target could be one of their sister boats, hunting out there in the night just as *Batfish* was doing, and either its gear was seriously out of calibration or the other boat was close enough that its radar spilled over onto the Japanese wavelength.

Fyfe idly scratched the stubble of a beard that had popped out since he had last taken the time to shave. If he hesitated too long, a plump, juicy warship could swim right off and leave them. Or the Japanese could wake up and realize they were being tailed and start shooting first.

If he wasn't careful, though, *Batfish* could send one of her own to the bottom.

The skipper had no choice. He would have to chance that the Japanese—if they were Japanese—weren't listening for enemy radio transmissions in these waters. And if they were, that they would not have time do anything about it once they heard the signals so close by.

"Prepare a message for our boats," Fyfe ordered, and then winked. "Let's make sure we aren't about to blow one of them to hell. That wouldn't look too smart on an attack report."

The radioman quickly composed and read his message back to Fyfe. The skipper gave the okay to transmit. Within minutes, replies came in from all five of the other boats in their wolf pack. To a man, they reported, "Not me."

It was confirmed. The target was the enemy.

And their signal was still saturating the detection equipment, their pip was as prominent as ever on the SJ radar scope.

Fyfe gave the command to pick up speed a couple more knots. He also began maneuvering to get into position to fire a complement of four Mark

18-2 torpedoes from the forward tubes on a 130-degree starboard track, each set to run at a depth of six feet and at a two-degree spread.

But suddenly, the vessel they were trailing made a radical turn to port.

"You think they heard the radio transmission and got spooked?" Sprinkle asked. The XO had never dropped his glasses from his eyes, despite the fact that he still had not seen anything out there but inky-black night. They really wanted a visual contact before launching an attack. If they didn't get it, they would shoot anyway, based on the radar and sound data.

"I doubt it," Fyfe answered. "They're probably just turning to go west of Fuga. They get out into the straits, though, and they might steam right off and leave us with nothing."

Word from below was that, despite the abrupt course shift, the target's radar was still booming, still giving Batfish all she needed to keep the vessel in her sights. But the speed had not varied. He didn't seem to be running from them at all. Probably the Japanese boat's skipper was more concerned about an aerial attack than one from another submarine. The radar signal was, if anything, stronger than before. Range to the target was dwindling. Soon, they were going to be able to drive right up next to the guy, close enough to wave and say, "Good morning!"

"He's sure being cooperative," Sprinkle observed. "They might as well turn on all the lights and have a dance out there on the deck."

Fyfe grinned for the first time in a while.

"Yeah. Bless their hearts."

The captain, too, continued to stare through his own glasses, but there was still no sign of anything out there in the darkness. He had to trust radar and sound to tell him where the enemy was, where he was headed, and how fast he was going if he wanted any chance of blowing him out of the water.

Now the target seemed to be maintaining the new course, likely headed for the island of Formosa, off the mainland Chinese coast. The target was swimming exactly as the intelligence had indicated he would be.

"Right full rudder," Fyfe barked. "All ahead flank."

Batfish was moving in for the kill. Everyone aboard, whether he heard the command or not, felt the big Fairbanks Morse diesel engines rumbling deeply on their mounts in the engine room. No matter how many times he had heard those words from the bridge or conn, no matter how often he felt the boat respond to the command to give chase to an enemy vessel, it still sent a thrill and a good shot of adrenaline through every sailor aboard.

This was what this vessel had been designed and built to do. This was what each of these men had signed on for and been trained to do, too.

At eleven thirty p.m., with the target at a range of 1,850 yards, just a few degrees off the starboard bow, Captain Jake Fyfe sang out, "Fire one!"

Everyone on board could feel the kick of thrust as the first torpedo was flushed out of the tube with high-pressure air, and then its own internal electric motor spun up, sending it quickly off toward the target.

Twelve seconds later the skipper sent the second torpedo whooshing away. Two more followed, twelve seconds apart. Four fish were gone and were running toward the enemy boat at better than twenty knots. Three hundred fifty yards after leaving *Batfish*, the torpedoes armed themselves, ready to detonate upon impact with the hull of the stalked enemy submarine.

The torpedoes were set to travel at a depth of six feet, plenty shallow enough to ram a surfaced submarine in the flank, explode, and do the most damage. The nose of each fish was aimed slightly to the left of its predecessor in what was termed a two-degree spread, all to help increase the likelihood that at least one of the weapons would strike its target. In most cases, with a target of this size, one successful hit was all it took to accomplish their goal.

Below the bridge, in the conning tower, the sailor designated to be the counter stared intently at a stopwatch. He listened hard for the explosion that would come when the powerful Torpex warhead on the first torpedo butted against the steel hull of the Japanese warship. He knew from experience when that boom should erupt, ripping apart the still, dark night and sending a flaring fireball into the black sky.

The young sailor listened, watching the maddeningly slow movement of the stopwatch hand.

Listened, watched.

All he heard was the ticking of the watch and the anxious breathing of the men on duty around him.

Jake Fyfe didn't need a stopwatch. From his perch on the bridge, he knew that too much time had gone by already without the anticipated boom and inferno.

All four of his torpedoes had missed. A full eight minutes later, the men aboard *Batfish* clearly heard four explosions, a neat twelve seconds apart, when the fish finally found ground on distant Fuga Island and detonated harmlessly on the beach there. The only damage would be to sand and mangrove.

Surely the submariners aboard the enemy vessel heard the explosions, too. They would now realize that somebody was shooting at them from behind. The Japanese boat was much closer to the island than *Batfish* was. They would surely begin evasive maneuvers now. Or line the boat up and start shooting back with their own complement of deadly torpedoes.

But the report called up from the conning tower and control room didn't back that expectation at all.

"No change in course or speed," radar reported.

"They probably figure it's nothing more than another bombing run on Fuga," Fyfe deducted, at a loss for any other explanation for the target's nonchalance.

"They still don't know we're here, then," Sprinkle said, pursing his lips.

The skipper took a deep breath, then exhaled slowly.

"Yeah, and that means we've been granted a second chance," Fyfe said through clenched teeth, his jaw set firmly. "We don't get too many of those in this war, XO. We don't want to waste it. And damn it, this time we're going to eyeball the son of a bitch before I waste any more of our fish on his sorry ass."

And with that, Fyfe dropped out of sight down the hatch. When his feet hit the decking in the conning tower, he stepped straight to where the attack officer stood over the plotting board, idly scratching his head, a puzzled look on his face as he studied the markings scrawled there. The skipper didn't even have to ask the obvious question when his shadow fell over the plot.

"We had her speed wrong," the attack officer said without looking up at his captain. "I'm not sure how, but we did. She's doing fourteen knots, not twelve. We missed astern."

The fish had swum where the target had recently been.

Fyfe considered the complicated geometry of what they needed to do to get into position to make another attack on the enemy boat. It never crossed his mind to pull back from the dangerous pursuit.

"How sure are you about fourteen?"

The attack officer didn't hesitate.

"Sure as I can be."

"Then let's go take another shot at the son of a bitch before he gets all the way to Formosa."

FIFTEEN

Hot Run!

February 1945

"Let's see if we can get in visual range, XO," Jake Fyfe said matter-of-factly, as if he were simply idling over for a closer look at the ladies on the bathing beach at Fremantle, not cozying up to what was most likely an Imperial Japanese Navy submarine with a swarm of restless torpedoes in her tubes. The skipper still stood on the bridge of his vessel, peering through his binoculars. And it was just as dark as ever.

After the four-torpedo miss, they had pulled out to five thousand yards and were running all-out, trying to make an end run around the same target they had failed to take before. In the meantime, the torpedomen in the bow room were hastily reloading their tubes.

It was a risky thing to do, this full-speed run. So far, the Japanese submarine appeared to have no inkling that they were being stalked, but *Batfish* was certainly being noisy and clumsy enough to be detected if the Japanese were only listening. Besides, the enemy boat was still running on the surface, where they could very well spy *Batfish* if Fyfe and his boat drew any closer. Still, firing at a target that could be seen was the best way to shoot to kill, and Fyfe did not hesitate to continue the assault.

They were going after the bastards. And this time, Fyfe wanted to get close enough to see what he was shooting at.

Below, the crew members could feel the electricity of the chase once more. The intensity of it all was actually heightened by their first near miss. Now, as they raced to get ahead of the Japanese vessel, the men were all too busy to think about what had gone on before. Or even to arrange the usual pool on the outcome of the attack. There was also the element of mystery to add to the thrill of the chase.

What if the boat they were shadowing was really full of Japanese generals? Crammed with top-secret documents? Carrying purloined gold?

Hell, it didn't matter if it was a damn garbage scow, as long as it carried the rising-sun flag!

By midnight, they were in place, within fifteen hundred yards of the radar pip they had been pursuing for over two hours.

"I see her," one of the lookouts in the shears called out. "Two points to the starboard of the bow."

"I see her, too," Clark Sprinkle said quietly.

There was no longer any doubt. It was the unmistakable profile of a Japanese submarine, possibly an I-class. A submarine that still, amazingly enough, appeared unaware of *Batfish*'s presence. Or maybe that was only a bluff. She just as easily could be, at that very moment, aiming torpedoes at her stalker, getting ready to blow *Batfish* out of the water.

Jake Fyfe pressed the bridge intercom button.

"We have visual on a Japanese submarine . . . range one thousand yards. Prepare to fire."

In the forward torpedo room, each man stood poised, sweating as much from the tension as from the heat in the compartment, though they were blessed with plenty of both. They were awaiting the final data before they sent their deadly fish away. Torpedoes were in the tubes, ready to be flushed.

In the conn, the firing officer calmly and deliberately fed data from Captain Fyfe and the radar operator into the TDC and relayed the results from the machine to the torpedomen up front via intercom.

Then came the call from Fyfe.

"Clear the bridge!"

The XO and lookouts bounced down from their perches and, in one motion, slid down the ladder into the conning tower below, their feet never touching the rungs of the ladder on the way down.

Taking the lookouts out of the shears now was a risk, too. Once they went below, their night vision would be ruined for a while, and they would be useless topside. But Fyfe also wanted to be able to dive instantly should this attack go sour, or in case someone uninvited decided to crash the party.

Batfish's commissioning party, August 1943, Portsmouth, New Hampshire. Captain Wayne Merrill is at center, smiling broadly. (ROBERT FULTON)

The three World War II skippers of *Batfish*. Left to right: Captain Wayne R. Merrill, Captain John K. Fyfe, and Captain Walter L. Small. (U.S. NAVY)

Commissioning officers for *Batfish*. Left to right: Ensign O. A. Morgan, Ensign W. L. McCann, Lieutenant D. A. Henning, Lieutenant Commander Wayne Merrill (CO), Lieutenant R. L. Black, Lieutenant J. M. Hingson, and Lieutenant Commander P. G. Molteni. (U.S. Navy)

Batfish at Pearl Harbor, Hawaii. (U.S. Navy)

Seeking visual contact on patrol in the Pacific. (U.S. Navy)

Machinist's mate Robert "Steamboat" Fulton on watch aboard *Batfish*. He served on the submarine for all seven of her World War II patrols. (U.S. Navy)

The control room diving station. Diving officer Herman Kreis watches the pitch carefully while crewmen James Garnet and Robert Craig operate the stern and bow plane controls. (U.S. Navy)

Lookouts in the shears scan the horizon for an enemy target. Skippers preferred to use their youngest crewmen as lookouts, assuming their eyesight was keener. (U.S. Navy)

A *Batfish* sailor on watch in the boat's electrical control room. (U.S. Navy)

Captain John K. "Jake" Fyfe on the bridge. Fyfe was awarded the service's highest honor, the Navy Cross, for his leadership in sinking three enemy submarines in an astonishing seventy-seven hours. (U.S. Navy)

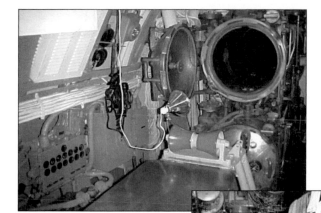

Close-up of one of the submarine's torpedo tubes and the assembly used to load the 1.5-ton weapons. (BRUCE BROTHERTON)

An unidentified *Batfish* crewman prepares the battle flag to fly from the periscopes as the boat returns from her sixth patrol. (U.S. Navy)

Batfish officers at about the time of the sixth war patrol. Front row, left to right: Lieutenant Reuben Pepper, Lieutenant Clark Sprinkle (XO), Commander John Fyfe (CO), Lieutenant Gerson Berman, and Lieutenant Herman Kreis. Back row, left to right: Lieutenant John From, Lieutenant Wayne McCann, Lieutenant Richard Walker, and Lieutenant John Ditwig. (U.S. Navy)

The crew of the sixth patrol celebrates after an historic run that added three more patches to *Batfish*'s flag. (U.S. NAVY)

Batfish crew assembles on deck to receive commendations. The crew of an unidentified nearby submarine watches the festivities. (U.S. NAVY)

Gala party thrown for the crew's family and friends in San Francisco, prior to embarking on her seventh and last war patrol, May 25, 1945. (ROBERT FULTON)

Batfish returns to San Francisco at the end of the war, September 1945, ready to be decommissioned. (U.S. Navy)

Tethered to the bank of the Arkansas River in Muskogee, Oklahoma, *Batfish* is threatened by floodwaters during the spring of 1973.

(Robert Fulton)

Representatives of the Oklahoma Maritime Advisory Board inspect the *Batfish* in New Orleans in September 1970. Albert C. "Ace" Kelly, the board's chairman at the time, is the gentleman in sunglasses. (Robert Fulton)

The 310 boat resting in her shallow moat in the middle of what was once a bean field 1,300 miles from the nearest salt water. (Bruce Brotherton)

The boat's conning tower on display. The large structure in the middle of the photo is the periscope. (Bruce Brotherton)

The submarine as she appears today, in a former bean field in Muskogee, Oklahoma, in the heart of what was once called the Dust Bowl. (Bruce Brotherton)

"Set the fish in tubes one, two, and three to run from a hundred and seven to a hundred and twenty-five degrees, four feet, two feet, and two feet," the captain ordered the men down in the torpedo room.

Fyfe could feel the gentle motion of his vessel as the doors on torpedo tubes one, two, and three opened and were flooded with seawater.

"I still can't believe they haven't seen us," Fyfe said to himself as he kept his binoculars aligned on the stain on the horizon, now only nine hundred yards away from them.

"Ready to fire," Sprinkle finally reported from below.

Fyfe watched for any indication that the target might suddenly make a move in some other direction. Or that she might decide to dive. No sign of any change in course or speed, and the sub was still riding on top. The enemy vessel steamed ahead at a steady, dependable, seemingly carefree fourteen knots.

Fyfe scanned the sea between the two submarines, looking for any sign that the other sub might have launched its own array of torpedoes.

Nothing. But that didn't mean anything. The enemy torpedoes wouldn't likely be visible until they landed an uppercut on *Batfish*'s chin. Then it would be a bit too late to duck the punch.

"This is it," the skipper said, and pressed the intercom button again. "Bridge to conn. Fire when ready."

He could easily hear the voices through the open hatch that led down into the conning tower as the message was relayed to the forward torpedo room. They were about to attack those brother submariners over there for a second time. There would almost certainly not be a third chance, regardless of what happened.

"Fire one!"

He waited, but oddly, there was no recoil in response to the command. No sign at all that the torpedo was away.

Something was wrong.

A Mark 18 torpedo weighed close to three thousand pounds—a ton and a half—and had the kick of a Missouri mule when it whooshed away and quickly accelerated to nearly twenty knots.

But this time, there was nothing.

Nothing but a frantic cry from the forward torpedo room.

"Hot run in tube one! Number one failed to fire, Captain! She's stuck in the tube. About six inches of her nose is outside."

A whirlpool of thoughts swirled through Jake Fyfe's head in the next few seconds.

Torpedoes were not armed to explode immediately upon being forced from their tubes and sent on their way toward an enemy vessel. To protect the shooting vessel, a wire umbilical was snapped at launch, and that allowed the arming vane in the weapon's nose to begin spinning as it plowed through seawater. A fish typically traveled about 350 yards before it became "live," the vane aligning the detonator with the weapon's charge at that point—hopefully a point well away from the shooting vessel. Then the torpedo would be ready to explode on contact with anything it might encounter in its path.

Such as contact with an enemy target.

Or maybe contact with a wall of seawater or the door at the mouth of *Batfish*'s number one torpedo tube.

It was certainly possible that the umbilical had been snapped and the arming vane might be spinning away on the nose of the stuck fish at that very moment, getting closer and closer to making the weapon "live" in the boat's forward tube, ready to blow at the slightest contact.

The torpedomen in the forward compartment knew what they were up against. They had the nose of a live and potent device stuck out of tube one and not budging. The weapon would almost certainly do mortal damage to the submarine should it explode in the tube, so close to the sub's hull. And it would certainly be enough of a bang to let everyone in this part of the ocean know they were there.

Such things had happened before. USS *Tang* (SS 306) had been lost north of Formosa the previous October when one of her torpedoes went crazy, circling back and striking her at the stern. Seventy-eight men died. Nine survivors were rescued by the enemy and spent the rest of the war in a Japanese prisoner-of-war camp. That little mishap also ended the most productive submarine patrol of the war.

Tang fired twenty-four torpedoes on the trip. Twenty-two hit enemy ships. One missed everything. The twenty-fourth sank the *Tang*.

"Fire it again—manually!" Captain Fyfe yelled into the intercom, and then added, with equal force in his voice, "And fire number two when ready!"

They had the perfect setup on the enemy target. Even if they were about to be racked by their own torpedo, they could still take the other guy down, and maybe do it before he could get off a shot of his own.

"Fire two," Sprinkle acknowledged, cool, calm, workmanlike.

This time everyone on the boat plainly felt the welcome shove as the fish vigorously swam away through the black sea. And everyone on board held his breath, wondering if merely that little kick would be enough to ignite the hot run that remained lodged inside tube one.

Fyfe kept his glasses on the target and tried not to think about the ticking time bomb aboard his vessel. If the Japanese happened to turn around and look, *Batfish* was clearly in sight. If the bastard wheeled around now and came after *Batfish*, they would have a hard time evading, what with a hot fish in one tube and two other forward doors open to the sea.

Below and ahead of the skipper, in the forward torpedo room, the torpedomen had already told everyone else to evacuate the compartment and to close the hatch behind them. Now they were working feverishly, trying to break the bulky torpedo free with repeated blasts of compressed air, but the weapon seemed hopelessly stuck. They were doing little more than making plenty of bubbles on the surface. The torpedoman hit the "fire" button three, four, five times.

Nothing.

The torpedo was still there, apparently not yet armed. But it was there nonetheless, its nose sticking just out of the end of the tube and not willing to answer their pleading prayers and go any farther.

Twelve seconds had passed since number two had disgorged its weapon.

"Fire three!" Captain Fyfe barked from the bridge.

The satisfying kick verified that this torpedo was safely away as well.

"Three away!" the torpedoman said into the communicator microphone, confirming that a second fish was on its way toward the enemy submarine.

Thank God for that, at least, Jake Fyfe mouthed silently.

In the conn, the assistant attack officer was staring at his stopwatch, marking time since the firing of the weapon from tube two, waiting for the boom that told him they had struck their target. Or for the telling silence that screamed that they had missed the bastard again.

Up on the bridge, Jake Fyfe was keeping his own count, an eye in the direction of the target, praying for a detonation. But the skipper couldn't avoid worrying about the hot run in tube one.

"What do you recommend we do?" he finally called down to the men in the forward torpedo room.

"Captain, I don't think we can build up enough pressure to get it out without closing the door. And the damn thing is sticking out beyond the mouth of the tube."

"Can you tell if she's armed?"

"No, she didn't get out far enough to arm."

"Then try to close the door," Captain Fyfe said. He wanted more than anything to feel the nudge of tube one being flushed clean, but he kept his stare on the target instead, hoping he would see the detonation there momentarily. Hoping they had not misjudged speed or range again.

"Captain, you know hitting the nose of that thing might do enough damage to set it off," the torpedoman responded meekly.

"We've got to get it out of the tube or back inside. We'll have to close the door in case we have to dive. Try to close the door!" Fyfe ordered, leaving no doubt as to how he wanted to handle the problem.

The skipper agreed that it would likely be difficult to get enough pressure in the tube to finally expel the hot-run torpedo if the door remained open to the sea. He could only hope that the tube door banging on the nose of the weapon wouldn't be enough to make it explode.

Up front, the torpedomen looked at each other wide-eyed and simply shrugged. Then, without even thinking about it any longer, the senior torpedoman hit the button to close the door to the number one tube. It clanged hard against the nose of the stuck torpedo, but the stubborn bastard didn't budge a bit.

"I'm gonna need new underwear when this is over," the second man noted dryly, swallowing hard.

"Let's hope there's enough of you left to need underwear," the other torpedoman said as he punched the button again. This time, the door clanged hard against the torpedo, then nudged all the way closed, sliding the hot run backward into the tube.

The two men held their breath as they forced compressed air into the tube behind the weapon. They had to be careful not to raise the pressure too high or the tube might rupture. That was not a good thing to have happen either—the compartment would certainly flood and the two sub sailors would drown. It would also be difficult to submerge with the front room filled with water.

Once again, the torpedoman opened the tube door to the sea.

"Here goes," he said, and with an exaggerated flourish he hit the firing switch once again.

Whooosh!

Up on the bridge, Jake Fyfe felt the most wonderful, subtle jolt. And an instant later, he heard the welcome confirmation.

"Number one fired manually!"

It was too dark to see any sign of the thing swimming away. No telling where that fish would go, but right now, it didn't matter. It was safely away from *Batfish* and swimming in another direction through the black water. The collective outflow of held breath was audible throughout the boat.

Jake Fyfe swallowed hard and then sucked in another deep breath. They still had two other torpedoes away, hopefully bearing down on the IJN submarine at killer speed.

"Conn, come left to bearing two-seven-zero," he ordered. This new tack would carry them away from the target, driving them clear in case they missed again and the enemy skipper finally realized he was under attack. Fyfe was more than willing to go at the Imperial Japanese Navy sub once more, but if he did, he would have to start the hunt all over again, after running away to hide for a bit.

But just then, at the very moment the bow of *Batfish* began swinging to the northwest, a thousand yards away across the calm sea, a hellish, bright sun of concussion suddenly illuminated the dark night. A column of fire climbed hundreds of feet into the black sky. Jake Fyfe felt the shock wave of the blast on his face and chest. He was blinded by the corona of it before he could shield his eyes.

Below, the men around the radar console watched as the single pip they had been watching on their screen suddenly disintegrated into many tiny pinpoints of light, then disappeared altogether. Once the ripples of the blast faded, the sound operator could no longer hear the distinctive shimmer of the target's screws that he had been listening to for the last six hours. They had stopped dead. There were only the anguished groans and creaks of a vessel breaking up and sinking.

Fyfe blinked, trying to get his eyesight back. There were still smaller blasts occurring near the surface where the enemy submarine had been, secondary explosions as other ordnance aboard the vessel decided to blow up.

"Permission to come on the bridge?" Clark Sprinkle inquired from below.

"Permission granted."

The XO climbed up quickly and stared at the fireworks barge that had once been an IJN submarine. He couldn't keep the grin off his face.

Now there was a chorus of "Permission to come to the bridge?" from below. Fyfe aye'd most of them, then watched as his crew assembled around him in the cramped confines of the bridge and along the cigarette deck, slapping one another on the back, shaking hands, laughing out loud like a victorious football team.

He wished he had cigars to pass out. It was that good a "kill."

The toughest task for a submarine was bagging another sub. Few of *Batfish*'s sisters had managed such a feat. Fyfe was proud of his men for responding after the previous disappointment of the evening. They had done their jobs despite the near disaster of the hot torpedo.

A few minutes later, everyone topside heard the crump of a distant but distinct explosion.

"How many hits did you count?" the skipper called down to the assistant attack officer.

"Just one hell of a big one," the sailor reported with a laugh. "It was number two, from the sound and timing of it. Looks like number three tracked dead-on, but she either went under her or through what was left of her. That's the end-of-run residual damage you heard. God only knows where number one went, but I'm just glad it ain't still in the tube!"

"Me, too, son. Me, too." Fyfe couldn't keep the grin off his face as he ordered, "Radio, tell the rest of the wolf pack we bagged a red one."

A minute later, word came up the hatch: "*Scabbardfish* sends her congratulations and says, 'Welcome to the club.'"

USS *Scabbardfish* (SS 397), under the command of Frederick W. "Pop" Gunn, had sunk an enemy submarine just off the main Japanese island of Honshu a bit over three months before, on November 28, 1944.

The other boats quickly radioed their well-dones, but Fyfe knew the fun was over for the moment. There was work yet to be done.

"Clear the bridge. Take her down and let's reload. There's supposed to be more of the sons of bitches swimming around out here, and I'd prefer we see them before they see us. Let's be ready for them."

And with that, the brief celebration was over. With her hatches shut and dogged, *Batfish* slid smoothly beneath the dark sea. Slipping through the oil and flotsam from a prized Imperial Navy boat, and whatever mysteries she may have been carrying in her holds below, *Batfish* quickly disappeared below the black surface of the sea.

Although it was a harrowing experience for everyone on board, having a torpedo become stuck in a tube was not an unusual occurrence during the Navy's many sorties in the war. There is no evidence of the Americans losing any boats in this manner. Still, it did not make those harrowing minutes, facing any number of possible deaths from a potentially live fish, any easier for the submariners.

It had also happened on the *Batfish* before—Blackie Lawrence, who was a torpedoman in *Batfish*'s after torpedo room on war patrols three through seven, remembers all too vividly a previous incident in which a "hot run" gave them a fright. Lawrence and his fellow torpedoman banged the door into the nose of a potentially armed weapon, risking explosion, until they were able to drive it back deep enough into the tube to close the two-hundred-pound door.

Earlier in the war, a German torpedo that had failed to explode ran aground and was recovered on the East Coast of the United States. The Navy was quite interested in its design, since the Nazi U-boats were enjoying uncanny accuracy with their torpedoes. It was soon apparent why—their particular electric-powered weapon used an advanced sound-detection device in its nose and was designed to home in on the racket made by the targets' engines or their screws churning the water. The decision was made to build a version for use on American submarines and other vessels. A rush program developed a similar sound-guided torpedo, and *Batfish* was reportedly one of the first to get an experimental version to try out in actual combat situations.

Prior to patrol, torpedomen from the boat attended a top-secret ordnance instruction school in Hawaii, and then four of the weapons were loaded aboard in the dark of night, mysteriously draped and under heavy guard, just before they left port to return to the war. These experimental electric-propulsion models were dubbed Mark 27s, though torpedomen quickly nicknamed them "cuties" because of their smaller size in relation to standard torpedoes, as well as for their acoustical target-seeking characteristics: "Acoustical" was distilled down to "cutie." It was also the first submarine torpedo developed that was designed to "swim out" of the launching tube, rather than be flushed out by compressed air.

The *Batfish* sailors who saw the torpedo had their own opinions about the design of the device. They thought it was poorly crafted, in several ways. The worst part was that it had a single screw. That meant the battery had to be mounted off center to counteract the instability generated by the torque of the lone screw. The off weight made the weapon awkwardly unbalanced and hard to handle when moving it or loading it into the tubes. The *Batfish* crew had already managed to spill the corrosive acid from the battery on at least one occasion while moving one of the boat's cuties.

There was another design problem: At nineteen inches in diameter, the torpedo was two inches smaller than the Mark 14, the Mark 18, and other conventional weapons that were being used at that time. To make it fit snugly into the torpedo tubes on the submarines, wooden wings were designed to attach like shims to the torpedo's sides. Speculation about Lawrence's earlier misfire is that the wood swelled with exposure to seawater while the Mark 27 was waiting in the tube.

Another point: It is important to note that the radar signature on an unusual frequency that *Batfish* detected that night from its Japanese counterpart and then reported to the Navy turned out to be an invaluable bit of intelligence. It would prove useful to the Allies during the remaining days of the war. At the beginning of the conflict, Japanese navy vessels had no radar at all. As the war continued, though, they developed several systems, some of which would rival the gear used by the American warships. Simply by detecting and reporting the unique signal that she intercepted that night, *Batfish* gave the Navy valuable information about the signatures of subs in the IJN.

Even today, sixty years later, there is still speculation about which Japanese submarine was the first vessel sunk by *Batfish*. Japanese war records indicate it was likely *I-41* under the command of Lieutenant Commander Fumitake Kondo. Others maintain it was *RO-115*, a *Kaisho*-class fleet boat that typically carried a crew of thirty-eight men. Still others don't think *Batfish* sank a submarine at all. Jake Fyfe's vivid description of the explosion and the oil slick and debris they saw that night make it almost a certainty that it was an Imperial Japanese Navy submersible vessel that "the submarine-killer submarine" sent to the bottom.

Today, most naval historians agree with Fyfe's report, and they generally say it was *RO-115*. We may never know if the enemy submarine carried gold, collaborators, mistresses, secret documents, or the other rumored cargo. But we do know *Batfish* had struck another blow against an enemy that was beginning to lose its momentum in the Pacific theater.

SIXTEEN

Wrong Sub?

May 1972

Batfish had been sitting at the Port of Muskogee for almost three weeks before a contract was finalized with Midwest Dredging Company to cut a channel for her in the river bottom. The channel would allow them to move her to what was planned to be her interim berthing spot at the edge of the Arkansas River, a place where they could prep her for real tourists with real money to begin paying to come aboard. The Army Corps of Engineers had graciously issued a temporary permit to allow them to moor the submarine at the river's bank until September 15, 1972, but she would need to be taken into her permanent resting spot, proposed to be a moat several hundred feet inland, immediately before that date arose.

A few curious people wandered over to the port to look at the odd sight of a submarine lashed between a phalanx of barges, gently resting there in the river current. Some of them asked port workers when they would be able to climb aboard and take a look at her. No one really had an answer to their questions. But most who saw her agreed that she still looked a bit shoddy for a vessel that had supposedly enjoyed such a storied war record.

Based on the promise of bond money and more bank loans, Maritime Advisory Board executive director Karl Wheland (Wheland had resigned as chairman and had become executive director back in January, and Ace Kelly had been named chairman) signed the contract with the dredging company on May 25. It called for a 1,250-foot-long, 120-foot-wide channel to be gouged out of the bottom of the river to its south bank, near the site for the proposed new War Memorial Park. The agreement promised that the board would pay twenty-five thousand dollars for the removal of thirty thousand cubic tons of mud, plus fifty cents a cubic yard for any additional silt that had to be dug up. And it agreed to pay the amount in full within fifteen days of the completion of the work.

There was also a small contingency in the first of the contract's exhibits: The dredging was not to be conducted anywhere near the Port of Muskogee industrial park. If the work spilled over into that territory, it would invoke a union contract covering any work done there, causing the labor fees to grow. Given the nature of the financing, it was imperative to save money anywhere they could.

As May gave way to June, politics surrounding the *Batfish* project heated up as surely as the late-springtime weather in eastern Oklahoma.

The state legislature had done away with the Oklahoma Industrial Development and Park Department, the agency under which the Maritime Advisory Board was chartered. The board was moved under the jurisdiction of a new state entity, the Tourism and Recreation Commission.

As far as its members could tell, the board, with her slightly murky setup and nonexistent funding, would continue as it always had. But there was a problem. A big one. The new Tourism and Recreation Commission came under the control of the state's lieutenant governor, George Nigh. And the lieutenant governor had made it known already that he was concerned about the freewheeling style and tangled financial ways of several groups operating out there under state jurisdiction. One of the main ones mentioned was this submarine bunch that had just been moved over into his bailiwick.

Ominous as it was, that political development was compounded by turmoil that struck the Maritime Advisory Board just about the time that the dredging operations began.

Albert C. "Ace" Kelly had been de facto head of the board since its inception, regardless of who was officially the chairman or executive director. He had controlled the submarine veterans on the board since the time he had arranged for them to be appointed members in the first place. It was no accident that the sub vets outnumbered nonsubmariners on the panel. That meant that Kelly had pretty much run the operation the way he saw fit, often without conferring with Karl Wheland, who was now the board's executive director, or anyone else.

The take-charge style of Ace Kelly was fine with the sub vets. It had been Ace's idea from the beginning. And Kelly had been the one with the political clout necessary to get the board formed and to realize its goal of getting a submarine and parking it in a Dust Bowl state. Had he not done exactly what he had set out to do? Could they not look out the window at their board meetings, held at the Port of Muskogee, and see the awe-inspiring sail and beautiful profile of their diesel submarine, tied up and soon to be moved into her next resting place?

However, Wheland and the other members had grown tired of the loosey-goosey way things were being done. Finances were a mess. Everything had cost more than estimated. Delays were keeping them from allowing visitors, and they had expected to realize that income when they signed off on all those expensive contracts. They owed everybody and his brother and were still going into debt at a rate of one thousand dollars a month. And there were no real prospects of having any significant revenue coming in anytime soon. Certainly not enough to pay back the banks and get all the contractors off their backs and still get the submarine shipshape enough for a public opening.

A special meeting of the board was called, this one to be held up the turnpike in Tulsa. Not in Muskogee, near the boat, as was the usual custom. The intent of the meeting was to remove Ace Kelly as chairman. Most of the sub vets in the group saw this as a coup and backed their leader. When the hands were counted, the motion to replace Kelly was defeated by a lone vote. The old sub skipper, Karl Wheland, promptly resigned as executive director. He knew a successful mutiny when he saw one.

At the board's final meeting for fiscal year 1971–1972, on June 10, 1972, a long litany of overdue bills was read to the group. They would have to have money to pay for the dredging as soon as the work was done—the best estimate for that job was now between forty thousand and fifty thousand dollars, including towing the submarine into place. The folks at Avondale Yards down in New Orleans had grown quite impatient about the money owed them to raise the sunken barge from the encounter with *Silvermain*.

The latest correspondence from the Crescent City suggested rather strongly that someone in authority come down to New Orleans and take care of the matter posthaste. Those letters had gone unanswered so far. Williams Brothers had always been very understanding about money owed them for bringing the boat upriver, but their patience had now just about worn out as well. They were proud they could deliver the submarine to the folks of Muskogee, but they had men to pay and equipment that had been tied up for the trip. The board also owed Ora Lamb, the president of the First National Bank and Trust Company of Muskogee, a hundred thousand dollars, and though Lamb had not been pressing for payment, everyone knew they would have to pay it back sooner rather than later. They even owed money to Dick Fogle, a volunteer and former submariner who had been spending some of his own money just keeping *Batfish*'s condition status quo until she could be moved.

The members of the board okayed a motion to name a new paid executive director to replace Karl Wheland. It just so happened that Roy Smallwood, a high school math teacher and coach, a 1939 Annapolis graduate, a former naval officer, and a resident of Wilburton, Oklahoma, was present at the meeting, and he expressed an interest in the job. There was one snag: There was no money to pay him a salary. A member made the motion to hire him anyway and work out the details later. The motion was seconded and passed unanimously. The group had themselves a new exec.

There was one other note of harmony that came out of that meeting. Ace Kelly proposed that since Karl Wheland was no longer the board's executive director, Wheland could be renominated as a member of the body. Everyone agreed. Kelly promised to make sure the governor knew how anxious the board was to have Wheland back aboard and, as the minutes of the meeting stated, "The members wished Karl Wheland to be aware of and know how much his acceptance and work as executive director was appreciated."

Never let it be said that sub sailors didn't stick together, even after the most bitter of family squabbles.

Finally, at the end of June 1972, *Batfish* made the short journey from the Port of Muskogee along the newly dug trench, and was tied off along the riverbank near where plans called for a park and museum to eventually be

constructed. Joe Chambliss had come through with a gangplank borrowed
from the naval depot that could be used to span the water between the bank
and the sub. But the Navy man also expressed serious misgivings. He was
afraid that the proposed opening to the public on the Fourth of July would
be premature, that it would not show the submarine in its best light, and
that it could actually be dangerous to the visiting public.

Nobody listened.

Karl Wheland had sent out a press release on his own, telling the world
that USS *Batfish* would be open to the public on Independence Day. Kelly
and others agreed it was the perfect day to unveil their hard-won submarine
to the citizens of Oklahoma. Besides, they needed in the worst way the anticipated revenue from admissions to start flowing in.

When it became obvious to even the most optimistic among them that
Chambliss was, in the end, correct that the boat would not be in the best
shape by July 4, they decided to go ahead with the plans to let the public
tour her anyway. There had been too many ups and downs on the project
already, and it was important to show the citizens of the state that they
could, even after all they had been through, allow visitors to tour the boat
when they had promised that she would be ready.

On July 4, 1972, the USS *Batfish* was officially opened to the public.
There was little ceremony, still no official dedication. Everyone agreed that
formality could wait for another day.

Several hundred people paid a buck apiece to go aboard. To get there,
they had to navigate a dusty dirt road filled with potholes, park in a rough
parking lot covered with weeds and thistles, climb up a steep, sandy hill,
and cross the borrowed aluminum gangplank that passed over swirling,
muddy river water.

The boat herself was not so cosmetically impressive either. Sub vets had
donated hours and hours of their time and brought tools and paint. They
spent the last few days before Independence Day scraping, painting, in-
stalling a rough ventilation system, reattaching equipment, padding door-
ways, and doing all they could to make the boat realistic and reasonably
safe to wander through. They had done their best, but she was still a bit
rough.

Joe Chambliss was so concerned about the premature opening and the imprudent actions of his fellow Maritime Advisory Board members that he dashed off a hot memo to the board's executive committee. He was troubled about the inner workings of the group, its "organizational divisions, lack of teamwork and inadequate planning," and called upon the executive committee to stop members from acting as individuals without consulting with other members first. But he was most upset about the rush to open the boat before she was ready for visitors. It was a decision that he felt perfectly demonstrated the chaos within the panel.

"I visited the *Batfish* on 4 July," he wrote, "and in short, the public opening was premature. The sub was simply not ready despite commendable and Herculean efforts of many. Obviously, it was not ready appearance-wise and from a safety standpoint."

Chambliss was still an active naval officer, and he took that association seriously. He felt the boat's appearance would be blamed on the U.S. Navy and that visitors would not understand she was now under the control of the state of Oklahoma. He didn't want her shoddy condition to reflect on his Navy.

By the time of the board's executive committee meeting in July, Captain Smallwood, the new and still unpaid executive director, had gotten a good look at the group's financial straits. He couldn't believe what he saw. The books were rockier than any South China Sea shoals.

The Muskogee bank, which had been remarkably patient, was growing ever more restless. The Tourism and Recreation Commission was balking about fulfilling any previous promise of issuing bonds. Lieutenant Governor Nigh had raised the prickly issue of the Maritime Advisory Board's ever having had any right under the statute that created the panel to borrow money or execute contracts, even though the members had gone right ahead and done plenty of both.

The committee that day did vote to reimburse Dick Fogle a thousand dollars for his out-of-pocket expenses incurred as he kept the boat together while she awaited her move. Fogle was not collecting a salary either.

It was the middle of September before Smallwood was able to come up with a proposed budget for the fiscal year, which had begun three and a half months before. He could see some blue sky, though, and he made a strong pitch for an ambitious budget.

In a sea of negatives there were some plusses. Since the opening in July, over eleven thousand paying visitors had somehow found *Batfish* and toured her. They weren't all local folks, either. There had been visitors from some of the other states and even a few from foreign countries, such as Lebanon, Japan, Australia, and Mexico.

Smallwood boldly predicted revenues of almost a hundred and forty thousand dollars for the fiscal year. That included paid admissions, profit on souvenirs sold in the gift shop, the sale of the proposed bonds, and a settlement with the insurance company for the damage done by *Silvermain* while the boat was still in New Orleans. He, too, cited the success of the USS *Drum* in Mobile, Alabama. If they did only a fraction of the business the folks down there did, everything would be all right.

In fact, the picture looked so rosy that Smallwood proposed that the board begin paying him a salary of $10,250 for the balance of the year and that they hire an administrative assistant/secretary at a salary of $4,500. He already had a line on a retired Navy yeoman, "qualified in submarines," who could fill the position nicely. The sub vets were adamant about hiring only submariners to work at the boat.

Smallwood also proposed retaining "a retired Navy chief petty officer" to oversee "the preparation and development of the *Batfish* as an interesting exhibit."

Dick Fogle had some ideas of his own. For example, he suggested to everyone that they get some sea lions to put in the moat around the submarine. The animals would offer a nice addition to *Batfish* and remind visiting sub vets about their days spent near San Francisco Bay.

Despite the mountain of debt and the rough political climate, things were looking up now that the old boat's hatches had finally been unsealed and she had been opened to visitors.

Enter the state of Oklahoma and her examiners.

They were not nearly as impressed with the board's finances as were Smallwood and the members. Payroll taxes for the few employees who were actually getting paid were already over a thousand dollars in arrears. There was the not insignificant matter of the bank loans, the growing morass of unpaid bills, the threat of lawsuits from the dredging company and Avondale Yards, and the poor folks at Williams Brothers, the go-betweens between the Maritime Advisory Board and the various companies to which they were indebted, not to mention the almost sixty thousand dollars that was still owed to their own company.

The state accountants were also confused about why all those bills and contracts they were examining mentioned a submarine named *Batfish*. The law under which the acquisition of the submarine had been accomplished gave the authority to obtain and move a sub named *Piranha*. Where did *Batfish* come into the story?

The examiners rushed to inform Lieutenant Governor Nigh of the mess they had found down there in Muskogee, and in one of the divisions of Nigh's newly minted Tourism and Recreation Commission. At about the same time, Nigh received a request for an audience with attorneys from the firm of Sanders, McElroy, and Carpenter in Tulsa, representing the good people at Midwest Dredging. Quite simply, they wanted the state of Oklahoma to honor the contract Karl Wheland had signed and to pony up the long-past-due cash that was owed to their client for the big ditch they had dug in the Arkansas River.

The lieutenant governor promptly informed everyone who would listen that neither the taxpayers of his state nor anyone on his commission were even remotely responsible for any of the *Batfish* contracts or debts. If anyone was, it would be the submarine veterans and the individual members of the Oklahoma Maritime Advisory Board as private citizens. After all, they were the ones who had signed all those notes and contracts, on their own and without statutory authority.

Nigh put his sentiments into a press release, sent out under his name and that of the state's attorney general. The headlines in the state's newspapers the next day were damning: "Wrong Sub in Memorial? Debt Not Authorized Either."

Nigh was quoted as saying, "Legally, the taxpayers or the Tourism and Recreation Commission are not obligated for one penny. I'm embarrassed to report, though, that we find ourselves in a pretty bad situation."

The lieutenant governor went on to point out that the Maritime Advisory Board was set up only to, as its name clearly stated, *advise*.

"They never advised us. I advised them that they could not go into debt. If they default, there's a private citizen in Muskogee who has to pick up the tab." Then Nigh made his and the state of Oklahoma's position on the *Batfish* even clearer. "At no time can the banks look to the Tourism and Recreation Commission for money."

The hullabaloo also pretty much brought to an end any possibility of the Tourism Commission's issuing bonds to finance any part of the *Batfish* project. That caused a great deal of consternation among the banking community in Muskogee, most of whom had been under the impression that the bonds would go to repay the several hundred thousand dollars' worth of loans they had made already to the people who had brought the boat upriver.

So there they were, at the end of September, an optimistic budget before the Maritime Advisory Board, a small but constant stream of visitors climbing up the nearly vertical sandbank and across the long, borrowed aluminum gangplank to access the boat, and big plans for a sacred memorial park to pay homage to veterans from all wars and all branches of the service.

And on the other side, a state government that had washed its hands of the entire boondoggle, a whole convoy of bill collectors, queued up and hungry for what they were rightly owed, and headlines in the newspapers telling the whole state just what a muddy mess things had become down there on the banks of the Arkansas River at Muskogee.

Did the sub vets and members of the commission cower in the face of such withering fire? Of course not. They felt they were still simply doing their duty, bringing their submarine home, and steaming around whatever navigational hazards got in the way of their course.

Roy Smallwood issued his own press release in response to the lieutenant governor's. He confirmed that yes, it was true that finances had been a little rocky on the project so far, but the process was continuing to give Oklahomans something of which they could be proud. By spring, *Batfish* would be contained inside an inland berth, circled by a moat with greatly improved access for visitors, and perhaps even a contingent of sea lions. Landscaping, lighting, walkways, and security fencing would be completed by May, just in time for the peak tourist season the following summer. A museum was to be completed in 1973 as well. There would also be displays of other military armament, a combat art exhibit, World War II memorabilia, and more. A four-hundred-slip marina for the area was already on the drawing boards, and plans were well under way for a motel on the property. There was also a quarter-million-dollar federal grant that was all but assured, and that money would give the park a considerable shot in the arm.

Ace Kelly chimed right in with his own statement.

"The memorial's financial prospects are excellent," he told the press with a straight face. He wasn't lying. There was no doubt he believed completely what he was saying. He also addressed the rather controversial subject of the on-again, off-again bond issue.

"The bonds are in the final mechanical stages of preparation and should be issued anytime," he maintained.

The gathering storm clouds and impending flood of troubles didn't faze this group of old submariners. They had been dive-bombed and depth-charged far more viciously than this. They'd survived much rougher seas and far more biting gales than this little dustup. They'd make Lieutenant Governor Nigh see the worthiness of what they were doing and convert him into one of their biggest supporters. Creditors would wait just a bit longer once they understood the virtue of what the sub sailors were trying to build out there on the riverbank. They had not come this far to let a few minor accounting discrepancies, a gob of government red tape, and some bad press get in the way of doing this thing the right way.

SEVENTEEN

What Makes
Them Tick

Cherokee Indian law demanded a strict liability for any killing. A murder, to their way of thinking, created an imbalance in nature that had to be corrected. Righting that imbalance required revenge. Revenge would then restore harmony. It was the obligation of the clan of the murderer to admit and accept responsibility for the wrongful killing. Then the clan was expected to pay the cost.

Quite simply, even to a peaceful and civilized people like the Cherokee, blood called for blood, or harmonious nature would remain off-key until the score had been settled.

February 1945

The electric thrill of their success against the Japanese submarine ran throughout the *Batfish*, the excitement of it almost palpable enough to touch and taste. Up front, the torpedo room crew had hastily reloaded the tubes, just in case another target presented itself. Torpedo tubes didn't stay empty long in this part of the world.

As they worked, the men laughed easily, joking about the looks on the faces of the Japanese sub sailors when they felt the first *whoomp!* as the Torpex in the Mark 18 went all to fire and concussion.

An hour after unleashing the firestorm in the pitch-black sea, Fyfe ordered the boat back up top. They would look for survivors, for debris that might confirm the identity of their victim, and for souvenirs.

The second he popped the hatch at the top of the ladder from the conn to the bridge, an almost overpowering odor of diesel fuel poured down the opening. The skipper's eyes stung as he climbed on out into the black night.

The searchlight was quickly rigged and shone around the surface, looking for anything that might be floating there that could be retrieved. Sure enough, a thick, sticky oil slick stretched as far out from the boat's hull as they could see before the light was eaten up by the hungry darkness.

"We're a good two miles east of the spot where she went down," Clark Sprinkle noted from somewhere to the left of Fyfe's elbow. With his vision temporarily ruined by the brightness of the searchlight, the skipper could hardly make out the shadowy form of his XO standing there next to him on the bridge.

"Yeah, if we made this big a mess, that thing's on the bottom for certain."

"You want to look around some more, Captain?" Sprinkle pointedly asked.

Fyfe flashed him a crooked grin that the XO had no chance of seeing.

"What do you think, Clark? We've done nothing but ruin our night vision with that spotlight, and we're doing a damned good job of advertising to the whole IJN that we're still out here, waiting for them to take their revenge. We can come back at daylight and see what we can see."

He gave the order to pull the plug and dive back down to the safety of the deep.

It wasn't long before the jubilation among the crew over the sinking of the target had run its course. Raw fatigue settled in, as it always did when the adrenaline of the attack was spent, leaving flop sweat and aching muscles and eyelids that grew heavier and heavier.

And there was something else they felt this time, too. Something akin to melancholy. None of them mentioned it to his shipmates. They simply went on about their work or, if they were off watch, they headed to the galley for a cup of coffee or squeezed into a bunk for a few hours' shut-eye.

As he sank wearily down at the tiny desk in his stateroom, Jake Fyfe felt the same odd emotion. But he knew exactly what it was that he and his crew were experiencing. Nobody had to lay it out for him. They had sunk surface vessels before, and the usual elation, followed by the inevitable fatigue, had been there each time. But this was different.

Batfish had sent a boat full of fellow submariners to the bottom. Enemy or not, there was a kinship there, and though it was not openly acknowledged, it was not to be denied either.

Fyfe touched the lead of his pencil to his tongue and made an entry into his log, timing it at 1:50 A.M. He ended his notation with: "I would still like to salvage some Nip submariners and see what makes them tick."

Three hours later, after the crew had had some sleep and high-octane coffee from the galley, the mood of the boat was back on a high. Fyfe tried a couple of times to bring them back to the surface, but when they got to radar depth, it seemed the sky above them was swarming with airplanes. One time they succeeded in breaking the surface, but before they could open a hatch, a low-flying plane came at them from the east, out of the brightening overcast. They immediately headed right back under. Whether they were friend or foe was immaterial: They had to stay down.

It was almost ten o'clock in the morning on February 10, 1945, before they came back to periscope depth, scanning to see if it would be safe to come up and look around. Fyfe desperately wanted to look for survivors. He did see a covey of what were clearly U.S. Navy planes, a Black Cat torpedo bomber and four fighters, about four miles out and approaching from the direction of the mainland. He watched through the scope as the bomber peeled off and came low, probably inspecting the oil slick.

"Good to see friendly faces up there," Fyfe said, "but I don't want those flyboys to think we're IJN and start dropping things on our heads."

He had his mouth open to give the command to come fully to the surface when the sound operator yelled, "High-speed propeller! Sounds like a torpedo. I heard it splash when it hit the water. Bearing oh-nine-oh and closing fast!"

"Dive!" Fyfe bellowed. "Take her to two hundred feet!"

They were at ninety feet when they all clearly heard the pulsing of the torpedo motor passing directly overhead.

At the stern, in the aft torpedo room, Blackie Lawrence and Bob Oswald exchanged nervous glances.

Please, God, they thought, *don't let that plane be dropping cuties on us now!*

They listened especially hard to the torpedo's motor, hoping not to hear it avert, circle, and come back, homing dutifully in on the slight sound of *Batfish*'s screws.

It was several minutes after the telltale nose of the torpedo screw faded before the two torpedomen allowed themselves to breathe a sigh of relief.

"Level at two hundred feet," came the call from the conn.

Fyfe grinned, but there was sweat on his upper lip. What was it with this boat and the friendlies always doing their best to sink her?

He would later write in his patrol log: "[It was] a tender moment, and if these actually prove to be blue [U.S. Navy] planes a very unfriendly act." Fyfe theorized that the Black Cat launched the weapon after one of the fighters that were serving as its escort spotted *Batfish*, swimming along happily at less than sixty feet deep, periscope and radar depth. In a clear sea, with plenty of daylight, their track would have been easily visible to the airplanes.

"If the Japs don't get us, some swabbie in a plane will!" he said with a weak laugh. "We might as well stay down until dusk. Then we'll go back up and see what we can see."

The chances of locating a survivor were likely nil, but maybe they could get some clue as to the name of the boat they had sunk.

Submarines like *Batfish* could stay submerged for half a day with no ill effect. Much beyond that, if they didn't surface and refresh the supply, the air inside the boat would start getting stale and difficult to breathe. Still, if somebody was shooting at them every time they poked their head up, breathing fetid air was a better choice than going to the surface and offering a fat target.

When Fyfe finally brought *Batfish* back up, the sun had already dropped into the ocean and the air had cooled. Best of all, the sky was empty except for a few wispy clouds tinged orange by the dying sun, and the first shimmering stars of the tropical night.

The fresh air felt good as Jake Fyfe took in as much of it as he could. The sea was clear of debris and oil, too. They were too far from the previous night's success to hope to find anything. It would have been something if they had been able to retrieve paperwork or any evidence that might have given them a clue as to who they had sunk. Fyfe wondered if he could steam back to the area, if there might still be a Japanese submariner treading water back there that he could ferret out and take back home like some kind of living, breathing trophy.

The squawk of the bridge speaker interrupted his thoughts.

"Captain, ComSubPac has a message for you," reported the radio operator, nineteen-year-old Stan Javorski.

The brass had ordered three of the subs patrolling these waters with them—*Seapoacher*, *Plaice*, and *Scabbardfish*—to go hunting elsewhere. That left *Batfish*, *Blackfish*, and *Archerfish* to continue to swim around the Babuyan Islands together, seeking out prey.

Fyfe had mixed emotions about this development. Their little part of the ocean wouldn't be quite so crowded anymore, but it also left them with half as many friends in the territory if they needed help. Anyway, they were still "Joe's Jugheads," named after Joe Enright, the skipper of *Archerfish* and the wolf-pack commander for this operation. And they were still on the lookout for any possible target, but especially for the IJN subs that were supposed to be aiding the evacuation of the Philippines.

Joe Enright and *Archerfish* were fresh from making their own bit of naval history. The previous November, he and his crew had caught the gargantuan Japanese aircraft carrier *Shinano* as she emerged from Tokyo Bay on her maiden voyage. In a classic example of naval warfare, they stalked the supposedly unsinkable vessel and sank her with one spray of six torpedoes. The *Shinano* is still the largest vessel ever sent to the bottom by a submarine.

At about one the next morning, Enright sent Fyfe an order to move north of the nineteenth parallel, toward Calayan Island. It was too late to try to get there before daybreak, so they spent most of the rest of the night and all the next day at periscope and radar depth, patrolling, seeing little if anything.

Fyfe saw that the crew was getting restless. They had tasted blood. They were hungry for more.

This hiding, waiting for the sun to set, was grating on their nerves. They wanted to sink something else vital to the Japanese.

Finally it was dusk again. As they came back to the surface, a couple of planes showed up in the distance on radar, twelve miles out and closing. Fyfe almost reached for the klaxon, ready to order them right back down one more time.

But something made him wait. Some internal voice suggested that he not be so hasty to duck. Not yet. That mysterious voice in his head convinced him not to.

The planes made a sweeping turn, eventually droning away from them and posing no threat.

Only a few minutes later, the bridge speaker crackled with a new heads-up.

"Captain, radar signal on a hundred and fifty-eight megacycles," came the report. "She's weak but increasing steadily."

The same kind of signal as their previous encounter with the Japanese sub. Same frequency as before. If they had dived to get away from the latest patrol planes, as he had been about to do, they would never have intercepted this new radar sweep.

"Swing the boat around slowly," Fyfe told the helmsman. "Let's find the null and see what its bearing is. We may have ourselves another pig boat!"

Batfish's SJ radar probed the deepening darkness, looking for the shape of another enemy submarine out there somewhere. If the first boat had ignored them as they stalked it and shot it dead, maybe this one would, too.

"Got her!" came the call up the hatch from the conning tower. The radar had revealed to them in which direction the new target was and how far away.

"Report!" Fyfe sang.

"Three hundred and ten degrees true. Range eight thousand yards."

Fyfe grinned at Sprinkle and winked broadly.

Then the skipper gave the order to man battle stations.

Batfish had just caught another luscious fly in her web.

EIGHTEEN

Gateway to the Underworld

February 1945

Captain Fyfe was only too aware of the dangers of his occupation. The Annapolis graduate knew the many ways the sea could claim a man's life. He also knew how vulnerable a vessel like his submarine was. Certainly it was designed to sink, its stealth giving it a better opportunity to escape danger than a surface vessel had.

But there was danger in submergence, too. Danger at every step. That was why a submarine's crew was so well trained, and why the process of becoming part of the "Silent Service" was (and still is) so selective in the first place. Why each sailor who earned his dolphin pin by qualifying in submarines (gold pins for officers and silver ones for enlisted men) could theoretically take any station on board at a moment's notice and perform the job without fail, whether it was repairing a toilet or driving the dive planes. Why the old saying was, "There's room for everything aboard a submarine . . . except a mistake." One man not performing his job properly in a crucial situation, one malfunction of a boat's complicated systems, and she and her crew could sink to the bottom forever.

It's not theory. It has happened too many times to boats with names like *Squalus, Thresher, Scorpion,* and *Cochino.* And those were boats that didn't have anybody shooting at them, dropping depth charges on them, or launching torpedoes at them at the time of their tragedies. All were lost due to mechanical malfunction or human error.

But it was Jake Fyfe's nature not to worry about such things. He trusted his crew. He liked them, believed in them, and had bet his life on them almost every day since he assumed the command of *Batfish* from Wayne Merrill under a rather ominous cloud in May of 1944. He knew his boat, too, and how to get the most from her. He had never been the studious type, not even at the academy, but the Naval Academy yearbook, the *Lucky Bag*, noted, he didn't even have to work hard to stay "sat," or satisfactory. And as the annual described him, "He's one of the boys!"

To this day, former crew members who served under Fyfe have nothing but good things to say about their skipper.

"Great guy."

"Solid."

"I would have followed him anywhere."

When he first took command, he told his crew precisely what he intended to do: close in on and kill the enemy. So far, that was precisely what they had been doing. For some, it was a welcome change. Captain Merrill had been fine. Most everyone liked him, and still had good things to say about him as well. But they also appreciated their new skipper's aggressive nature.

Now, here they were, less than two days after achieving one of a sub's most daunting tasks—sinking another submarine—and they were lining up to take a shot at a second.

As he took his familiar pose on the bridge of his vessel, Captain Fyfe couldn't help but think how close they had come to not even encountering this latest enemy sub. They had been ordered to move to another patrol box, but the almost constant air cover and the threat of trying to run in broad daylight had postponed their trip to their new mandated coordinates. If Fyfe had ordered the dive in deference to a distant covey of aircraft, they would most likely never have known anyone else was in the area.

Only a half hour after finally gaining enough darkness to start moving, and after seeing the patrol planes disappear a dozen miles away, they had encountered the latest telltale radar signal on 158 megacycles.

Batfish's SJ radar soon had a pip on its screen, too. It was eight thousand yards out, at a bearing of 310 degrees true.

Once again Fyfe's executive officer, Clark Sprinkle, was at his elbow. The skipper shared his thoughts with him.

"XO, I say we stay topside and do a surface attack again."

Sprinkle studied the black sky in all directions.

"If anything it's darker tonight than it was the last time. Maybe we can get close enough to at least see what class this one is before we blow her to hell and back."

"If his radar ain't working any better than the last guy's, we'll be able to get close enough to smell what they're having with their rice for supper," Fyfe said with a chuckle. Then he sang out, more than loud enough for the crewmen below in the conn to hear, "Man battle stations! Commence tracking!"

Again an electric thrill shot through the boat. No matter how many times this mostly experienced crew heard those words, they had the same effect. Throughout the length of the boat, each man on watch was quickly at his post.

"It's another Jap sub," someone whispered, and the news spread throughout the close quarters of the boat just as surely as if it had been broadcast on the intercom.

"Another one?"

"Damn! Another one!"

"Can you believe our luck?"

"We gonna sink two subs in two days! Hot damn!"

Topside, Fyfe and Sprinkle listened to the distant throb of *Batfish*'s huge Fairbanks Morse engines and the pronounced hiss of seawater as it slid down the boat's smooth sides.

"Range six thousand," the conn reported.

"All ahead flank!" Fyfe ordered in response.

They could all feel the engines growl even deeper as the boat kicked ahead noticeably. Now cool spray broke across her brow, thrown high enough that the damp mist blew into the faces of the skipper, his XO, and the lookouts in the shears above. They all stared at the spot on the horizon where their radar proclaimed that their latest quarry was supposed to be, meandering along as if she and her crew were on some kind of pleasure cruise.

Everyone topside knew that it would be difficult to spot a low-profile vessel like a Japanese submarine in this darkness, but they had no doubt that if they got close enough, they could spot the target. And they also knew the enemy boat would likely have lookouts who could just as easily spy *Batfish* as she raced in their direction.

"Skipper, you have the feeling we've done this before?" Sprinkle asked.

"Yeah. Only thing is, we'd just better not miss this time."

There was little humor in Fyfe's answer.

They rode along for a bit, no one saying anything. It was almost a shock when one of the lookouts yelled out, "Jap sub, dead ahead!"

Fyfe moved his glasses slightly to the right, to where the lookout had reported his sighting. Sure enough, there she was. A slightly smaller submarine than the previous one. No sail to speak of, riding lower than expected in the water. Still, every man who saw the enemy boat knew how lethal it could be, small vessel or not. Their sister boat, *Archerfish*, was the same size as the IJN sub in front of them, and the *Archerfish* had sent the massive, unsinkable aircraft carrier *Shinano*—all 72,000 tons of her—to the bottom. Size didn't matter when it came to the lethal capacity of submarines.

"I see her, too," Sprinkle said. "She's following a straight course. No zigzagging that I can see."

The bridge speaker squawked the confirmation: "Radar bearing dead ahead, range thirteen hundred yards."

Jake Fyfe was already doing the math in his head, calculating the vectors. He decided to wait until the enemy sub was precisely where he wanted it, until the attack angle was perfect, and then he would launch hellfire at the bastard. There didn't appear to be anybody else lurking around to get in their way. For once, it appeared he had the luxury of being discerning when it came to choosing the time and place in which to launch the attack.

And that moment and spot were quickly approaching. A few more seconds and the enemy boat would be in his sights. He'd have the craft dead to rights.

Jake Fyfe opened his mouth to give the "Fire!" command.

And that was when the target disappeared.

The signal that had been growing stronger and stronger and approaching saturation on the radar set just down the ladder in the conning tower was extinguished like a doused fire.

The Japanese submarine had pulled the plug.

Fyfe's first emotion was anger. Anger at himself. Here he was, trying to maneuver for the damn perfect shooting angle, and now he had let his prey slip right out of his web. It didn't take him long, though, to decide he wasn't going to allow the Japanese submarine to float out of his reach that easily.

"Come left ten degrees," he ordered, and then he gave the command to speed up. He'd try to get ahead of the other boat, just in case the enemy decided to stick his head up again.

"You think he saw us?" Sprinkle asked.

"If our lookouts could see him, then I reckon theirs could see us," Fyfe reasoned, the frustration obvious in his voice. "As much racket as we're making these days, it's a wonder they don't hear us all the way to Tokyo." It was true. *Batfish* had plenty of miles on her since the last trip to the yards. Her sound signature was likely as loud and distinctive as anything afloat. "Fact is, XO, we'll never know why he went away."

It didn't really matter now, though. If the enemy boat had spotted *Batfish* and dropped beneath the dark sea surface, the skipper and crew on the target vessel could be doing either of a couple of things—one disconcerting, the other downright frightening. They could be making a turn, driving away from danger as fast as their engines would carry them while submerged. If their mission was to tote contraband and officers home from the Philippines, they might be willing to do all they could to avoid a fight, and might not even be armed.

That, or they could be lining up at that very moment, getting ready to shoot their stalker right between the eyes.

That was one of the reasons why Fyfe had ordered the turn and the increase in speed. If the other sub was running, they'd have a tiny chance of keeping up and reacquiring the target, so long as the Japanese were cooperative enough to maintain the same heading. The IJN sub couldn't make much speed submerged, and thus couldn't get too far away.

And if he were lining up his own perfect shot at *Batfish*, he'd have to try to hit a rapidly moving bogey.

"You see anything?" one of the lookouts asked, just loud enough to be heard over the rumble of the engines and the splash of seawater against the boat's sleek sides.

"Naw, he's still under or we'd have him on radar before—"

"No, dumb-ass, I mean anything that looks like the wake of a torpedo coming this way."

The other lookout didn't answer. He merely dropped the angle of his gaze ever so slightly.

A tense half hour passed. The men in the shears and on the bridge widened their gaze, searching the horizon in a broader sweep, hoping to catch a glimpse of the enemy boat poking its sail out of the water, of the slightest bit of sea spray trailing from a periscope, tentatively stabbing upward from beneath the sea.

"Captain, I hear swishing," came the call from Sound. "He's blowing his ballast tanks."

Fyfe checked his watch: 9:06.

"We've got the signal back, Captain," Radar reported a half minute later. "Weaker signal than before. Eight-six-five-oh yards, bearing eighteen degrees true."

Captain Fyfe later wrote in his patrol report, "Whether the target heard us or thought he heard us; saw us or thought he saw us; had us on his radar or thought he did, or just made a normal and routine night dive I don't know, but I do know that unless he has a radar detector that will intercept our SJ, he's going to have a hard time finding us this time."

Whatever had made the Japanese skipper decide to dive, he had obligingly brought his boat back to the surface now. But who knew for how long? Everyone was still at battle stations, and Fyfe was ready to chase the guy down and shoot, perfect setup this time or not, before he pulled the stopper once more.

"Let's go get him before he decides to drop out of sight on us again. All ahead full!" he shouted. "Everybody be ready. We'll do an end run and pop the bastard first chance we get."

One thing became very clear: The target had sped up since he came back to the surface. He was making a good twelve knots now, running a true course of 120 degrees. It took *Batfish* a full forty-five minutes to get to a point where they had any chance at all of shooting torpedoes at the enemy boat.

"Range six thousand yards," Radar sang out. They were slowly gaining on their quarry. And there was no indication at all that the enemy captain had any idea that he was being tailed.

Fyfe finally figured that he was close enough to do some damage to the enemy submarine. It wasn't the perfect shot by any means. But he didn't want to risk losing the contact again.

"Clear the bridge!" He pressed the klaxon button hard. "Dive to periscope depth! Dive! Dive!"

The lookouts fell from the shears and dropped down the ladder into the hole in the deck in one smooth, well-rehearsed motion, like a choreographed dance routine. Clark Sprinkle followed right behind, and then Jake Fyfe was through the hatch as well, pulling the cover over on top of him as he descended, getting out of the way so the quartermaster could twist it tightly shut. He headed straight for the attack periscope and quickly brought it around to the last bearing of the boat they were chasing.

Beneath the deck on which he stood, its angle now tilting noticeably downward, he could feel the big diesel engines below wind down as the boat switched over to the almost silent electrical drive. It was now batteries that energized the motors that drove the screws and pushed them forward.

"All ahead one-third," the skipper ordered. "Bring her right to one-two-oh." Seconds later they were lined up, steady on course and just deep enough so that only the periscope protruded above the surface. "Set torpedo depth at four feet," he spoke into the intercom that went to the forward torpedo room.

Fyfe looked hard through the eyepiece in the scope. There was nothing but darkness up there. It was so dark he could hardly make out the horizon. The target might just as well have been invisible.

But the radar didn't have any night-vision problem. It still showed them a picture of exactly where the other boat was. And he was still on the surface, still making twelve knots, still on his same course . . . and swimming right into the kill zone of *Batfish*'s torpedoes.

"Angle on the bow starboard, one hundred. Bearing one-two-oh," the radar operator said matter-of-factly, so there was no mistake when the numbers were dialed into the torpedo data computer.

"We're ready," the TDC operator reported. His gizmo had done its work, and the information had been relayed to the forward torpedo room.

"Shoot!" Jake Fyfe growled.

The call came in sequence, just the way it always did when the command came to launch *Batfish*'s torpedoes.

"Fire one! Fire two! Fire three! Fire four!"

All four weapons were out of their tubes and away. That, at least, was a relief, after the anxious moments during the hot run on the previous attack. Four tubes emptied, their fish set on a one-hundred-degree starboard track, range to run calculated to be 880 yards, half a mile, and using a one-knot speed spread.

Once the fish were away, there was the inevitable nervous quiet that ran throughout the boat like a foggy chill. And that was especially true when they were below the surface, operating on batteries—the vessel was eerily quiet up and down its entire length. Sailors could hear their shipmates breathing. Sometimes there was whispered banter.

Other times, when they were shooting at targets in convoys, the anticipatory quiet was all wiped out as they launched their torpedoes, then hastily turned and fled to escape the possible wrath of protective destroyers or airplane cover. At those moments, the noise of their flight took over. Once the torpedoes were spotted by the target vessel or its escorts, or once there was an explosion when they hit the target, the enemy would quickly come looking for the submarine that had launched the attack. When that happened, it would be best to be deep and gone.

Not tonight. There appeared to be no one else but *Batfish* and her target in that corner of the Babuyan Channel.

Clark Sprinkle could hear the tick of the assistant attack officer's stopwatch as it counted off the seconds since the fish in forward torpedo tube number one was set loose. The XO kept his gaze on the skipper, where he stood with his eye a half inch from the periscope eyepiece. He saw the brilliant flash that jumped from the lens of the scope, illuminating Fyfe's sweat-streaked cheek. The captain had time only to blink once before the whole crew heard the awful thunder of a direct hit, as the torpedo sacrificed itself.

"Got her!"

"She blew apart!" Fyfe said, his eye stuck to the scope and his face split in a broad grin.

There were shouts and whistles from one end of *Batfish* to the other.

Then, just as suddenly as they had erupted, everyone hushed, listening for the next boom.

It came nine seconds after the first, but much more muted. The second torpedo had most likely hit a piece of the disintegrating Japanese warship, or it had been detonated by the whirlpool disturbance stirred up in the ocean by the first violent explosion.

Then, eight seconds later, they heard another muffled blast.

There were more whoops and cheers and wolf whistles from the control room below, from the torpedo rooms, from throughout the boat.

Two subs sunk in two days!

Jake Fyfe leaned his head against the periscope for a moment. When he looked up again, he had lost his grin.

"Down scope," he said, almost too quiet to be heard amid all the celebrating that had broken out around him. "Go to one-five-zero feet and level off."

They had just reached depth when the boat was shaken by a sudden, unexpected blast, one that was close enough to rock the boat hard. Most men stopped and looked up at the top of the rounded bulkhead above them, as if they could see through it, through 150 feet of seawater, to find what airplane was bombing them, what previously unseen destroyer was now dropping depth charges on their heads.

It was quiet for a moment, but then, just as they had settled again, there was a second crunching explosion, even stronger than the first one. Again *Batfish* shivered, shook violently, and then settled back to almost perfect stillness. There was only the sound of dripping water as it slapped the deck, the distant whir of the boat's screws, churning seawater, shoving them gently along, getting them out of the midst of the hornet's nest that they had just knocked out of a tree.

It was quiet enough that they could hear a distant rumble, like far-off thunder following a violent storm. That blast marked the end-of-run explosion of their fourth torpedo. It had either missed or there was nothing left for it to hit when it passed through the burning mass of what had most recently been an Imperial Japanese Navy submarine.

"Maybe the bastard was hauling ammo back to—" one of the men in the conn began, but before he could finish, there was yet another teeth-rattling explosion. The sub heeled as if she were bending against a sudden gust of wind.

There had been no telling splash and click of a depth charge. Radar had seen no other vessels or airplanes while they were near the surface. Sound had reported no whir of torpedo screws.

Up and down the boat, sailors speculated on what the three numbing blasts might have been. And whether or not there would be more. They braced themselves, just in case.

"You boys know what that was?" Fyfe finally asked those within earshot in the conning tower. "Whatever else she was carrying, that boat we just sent to the bottom was certainly loaded with something mighty explosive. Some stuff that won't get used against us and our friends. God only knows how many lives we saved tonight."

As Fyfe later recorded in his patrol report, "Explosion . . . very loud, which shook up the boat considerably. Thought at first it was a close bomb, but then realized it was the finale to the swan song of one Nip submarine."

He also noted that the sound operator on *Batfish* spent the next quarter hour after the hit on the enemy sub listening to and reporting the unmistakable noises of a dying vessel—the pop and crack of small explosions, the rending of stressed metal, escaping air, collapsing bulkheads.

But, of course, no screams of dying men. Anybody on the enemy sub was way beyond that by then.

At 11:41 P.M., an hour and twenty minutes after launching the first torpedo, the skipper cautiously brought his boat back to the surface. After witnessing the violence of the fiery explosion, listening to the sounds of the enemy boat dying, he had no illusions of finding any survivors of the attack. It was almost a habit, though. Almost as if it would give his own men hope of survival in a similar successful attack from the other side if they could find one Japanese submariner still alive, floating there, awaiting rescue.

But once more there was only an oil slick, punctuated occasionally by bubbles popping to the surface from way down where the remnants of the submarine now lay.

Before they had time to do much searching, a hurried call came from the radar operator.

"Approaching aircraft! Range five miles! Bearing zero-four-zero!"

Friend or foe, attracted by the brilliant explosion that was likely visible for miles around on such a dark night, there was no point in waiting to see for certain where this newcomer's allegiance lay. Fyfe sounded the klaxon before radar had completed the report, and the four lookouts in the shears above the bridge were down and past him before the raucous sound had died away.

"Clear the bridge! Dive! Dive!" he called, but there was no one left topside but him. He paused a moment as the angle of his boat changed noticeably beneath him, as she plowed her nose into the sea, left oily and nasty by the vanquished enemy boat.

More brother submariners gone. Two boatloads of them, wiped out in less than forty-eight hours. Gone at the hand of his boat, his crew, him.

Jake Fyfe felt an odd mixture of melancholy and elation wash over him, even as the clutching black ocean washed over the forward deck of his submarine and the deep proceeded to reclaim it.

The skipper shook his head hard to clear the odd thoughts, took one step, dropped quickly down the hatch, and pulled the lid over on top of himself.

Twenty minutes later, they came to periscope and radar depth, made a sweep of the area, and, satisfied there were no other threats anywhere close, *Batfish* shot to the surface long enough for Stan Javorski to get on his radio and brag to the rest of the wolf pack about what they had done now.

Then Fyfe ordered them to get going to their assigned area, to the duty station where they were headed when the Japanese boat had swum right into their path and invited them to attack.

And he also reminded them that they would continue to perform their primary duty, the reason they had come to this part of the war in the first place—to look for enemy submarines to sink.

They had bagged two. Hell, why not shoot for three?

NINETEEN

The Textbook Shot

February 1945

"Looks like another one!"

Jake Fyfe had been standing there on the bridge of his submarine, alongside Clark Sprinkle, talking quietly, listening to the whispers between the lookouts above them, the hum of activity from the conning tower below, the sibilant slap of seawater against the sides of *Batfish* as they steamed along in what appeared to be an empty sea. The weather had turned foul. Squalls raced past them, dropping patches of hard rain, and then they scooted on. The sea was choppy and the boat rolled beneath their feet. The cloud cover and passing rain showers made it even darker than the last two evenings had been.

Once again, it was the radar detection gear that spied what appeared to be their next target. The skipper checked his timepiece. Just after two a.m., February 13. He scribbled the information in his notebook.

"What you got?" Fyfe inquired.

"Radar interference, Captain. This one's on a hundred and fifty-seven megacycles, but it's not nearly as strong as the other ones were."

Not exactly the same frequency as the other two, but that still wasn't a channel that Allied radar would be using. Could it be another submarine? Fyfe didn't want to get his hopes up, but he could feel a shot of pure adrenaline anyway. His pulse kicked up with anticipation.

Even if it was an IJN pig boat, the signal was weak and could be in any direction from them, maybe steaming away from them already at a pace they could never hope to match. No use getting anybody's hopes up.

Still, wouldn't it be something if it were another one of the bastards? Three subs in three days! It was an unimaginable feat.

"Tell APR to find the null," the skipper ordered blandly, working to keep the excitement out of his voice. They needed to determine which direction to look through the gloom.

"Battle stations?"

"Not yet." Fyfe knew that before he could unleash his Mark 27s, he required visual contact. "Let's see him on radar first."

Sprinkle was already disappearing down the hatch to the conn to alert everyone on watch that they might have something else to shoot at soon. He didn't mention that it could be another submarine that they were contemplating going after. No use getting the crew's hopes up until they had more than a distant, wavering radar signal.

Meanwhile, the boat was already making a broad turn while the men below watched their glowing instrumentation, waiting for the instant when they could determine the likely direction from which the mystery signal came.

By the time they had found out and relayed to the bridge that the target vessel's bearing was 220 degrees—a matter of moments—everyone on the boat who was not asleep (and a few who were) had already heard the rumor that they were about to stalk and bag themselves another IJN submarine.

So much for not feeding anticipation.

"Bring her to two-two-oh degrees!" Fyfe sang out, an unavoidable smile on his face. "All ahead full!" He turned to look up at the rain-soaked boys riding in the shears, ignoring the drizzle in his face. "Keep a sharp eye, fellows. Be loud about it if you see anything."

Only one of the lookouts watched the direction that *Batfish*'s bow was now pointing. The others were turned in the other three directions—port, starboard, stern—to watch for any signs of somebody sneaking up on them while they were busy stalking the weak-signaled target.

The submarine ran full bore for twenty minutes through the pounding rain. It was totally dark all the way to the horizon, no matter which way the men topside peered. The rock-steady rumble of the Fairbanks Morse engines below was almost hypnotic, but the brisk, wet wind in their faces helped keep them alert. That and the familiar thrill of the chase. Still, they could see nothing but the white of the foam breaking over the bow and churning in their wake astern.

This was one of the best moments for Jake Fyfe—having a fine racehorse of a submarine under him as they galloped to what they hoped would be a good finish. A good crew, well trained, eager, doing exactly the jobs that they had rehearsed so many times. Sometimes he wished he could be down there among them in the torpedo room, the control room, the engine room, or the maneuvering room as the boat galloped after its prey. He wished he could watch them work, see the look in their eyes, the set of their jaws, hear what they were saying to each other in the dead minutes between detection and acquisition of a target. To take part in their hasty, good-natured betting pools on what kind of vessel they would find, how many fish they'd send out, how many of the torpedoes would hit the target, or whether or not the target would go down from the wounds they inflicted.

If these youngsters were nervous or scared, if they felt their own mortality as they raced to get closer to and within striking distance of a dangerous enemy, they hid it well with jokes, laughter, and with even more rapt attention to the fine detail of their jobs.

Fyfe appreciated the close-knit camaraderie that was so much a part of being a submariner. He loved his wardroom crew, too, but he wished that he could spend more time with the "rag hats." He enjoyed telling them jokes, hearing their laughter, watching their practical jokes unfold, but usually from a distance so he wouldn't dampen their spirits with his presence. Though he wasn't much older than some of them, he still felt like a proud papa watching his sons excel.

Being below during an attack would be a treat, for sure, but his true milieu was being up on the bridge when they began an all-ahead charge. Being in the conn was good, too, but it was nothing like being topside, in the open air. He loved feeling the awesome power of his war machine as she obeyed his commands, loved the sting of spray in his face as the sea broke hard over the bow and hung there in the air long enough for the boat's sail to punch a hole through it.

But the best part was the anticipation of the fight. He was about to match wits with another warrior. Even if they both did their best, there was a good chance one of them would not be going home. Luck. Skill. Crew.

Equipment. Mechanics. Whatever was the ultimate determining factor didn't really matter in the end.

One of them would steam away. The other would be at this spot on the ocean floor for eternity.

In most cases, *Batfish* and her captain had a distinct advantage over the surface ships that they trailed. They could sneak up and bite before the victim, riding high and unaware on top of the ocean, even knew they were there.

But shadowing another submarine was a different kettle of fish. He could run. He could dive. He could sneak right back and punch *Batfish* in the nose.

That was what had made those last two kills so special. Jake Fyfe had bagged quarry as slippery and elusive as he was. He hungered mightily to do it again.

About twenty-five minutes after the first detection of the weak radar signal on 157 megacycles, Clark Sprinkle leaned over the plotting board in the conning tower below. He had seen all that he needed to see.

The exec alerted his captain that SJ radar had detected a pip at 10,700 yards, still on the same bearing, and it was heading off at 120 degrees. The vessel that was spitting out all that radar juice was just six miles away. And it was all by itself in this part of the ocean.

Ten minutes after that, Sprinkle reported up to the bridge that the guy was still meandering through the sultry night at a leisurely seven knots, not attempting to run away from them or anybody else, even though he still doggedly painted the black night with his invisible radar beam. Either he had not yet seen a pip for *Batfish* on his radar scope, or he simply didn't care.

Fyfe was ready. As soon as he heard his exec's report, he shouted, "Man battle stations! Go to periscope depth! Dive! Dive!"

This part of the hunt was always an exhilarating experience for Fyfe. Punching the raucous klaxon, yelling, "Dive!", watching the lookouts as they fluidly dropped past him and vanished through the hatch. Sensing the sudden downturn of the boat's bow as her powerful pumps sucked in seawater and as the planesmen aligned the "wings" on each side of the hull to make her "fly" downward, disappearing into the depths. Being the last one off the bridge, slamming the cover hard behind him, leaving the quartermaster tightening the hatch cover above him as the first splashes of seawater doused the bridge and spilled inside the conning tower. A good crew could have a boat completely under in less than forty-five seconds after receiving a dive command.

"Contact bearing one-zero-five," Sprinkle announced as Fyfe pulled up the periscope. "Range seven-one-five-oh yards."

They had cut the range to two miles.

The skipper spun the scope around until the indicator on its base pointed to 105. Meanwhile, the firing officer dialed in the information using the knobs on the front of the torpedo data computer.

"We're in a great spot," Fyfe said, mostly to himself, as he peered through the eyepiece. Everyone in the conn knew it was true. The enemy vessel—almost certainly another submarine—was heading to the south. *Batfish* was approaching from off the IJN boat's port bow, quickly catching up to him. If the son of a bitch didn't zig or zag or make the one radical course change only a submarine can make—pulling the plug and taking her down—then they had a better than average chance to take some shots at him. And if everything lined up and they didn't mess up, they would soon have a perfect textbook shot.

Every man in the conn was thinking, *Fish in a barrel.* Nobody said it out loud, though, not wanting to jinx the opportunity.

"Damn good thing he's cooperating, too," the captain added. His exec, only a foot away on the other side of the scope, nodded in agreement. Sprinkle knew exactly what Fyfe was talking about. They didn't have many bullets left in their gun. Only two torpedoes remained in the forward room, and they were already loaded into their tubes. If they shot and missed with those, they'd have no more fish up front. They'd have to turn tail and fire "stingers," torpedoes shot from the after torpedo room.

"What have you got now?" Fyfe asked the tracking party.

"Speed seven knots, steady. Course remains one-two-zero."

It was almost as if Fyfe and his crew had the target on a string, like a cat's toy, playing with it until they decided to pounce.

Fyfe guided *Batfish* so they could bring her directly across the meandering target's apparent path, and then get ready to turn and fire both torpedoes in the forward room right down their own wake as the poor, unfortunate and apparently unaware bastard crossed it. The geometry of it all spun through the skipper's head, the moves that would culminate in their bagging an unprecedented third submarine in three days.

It was a near-impossible feat for one submarine to sink another, simply because of their stealth and maneuverability. *Batfish* had sunk two subs already, and done so in only a couple of days. And now, less than twenty-four hours after racking up their second, they were calmly and deliberately setting up for their third sub victim. It never occurred to Fyfe and his crew that what they were doing couldn't be done. They had another prized IJN sub in their range, and there was no time to think of the magnitude of their feat—they had an enemy boat to put on the bottom.

They were level at forty-four feet, periscope depth, easing along at three knots. And everything would soon line up.

"Don't turn on us," Fyfe prayed as he peered through the scope into blackness, broken only by the occasional lightninglike flash of phosphorescence. "Stay the course, Skipper. And whatever you do, don't do like that last one and—"

"Target's gone from radar, sir!"

TWENTY

An Orphan
Submarine

October 1972

It was a damp, dreary fall in the American Desert. During the week of October 30, heavy rains fell, and the Arkansas River rose over six feet where it flowed past Muskogee. When an employee came down to open up *Batfish* to visitors on November 7, he discovered that the sandy berm that had been built up to allow access to the deck of the submarine had caved in. It was now unsafe to try to walk across the gangway. Additionally, the tether attached from the boat to her mooring was loose, and there was a real fear that she could founder if she broke loose and drifted out into the flood current in the middle of the river.

While the sub herself seemed to be okay, she was temporarily out of business as any kind of a tourist attraction.

Executive director Roy Smallwood looked over the situation and quickly convinced a county commissioner to dedicate some of his men and equipment to come over and fix the access. A group of sub vets rushed down to help anchor *Batfish* to a sandbar and took the additional precaution of flooding her ballast tanks with river water to try to keep her from floating away or keeling over. Nobody wanted to see the proud old girl flipped over with her bottom showing.

A week later, they were able to reopen for visitors, even though the access needed almost constant attention now. The budget called for between twelve and fifteen hundred dollars per month in paid admissions in November and December. They couldn't afford to lose a single penny of that revenue.

The Corps of Engineers had been nice enough to extend the permit to leave the submarine moored at the riverbank, but they now warned that she would have to be moved by New Year's Day, 1973. The Corps was worried about more flooding during the rough winter weather and the possibility that the sub could break loose, get out into the main channel, and sink, causing a major navigation problem in the middle of their newly opened waterway.

It's worth noting that December 31 represented another deadline, one that most on the Maritime Advisory Board had been pointedly ignoring for quite some time. That was a crucial date specified in the original contract with the U.S. Navy by which the sub was required to be relocated to her permanent mooring. Nobody knew for certain what the ramifications of not meeting that deadline would be. But not even the most optimistic sub sailor in the group could make the case that the sandbank and borrowed aluminum gangplank would pass for a "permanent" resting spot for the historic submarine. Especially since that mooring seemed to get washed away every couple of days.

The Tuesday after Thanksgiving, the Honorable George Nigh, Lieutenant Governor of the state of Oklahoma and chairman of the Tourism and Recreation Commission, convened a meeting of the panel at the Will Rogers Memorial Office Building in Oklahoma City to once and for all settle the sordid, confusing matter of the USS *Batfish*.

Those present at the meeting included Mr. Nigh; John Devine, the director of the tourism committee; and several other members and staffers from the group. There were also three state senators, including John Luton from Muskogee; along with Captain Ray Smallwood, the executive director of the Maritime Advisory Board; and board members W. E. Battenfield, Nick Guagliardo, Ron Banks, Geen Gilmour, and Ace Kelly. Robert Lomax, the mayor of Muskogee, made the trip, along with representatives of the chamber of commerce and the Muskogee Port Authority. To the consternation of a few in the group, there was also someone there from the state examiner's office and from the attorney general's office, as well as a reporter from one of the Oklahoma City television stations.

Nigh went through the rather convoluted history of the Maritime Advisory Board, but most present had a hard time following the bureaucratic maze. Roy Smallwood made a presentation, speaking for the Maritime Advisory Board, reminding the assemblage of what a wonderful opportunity *Batfish* was for Muskogee, the state and beyond. "It is one of Oklahoma's most unusual, entertaining and educational attractions," he said. "It can become an attraction of national importance—perhaps a Naval Hall of Fame. This idea may sound a bit unusual for this inland state, but the United States is an island and a maritime nation, and many of our great naval leaders have come from its interior, hundreds of miles from the sea."

Smallwood nodded toward Kelly and the other sub vets in the meeting room, then reminded the group that the city of Memphis, Tennessee, was hauling in PT boats for a museum; Omaha, Nebraska, had already gotten its hands on a minesweeper and was going to build a thirty-seven-acre park around it. And he reiterated the success the state of Alabama had enjoyed with one of *Batfish*'s sisters, the USS *Drum*, sitting down there in Mobile with folks lining up on her decks to take a tour. Folks who had paid good money for the privilege.

"Muskogee has the lead," Smallwood pitched. "And she already has a submarine with a proud and illustrious history. And the planned location of the park is clearly visible from the Muskogee Turnpike."

He balanced his plea for approval for the permanent mooring and for a building for offices, a ship's store, restrooms, and a museum with an honest recitation of the group's financial situation. Bottom line: By the end of the year, the submarine would be $387,000 in debt. Deep water, indeed. A board that had no authority to borrow money or incur indebtedness was over a third of a million dollars in the hole.

"We are on the verge of something great for Oklahoma," Smallwood concluded. "It is my belief that this opportunity should not be lost."

The group discussed dissolving the Maritime Advisory Board and turning *Batfish* over to the Muskogee Port Authority. There were a couple of problems there. The board didn't have the authority to sign the boat over to anyone. Apparently nobody did. And nobody was certain the port authority wanted the orphan submarine, or could legally accept her if it did.

So, Oklahoma didn't want her. Muskogee wasn't sure they could take her. The Navy didn't want her back. And the Maritime Advisory Board, which had signed her adoption papers and brought her all the way from Texas, didn't have authority to possess her in the first place.

The lieutenant governor then proceeded to lecture Maritime Advisory Board members present, reminding them that the state had no responsibility whatsoever for any of the debt associated with the proud old submarine. And that the mess they were discussing was the fault of the board, who had not deemed it necessary to communicate with the tourism commission or its predecessor about their plans. Its members just went off half-cocked and did whatever they wanted to do, whether they had authority to do it or not.

"By statute, the Maritime Advisory Board was an advisory committee, though it certainly has never acted in that capacity," Nigh pointed out. "So why not advise the commission? What suggestions do you have?"

There really were none at that moment.

Nigh gaveled the meeting to a close with a request for a plan. Any kind of plan from anybody. And he wanted it by Monday, December 11.

Ace Kelly, speaking for the Maritime Advisory Board, sent a letter to the lieutenant governor on December 9, admitting that his well-intentioned group did not have the money to continue operating and maintaining the submarine. There was also the problem of security. Vandals had struck several times already, and thieves had carted off hard-to-replace equipment from the submarine. Sub vet volunteers—theoretically unarmed—now slept on the boat at night to try to prevent further larceny. They were worried that her value as a tourist attraction was being spirited off the property one piece at a time.

But Kelly wasn't totally surrendering. Neither were the other submariners. He and his crew simply steamed around the target and began an assault from a new bearing.

The letter urged Nigh to let the Tourism and Recreational Commission take legal possession of *Batfish* and the land that had been donated by the Muskogee Port Authority. It also urged that the state panel assume responsibility for maintaining and protecting the sub and her future surrounding acreage. And finally they strongly suggested that Nigh and his commission get busy issuing revenue bonds to cover all debts accrued so far while generating enough extra dollars to construct the thirty-acre War Memorial

Park the way it should be built, all so they could get about the business of honoring those who had fought and died for the country.

It was a bold and risky plan of attack—just the kind an old sub officer might devise. It only half worked.

Nigh did allow his commission to take custody of the orphan sub, but there was no immediate discussion of bonds or of constructing a magnificent park in honor of lost submarines and war veterans.

The lieutenant governor's first move, four days before Christmas 1972, was to relieve Captain Roy Smallwood of his command and lay off the couple of other paid employees at the submarine. He also ordered that *Batfish* be padlocked, shut off from the public. Then he talked the Army Corps of Engineers into extending the permit for her to moor in the river until March.

And that was it.

"The submarine-killer submarine" had run aground, apparently with no hopes of ever getting under way again.

TWENTY-ONE

In the Course
of Duty

The Cherokee, Creek, and Chickasaw Indians believed that the soul of a murdered man was forced to wander about the earth, not able to move on to the next world until his death was avenged. This led to imbalance. The murderer was required to accept responsibility for the death of a tribesman, then had to make the ultimate sacrifice for his transgression. Only then could the innocent ghost be freed and allowed to cross over into the next world.

February 1945

"Radar is still not picking up the target, sir!"

So here they were, *Batfish*'s sixth war patrol, the fourth with Captain Jake Fyfe in command. A great patrol—two enemy submarines and their crews erased from the IJN fleet—was now on the verge of becoming downright amazing.

But then the latest son of a bitch they had painted on their radar had pulled the plug on them. Gone, who knew where and for how long. And there was no telling what the sneaky devil was doing down there by now. Most likely running, if he had heard *Batfish* coming.

Or maybe he was doing the same thing Jake Fyfe and his crew would be up to if the roles were reversed. Captain Jake wouldn't run from anything if there was any hope of blowing it out of the water.

That was what had the *Batfish* crew worried.

Every man on that submarine stood still and listened with all his might for the whooshing sound of the enemy boat blowing water out of her tanks with compressed air, signaling to the world that the Japanese skipper was preparing to oblige them all by surfacing. They strained to hear the sound of the enemy boat's screws as she made a full-bore run at *Batfish*, just the way the American submarine had been preparing to do to the IJN boat only a few minutes before.

But every sub sailor aboard *Batfish* listened most intently for one specific sound: the metallic, telltale whir of a quickly approaching torpedo.

The radar operator's jaw was working tensely as he watched the scope in front of him. He was hoping for a solid reflection to appear, indicating that the target had returned to the surface. All the while, they monitored 157 megacycles, hoping against hope to see the reappearance of the other boat's radar sweep.

But there was nothing.

Jake Fyfe hugged the dripping-wet periscope, still looking at almost total darkness through the instrument's eyepiece.

Had he run his boat and crew right into an ambush?

"What was his last bearing?" he asked, his voice husky and low in the quiet of the conning tower.

"Zero-two-zero. Seven-one-five-oh yards."

Fyfe scratched his head. Could the Japanese skipper have heard them coming? Not likely. They were running quiet. That was why Fyfe had taken her down, put her on batteries, and ordered that she be rigged for silent running. If the enemy boat could hear *Batfish*'s screws, then they had possession of some far better gear than the American boats did, something new that the Navy and its spooks didn't even know about yet.

The sonar had not been pinging. They were too far away from the IJN boat for that. Radar had told them all they needed to know, and they had been using that judiciously as they shadowed the target.

The enemy couldn't have seen *Batfish*'s radar signature either. At least, Fyfe didn't think so. So far, the Japanese had not indicated that they had the necessary equipment to detect the Allies' new SJ signal. The radio set had not been keyed at any time during the approach, either. There was nothing to give themselves away there. They should have been invisible.

So why had the bastard suddenly decided to take a dunk?

"Hell, maybe he'll come back up in half an hour like his buddy did," someone in the conning tower offered. The last submarine they had tailed had dived and surfaced like a playful dolphin just before *Batfish* sent it to hell.

"We can only hope," Fyfe said wearily. "The other two boats sort of spoiled us, I guess, the way they made it easy for us. We expect them all to behave now. Let's surface and make a high-speed run. We'll try to get ahead of him and on his track, just in case he maintains the same heading and decides to play along with us and show his ugly head again."

Several of the sailors in the conning tower glanced at each other. It would have been easy just to sit there, hoping the target would surface again within radar range and give them something tangible to chase. And it would have been almost a sure thing that they would never see the boat again. No, their skipper was going to aggressively try to anticipate where the target would end up and go sit and wait for him to get there.

There was risk, of course. They were probably relatively safe, sitting there at periscope depth. Making a topside run to try to intercept the target would give the Japanese contact, as well as any of his friends who might just happen to be driving by, a good chance to catch *Batfish* on the surface and dispatch her to eternal patrol.

Fyfe had made known his predilection for what to do in situations like this plenty of times before. He didn't come out here to hide and hope somebody swam up his tailpipe. Not unless the hiding was just long enough to line up the tubes on a juicy target.

The skipper didn't hesitate as he gave the command to surface. They all felt the vessel tilt, her snout heading upward at a steep angle. Then, once they were back out in the night air, the big diesels shoved her hard forward, toward an imaginary spot on the surface of the sea ahead of them where they could sit and wait and hope the Japanese submarine would come idling conveniently close enough so *Batfish* could shoot her to death.

The better part of a half hour had already passed since the target went sinkers. If the other crewman's guess was right—that there was some kind of reason for the Japanese subs to periodically dive and stay down for thirty minutes—then they should be back on the surface shortly. If not, the hat trick was looking more and more unlikely.

They were nearing the point where they would have to break off the patrol and go home for fuel and refitting. They couldn't idle around out here forever. The enemy boat could have gone off in any other direction once she disappeared. She could already be making a clean getaway. Or she could be lining up a shot on her tormentor at that very moment, getting ready to shoot as soon as *Batfish* blithely paddled to a stop long enough to offer an easier target.

They had been fortunate so far. The other two boats, no doubt fully capable of mounting a vicious counterattack or preemptive assault, had been stalked and killed with no return fire.

Had Fyfe and his crew pressed their luck? Was this new contact about to exact revenge for the shipmates he had lost in the last three days?

"Go to radar depth," the skipper commanded. "Let's see if we can spot anything of him."

"Nothing out there," Radar duly reported a few minutes later.

Another maddeningly slow half hour crept by. The conning tower was so quiet every man could hear the shuffling feet of his shipmates; the occasional growling of a stomach, too long delayed from a late dinner; the plinking sound of ocean water from the periscope dripping onto the deck at their feet.

Every one of them jumped involuntarily when the soundman shouted, much louder than necessary, "APR contact! He's back on one-five-seven megacycles!"

"Got him on the SJ scope, too," Radar chimed in.

Over an hour after the enemy sub had decided to go swimming, he was back on the surface.

"Somebody tell me where he is!" the skipper barked.

"Range nine-eight-oh-oh. Bearing three-three-six true."

He was over a mile farther away from them than he had been when he dived. They were still in real danger of losing track of the target.

"Take her up!" Fyfe cried. They would have to get on top in a hurry to make yet another high-speed approach on this same bucket of bolts.

As soon as the hatch at the top of the conning tower had broken the surface, Fyfe was out and onto the bridge. It was still too dark to see anything that didn't want to be seen, so they relied on radar to confirm when they were within seven thousand yards—about four miles—of the enemy vessel.

Fyfe ordered them to dive directly across the path that the other oncoming boat would soon be taking. He wanted the stern tubes lined up so he could fire the torpedoes right down their wake when the enemy boat passed.

When they were finally in position, he told the diving officer to take them to radar depth and to get ready to line up for a point-blank shot when the poor, unsuspecting son of a bitch rode past where they would be sitting, waiting. It was like drawing a bead on a clay pigeon after shouting, "Pull!"

The dash across the enemy sub's likely track was a risky one, but it would leave *Batfish* with her stern tubes—the ones where they still had more than a couple of torpedoes available—pointed directly toward the approaching boat. Fyfe intended to seize every advantage he could get, and make every one of their few remaining fish count.

But as soon as they got to the desired depth, the sea suddenly became rough going. The high-speed flanking run had taken them into the relatively narrow pass between Dalupiri Island and Calayan Island, and the current was running something fierce here. It was all the crew could do to keep the boat steady, aimed with her ass end pointed in the right direction, and at the proper depth to continue the radar sweep while keeping the top of the periscope above water.

"Tide rips are making depth control and steering very difficult, and I hope they don't adversely affect the torpedoes," Fyfe wrote in his log. The current—just one more factor he had to add into the complicated equation.

He and his crew could feel their boat slewing slightly as the planesmen in the control room directly below and the men in the maneuvering room back toward the stern coaxed and finessed their controls to try to hold her steady in the considerable crosscurrent. It was like trying to hover a helicopter in a hurricane.

"Make ready aft tubes," Fyfe said. "Set the run to six feet, one-knot speed spread. Eighty-degree starboard track. And stand by to fire."

Fyfe was taking no chances. He was setting the torpedoes to run a bit deeper than normal. He didn't want them to breach in the strong current and either explode prematurely or be knocked off course. They should still be in a good spot to kiss that enemy sub's side tanks.

"Aft tubes flooded," came the report from Blackie Lawrence back in the aft torpedo room. The Mark 18-2s were loaded and ready. The tubes were flooded with seawater, the torpedomen ready, awaiting the command to flush out their weapons and send them off to an explosive rendezvous with their intended target.

The plotting board projected that the target was swimming cooperatively so far, meandering right into their crosshairs. If she didn't suddenly vary speed or course, and if she didn't once again decide to take a dive, they had her dead to rights.

"Stand by," Jake Fyfe said.

"Bearing steady . . . one-six-five." The skipper of the IJN boat had no clue the *Batfish* was about to spring closed the trap. "Range one-five-zero-zero."

The sailor operating the torpedo data computer reported, "We're all set." The numbers had been entered, the results calculated among the gears and sprockets of the TDC and then relayed to the torpedoes themselves.

Now the fish knew precisely where to swim.

"Fire seven!" Jake Fyfe commanded. There was a tangible nudge as the Mark 18-2 was shoved from its coffinlike compartment and spun away from its mother ship.

Fifteen seconds passed. A long, quiet fifteen seconds. Only the ticking of the tracker's watch broke the near-total silence in the cramped conning tower.

"Fire eight!"

Another jolt, another quiet span of time. Seventeen seconds this time, though it felt like tense, hot minutes.

"Fire ten!"

The last torpedo had been regurgitated from the sub.

"Torpedoes running straight and true," came the word from the sound tracker, listening to the hum of the weapons as they all three swam away.

Fyfe requested that the periscope be raised and, in the same breath, asked, "How long now?"

"Fifteen seconds to target, sir."

Fyfe put his eye to the eyepiece. Nothing, still, but the blackness of night.

The tracker began counting it down.

"Ten. Nine. Eight. Seven . . ."

Maybe it was getting ever so slightly lighter up there. Fyfe imagined he could see a hint of horizon. Or maybe it was only a reflection of something in the scope.

"Six. Five. Four . . ."

He could almost see the flash now. Hear the eerie, muffled roar, just like the other two.

He wasn't breathing. Even with all the times he had gone through these familiar, well-rehearsed steps before.

"Three. Two. One. Zero."

Nothing, except the incessant ticking of the stopwatch, the hand now advancing past where it was supposed to indicate conflagration.

Fyfe spun from the scope to try to get a quick look at the radar screen, to detect whether the IJN skipper had performed an unexpected maneuver.

Just as he did, the flash from the eyepiece of the periscope lit up the entire dark interior of the conning tower. A second later, they felt the shimmering boom of an awful explosion, hard and concussive, even though it had taken place almost a mile from where they hovered, fighting the current that ran between the two islands.

Batfish heeled slightly, then bounced up and down from the force of the blast. Throughout the boat, sailors leaned hard against anything solid, grabbing their ears if they could spare the hands, even as the grins broke over their faces and the yelps of elation sounded up and down the line of compartments.

"Target could be seen blowing apart on radar screen," Fyfe would report in the patrol report. "And the explosion was accompanied by a large yellow ball of fire as seen through periscope. The second and third torpedoes missed, not due to errors in data, but because target sank so quickly."

The captain was quiet as he watched the awful, billowing firestorm that he had stoked.

Jesus, he thought, contemplating the devastating carnage they had just visited upon the enemy. But a smile was playing at his lips, too. "Radar, you see anybody else up there?" he asked.

"No, Captain."

"All right. Take her up and let's see if we can find any survivors."

When the quartermaster unscrewed the hatch and opened it, Fyfe stuck his head up just in time to hear the distant end-of-run explosion of his second torpedo. By the time he was out on the bridge, there was the other one, thirty-five seconds later. He was a bit miffed that he had wasted two perfectly good torpedoes, but they had been the insurance. There had been no way to know that the first one would do all the damage they needed it to do.

The air was thick with predawn haze and a strong, breathtaking mix of diesel fuel stench and oil smoke. He guided the boat through a heavy oil slick that already blanketed the surface of the water. Bits of debris floated in the gooey mess, but they saw nothing sizable enough to make it worthwhile to try to fish it out.

There were no swimmers either, no life rafts bobbing in the slick.

The beam of the searchlight was too diffused to see much of anything, so they decided to douse it and stay on the surface and wait another hour and a half or so, until the sun gave them enough light to see what they could find. The radar would keep an eye out for patrol planes or approaching enemy vessels.

When there was enough daylight to see, they could make out chunks of wood and soggy paper but not much else. Certainly no Japanese submariner floating in the slime, awaiting rescue. There were apparently no survivors.

Then one of the lookouts called out and pointed to starboard. A sailor on deck, Dick "Hershey" Hosler, retrieved what appeared to be a box that had been floating there, almost lost amidst the thick oil.

It turned out to hold Japanese navigation equipment and a book of tables. Speculation was the order of the day. Maybe the navigator had come up on the boat's bridge after they surfaced, waiting for first light so he could take a navigational fix. Maybe that was why they had surfaced in the first place. What must have gone through the man's head when he suddenly felt the boat rise up beneath him and explode in flames? Fyfe thought.

If he lived long enough to even realize what was happening, that is.

There was a workbook in the box as well, and it indicated that the boat had most recently traveled from Nagoya, on the main Japanese island of Honshu, making its way down to Formosa. She was on her way to Luzon, one of the Philippine Islands, when she met up with *Batfish*. No doubt she was one of the evacuation boats they had been tasked to intercept. They had stopped her before she had a chance to pick up her passengers.

Sitting there on the surface, surrounded by tarlike oil and the flotsam of the enemy sub, Fyfe ordered the radio operator to report their accomplishment to the wolf-pack commander and to ComSubPac headquarters back at Pearl Harbor, and to get it done quickly in case they had to duck for cover. The report was straightforward, no gloating. Not even a mention that it was their third submarine sent to the bottom in three days. They figured

Admiral Lockwood and Admiral Nimitz could count to three all right without their help.

That done, they submerged at 0630. No sense tempting fate, lollygagging around the scene of their triumph until some Japanese patrol plane came screaming out of the morning sun and sent *Batfish* right down to where their most recent quarry now rested.

Besides, there were clearly no survivors. Nobody to pull, willingly or unwillingly, from the oily drink. Nothing could be done for those submarine sailors now.

The crewmen aboard *Batfish* who were coming off watch headed for the galley to get some eggs and bacon and some hot joe in anticipation of an uneventful day beneath the sea and an opportunity to get some serious rest after the night's tense excitement. Those just coming on watch were full of stories of what they had seen and heard during the attack and how their contributions had been the most important cog in the whole operation.

The squawk of the intercom system caused them to pause in midchew or leave a boast uncompleted.

It was the voice of their skipper, Captain Jake. The old man sounded a bit tired, as he well should have. But there was something else in his voice, too. Something hard to place. Pride, maybe. But something akin to sadness, as well.

Why? They'd just sent a couple score Japanese bastards to the bottom. But by the time he had finished his short speech, every submariner aboard knew exactly what his captain was feeling.

They may have never expressed it before. May not have known how to put it into words, even if they had wanted to. But they knew what Captain Fyfe was talking about.

"Men, within three days, we sank three enemy submarines." That statement seemed like something that deserved a cheer but, for some reason, there was none. Except for the slight echo down the length of the tube that was known as *Batfish*, there was silence. "There were no survivors," Fyfe continued, reading from the lines he had scribbled before beginning the arduous task of writing up the attack report while it was still fresh in his mind. "Those men aboard the Japanese subs who died as a result of our actions were combatant enemies. They knowingly risked their lives in war, just as we do. In the course of our duty, we attacked and sank them."

Up and down the length of the boat, sailors watched the reactions on the faces of the men who shared the cramped compartments with them. Surely one of the kids would break the mood with an ill-timed whoop. It didn't happen. Each man, first-timer and veteran sub warrior alike, listened in rapt attention to his skipper.

"Within our good fortune that we did not lose our boat or our lives, there is of course some sadness that these submariners have died by our hand."

Now, some of the sub sailors exchanged quick glances. Every man among them had, at some point, had the same thought, even if none of them had verbalized it. They faced an enemy who would kill them without question. But the men on those boats were also brother submariners, who endured the same hardships and shared the same camaraderie with their shipmates as did they. A comradeship as strong and as enduring as any a group of men could ever possibly experience.

Fyfe cleared his throat and wrapped up his short speech so that his men could get about their duties, finish breakfast, and catch some well-deserved rest after three days of almost continuous stalking.

"The only way that could have been otherwise in this war would have been for us to have died at theirs. Thank you for your excellence, and congratulations on your success."

Then the ovation began, slowly at first, but building to a crescendo up and down the length of the boat. A cheer that seemed to relieve all the accumulated cloud of tension from the previous seventy-seven hours.

With that, Jake Fyfe made his way up and down the length of *Batfish*, thanking each man personally for his efforts. And he had a gift for each of them. From his executive officer and wardroom crew to the rawest teenage sailor, each of them received the same thing. It was a page torn from the Japanese book of navigation tables that had been retrieved from the site of their latest destroyed target.

The next day, *Batfish* received a message from Admiral Nimitz and Admiral Lockwood, congratulating them on their astounding success, and thanking them for giving the Imperial Japanese Navy "a chronic migraine headache."

In honor of all the praise, and as thanks for their hard work, Captain Fyfe decided to give his boys a treat. The consumption of alcoholic beverages aboard a U.S. Navy vessel—surface or submarine—is strictly forbidden. Even so, most subs carried a supply of "medicinal alcohol." The skipper ordered that the stuff be broken out and that every man not on watch receive a ration. Those on watch could imbibe as soon as they were relieved.

The men toasted their captain. They toasted Admiral Lockwood and Admiral Nimitz and drank to the health of President Roosevelt. There was even a sarcastic toast or two to Emperor Hirohito, Tokyo Rose, and Adolf Hitler. The men exchanged pages of the IJN navigation book their captain had given them and autographed them for each other.

Slowly the party wound down as watch approached for some and fatigue overtook others. As the submarine sailors eased back on their tiny bunks or sat together at various duty stations, the mellowness from the drinks was heightened by the feeling of accomplishment.

They had done their duty. They had been sent out here on this steel war machine to do one thing: kill the enemy. They had accomplished that in spades.

There was a good chance, they knew, that nobody would ever know about their accomplishment. It was a small part of a very big war. And besides, most of it would be classified for years to come. Then, so far as they knew, when the story did come out, no one beyond themselves would care anymore. It would be old news, ancient history. That they understood.

But the crew of *Batfish* would know and care. They would know they had done their duty. That they had done their part to avenge the deaths of those men who were blown up in their bunks on the *Arizona* or who had drowned in the fiery waters of Pearl Harbor when they leaped off the burning deck of *California*. Know that they had made sure that the men on *Trout*, *Grampus*, *Grayback*, and the rest of the lost boats had not died in vain.

So be it if, in the course of doing that duty, they had sent some of their own—brother submariners—to eternal patrol.

A bit of harmony had been restored to a discordant universe.

TWENTY-TWO

Teamwork and Headwork

February 1945

The Navy knew *Batfish* was ready for some shop time after her sixth and most spectacular patrol. But the old girl still had some preening to do before she headed back to the beauty shop.

On February 21, the submarine arrived at Guam, a hard-won dot of dirt in the middle of the Pacific Ocean. As soon as she snuggled up next to one of her close siblings, USS *Aspro* (SS 309), in Apra Harbor, they were assaulted by a bevy of official U.S. Navy photographers. Also in the crowd was a particular admiral, Charles Andrew Lockwood, there to personally shake the hand of every single crewman aboard *Batfish*.

Lockwood had been a submariner since 1912. It's easy to see how far back he went with the pig boats when you learn that his first command was in 1914 in a submarine named *A-2* that carried the hull number SS 3. He had been ComSubPac since 1943. Lockwood, as well as his boss, Admiral Chester Nimitz, had a special affinity for the men who went to war in the submarine service. That was partly because they had a front-row seat to their performance against the Japanese. But it went deeper than that. Lockwood was a submariner. Nimitz, though the commander of all naval vessels in the Pacific, was a former submariner as well, and considered every one of them his brother.

It was clear, too, that they appreciated the significant accomplishment by *Batfish* and her crew in sinking the three IJN submarines. As soon as all the handshaking was completed, Admiral Lockwood spirited Jake Fyfe off the boat and took him to a debriefing. Fyfe later told his wardroom that heavy-duty brass from the Army, Navy, Marine Corps, and Army Air Corps were there. He also admitted that he thought he did okay answering all their questions—once his knees stopped shaking. Hughston Lowder later wrote, "It's odd what makes men's knees shake. In four war patrols, we'd never seen [Captain Jake's] battle-chatter."

When *Batfish* made her way on to Pearl Harbor, her crew was surprised again by the spirited welcome they received. There was a band playing and a sizable crowd gathered, cheering them on as they moored at the sub base.

Hell, they were famous! And all for simply doing what they went out there to do.

There was a special ceremony on deck, with the men in their dress whites lined up in a perfect pair of rows, and more brass than most of them had ever seen gathered in one spot at one time. Each man received the Submarine Combat Medal, and the boat and crew were awarded the Presidential Unit Citation with Bronze Star, presented by a special representative of Secretary of War James Forrestal. Someone from the Philippine government gave them the Philippine Liberation Ribbon with Bronze Star. And finally, Captain Jake Fyfe was awarded the Navy Cross, the U.S. Navy's highest honor.

It was difficult for the men standing there on that deck on a beautiful Hawaiian afternoon not to be aware of where they were, only a short distance from where the war had started. But for some of them, the magnitude of what they had done to help bring that war to a speedier close may not have been so obvious until the Presidential Unit Citation was read aloud, the words from the scratchy loudspeaker gently lifted on the sweet-smelling tropical breeze, drifting across the peaceful waters where so many had died only a few years before.

> For extraordinary heroism in action against enemy Japanese combatant forces during the sixth War Patrol in the South China Sea from December 30, 1944, to March 3, 1945. Persistent and aggressive in her search for vital targets, the USS *Batfish* relentlessly tracked down the enemy and in three separate, brilliantly executed attacks, launched her torpedoes with devastating speed and skill and demolished three Japanese sub-

marines. By the destruction of these formidable and threatening hostile Fleet units in a single War Patrol, the *Batfish* contributed significantly to the successful completion of the war. The courage, superb seamanship and gallant fighting spirit of her officers and men reflect the highest credit upon herself and the United States Naval Services.

ComSubPac's endorsement was even more glowing:

This illustrious patrol was outstanding and smart in every sense of the word. The splendid planning, judgment, and daring displayed in the attacks are best characterized by the unprecedented sinking of three enemy submarines. The [commander] congratulates the commanding officer, officers and crew on the brilliant teamwork and headwork displayed on the patrol and the severe damage inflicted upon the enemy.

The mention of the importance of both teamwork and headwork confirmed for Fyfe and the others that Nimitz and Lockwood, the old submariners who would appreciate such traits if anybody did, had had a hand in the wording of the endorsement.

The boat and her crew were able to stay in Hawaii and bask in the glow of their accomplishment for only a couple of days. On March 6, they were off again, this time heading for Mare Island, San Francisco Bay, for a long-overdue major overhaul and updating. The boat would be spending some time at Bethlehem Steel Shipbuilding yards. The crew was off on their own, headed home for thirty days of well-deserved leave.

Jake Fyfe was gone, too. He was reassigned as the prospective commanding officer of a new submarine that was already under construction in Philadelphia.

While the boat was undergoing all her changes, and while her crew was spread all over the country, word came on May 7 that Germany had signed articles of surrender in front of General Ike David Eisenhower. Japan could not be far behind. God willing, the end of a long, nasty, and brutal war was in sight.

With about half of its crew new, and with her third commanding officer, Lieutenant Commander Walter L. Small, in charge, *Batfish* departed San Francisco on the last day of May 1945. It had not been an easy time for the old girl in the yard. When they were ready to leave, a bad leak developed in the circulating water intake valve in the after engine room. Replacing it would take weeks. They would have to bide their time, awaiting their turn to go back into the Bethlehem yard. Every man aboard was anxious to get back to the war before it ended without him.

Someone came up with an ingenious fix. A diver went over the side, swam down beneath the waterline, and stuffed a standard Navy-issue pillow—yes, a pillow—into the breach in *Batfish*'s hull. Meanwhile, inside the boat, the nuts were loosened on the flange holding the valve in place and out it came. Standing by was a sailor with a wooden plug, whittled out to fit the hole where the valve had been, now plugged with the pillow, and another sailor stood with a sledgehammer, ready to drive the plug into place should the pillow give way. If both plugs failed, water would flood the engine room and it would have to be sealed off. The boat could go to the bottom of the harbor before they could get her back up, tow her to the repair facility, and fix the leak the recommended way.

That would have been a rather ignoble thing to have happen to the hero "submarine-killer submarine!"

But it worked. The job was completed in less than fifteen minutes, and they were able to leave Mare Island on schedule and get back to the war.

The crew might just as well not have worried about the war ending before they returned to it. Japan proved stubborn, determined to fight on. They seemed to be the only ones on the planet who didn't think it was all but over already.

The crew found their new skipper to be more than competent, but they also noted that he was much more "by the book" than Jake Fyfe had been. He was obviously intent on making admiral, as several other members of his family had done.

Walter Small was a tall, slender man. Because of his stature, the crew members dubbed him "High Pockets," a nickname only used when the old man was out of earshot. Several of them also learned from others who had served with him that he was a two-scotch-and-tonic man, that he would slug down the first drink, then sip the second one slowly until someone came along to buy him another one.

Batfish's first duty back at the war was to serve as lifeguard off the Japanese coast, in an area laughingly called "the Emperor's bathtub." American bombers pounded the Empire almost continuously, but the antiaircraft fire was not nearly as fierce as it had once been. There were only a few downed pilots to save and, no matter how spryly *Batfish* responded to the call, it seemed somebody else always beat them there. Sometimes they could hear the ominous drone of the American high-altitude bombers and catch a glimpse of them through the clouds, on their way to wreak havoc on the Emperor's homeland, but there were practically no enemy contacts for "High Pockets" and his boys.

For security reasons, *Batfish* and the other lifeguard boats—like her sisters *Sandlance* (SS 381) and *Spikefish* (SS 404)—were not advised in advance of those days when there would not be any bombing runs, days when they could range free and do some serious hunting for somebody to shoot at. They were required to stay on station, even though there would be no one to pluck from the water.

Finally, Captain Small became so desperate for targets that he attacked a town.

On July 24, Small brought the boat to the surface about three thousand yards off Yakushima, an island about fifty miles from the mainland. They proceeded to use the five-inch and 40mm deck guns to shell the tiny town of Nagata, giving about twenty people enjoying the beach there a real thrill and causing more smoke and dust than any real damage. A few buildings were seen afire, but there were no big explosions to indicate they had hit an ammunition dump or fuel storage facility.

Captain Small didn't typically have the dry wit of Jake Fyfe when he made his notes in the deck log, but he did show a flash of humor when he wrote, "Upon surfacing there were about 20 people on the beach, but they miraculously vanished before we got off our first salvo. Roughly 90% of the shells landed in the target area and four direct 5" hits were observed, some of which demolished a frame building in the camp area. After about the 10th salvo, smoke was so thick that further fall of shot couldn't be observed. This ended our diversion."

The official damage tally was logged in the patrol report as "Gun Attack #1." "One building destroyed, two and possibly more buildings and barbed wire entanglements damaged at Nagata on Yaku Shima. Smoke and haze prevented further observation of fall of shot."

Batfish did make one high-speed, ninety-mile run to rescue three downed pilots, floating in a life raft in near-typhoon conditions. Nathan Mangeno, James L. Van Epps, and Robert L. Bleicher, of the U.S. Army Forty-first Bomber Group, Squadron 820, plane 879, were all injured. They had bombed a bridge on the Japanese homeland's southernmost island, dropping their ordnance from a height of only five hundred feet. Somewhere on their pullout they were hit by antiaircraft fire. There may not have been the same amount of ack-ack over Japan that there once had been, but what there was could still be deadly. The pilots were forced to ditch in the ocean. The plane came apart on impact with the rough, rolling sea and exploded into flames. Three crewmen in the rear of the plane did not make it.

Once they pulled the airmen aboard, Small ordered their lifeboat sunk by gunfire so the enemy would never know they had been there, and so no other American vessel would waste time and risk attack while trying to rescue somebody from an empty boat. He then guided the submarine back toward their station while *Batfish*'s pharmacist's mate treated the airmen's wounds.

The injured men were informed that they would have to ride on the submarine for a while. As the boat could not leave its assigned area yet, they had to remain on station for sea rescue duty.

The downed fliers—as well as everyone else aboard the submarine—had some anxious moments a day later when a supposedly friendly B-25 aircraft, ignoring the flashes of recognition codes from *Batfish*'s bridge and screaming calls on the VHF radio, dropped bombs frighteningly close to them on the port beam, all in an obvious and damn near successful attempt to sink them. They could even hear the pilot talking on the radio about how he was going to sink a Japanese "cruiser" he had spotted.

The skipper managed to get the boat submerged before the wild-eyed pilot could circle and make another run at them. After things calmed down, the rattled bomber crew members promised to do all they could when they got back to their base to see who the bastard was.

They didn't have to. As they headed toward Iwo Jima to drop off the injured men, a message was copied in the radio shack. It said, in effect, that the pilot had admitted dropping bombs on a U.S. submarine, that he was quite pleased that he had missed, and that he apologized. The message concluded with "Pilot is no longer a pilot."

Later Bleicher and the other fliers learned that the pilot who had almost taken out *Batfish* that day had actually been in the same squadron with them when they bombed the bridge. Because of a fuel-consumption problem on his next mission, the pilot and his crew had pulled away from the bombing run and spotted *Batfish* as they were returning to base. Whether it was frustration at having to abort his mission or just a bit of overzealousness, the pilot mistook the sub for an enemy cruiser and tried to send her to the bottom.

Batfish was back on lifeguard duty on August 6 when crew members heard a short, calm message on the radio. The traffic came in an unusual form, plain text, copied from radio station NSS, preceded by a strange series of zeroes. Stan Javorski, the radio operator, couldn't believe what he was writing down. He sent "IMI," the code asking for a repeat. When it was resent, the message was still just as shocking.

An airplane had dropped a single weapon on the Japanese town of Hiroshima. That lone bomb had destroyed the entire city. It was described as an "atomic bomb." The message went on to say that as many as five thousand people had been killed. That figure would later be revised to over eighty thousand killed outright.

Javorski couldn't help it. He let out a whoop. Everyone in the area came running to see what he was so excited about.

"What's up, 'Ski? The Pirates win the World Series?"

The men looked at one another when he told them what he had just copied.

What kind of secret weapon was this thing? A weapon so powerful an entire city could be destroyed by one of the things, claiming five thousand lives in an instant of hellfire?

Then the realization hit them.

If the United States possessed one such terrible weapon, then it had to have more of them. Now, for certain, the Japanese would see the futility in continuing to fight. Besides, news from all over the Pacific was good for the Allies. What kind of people were these who didn't know when they were beaten? What would it take to convince them?

When the skipper got the paper copy of the message that was sent up from the radio shack, he promptly sent for Javorski.

"Is this the way you copied this message?" Small asked.

"Yes, sir."

"You have any idea what an atomic bomb is?"

It turned out Javorski did have an inkling. Back in Pittsburgh, he had heard from friends who worked for the big Westinghouse facility there about attempts to split the atom, and what such a scientific breakthrough would mean.

Still, the skipper had a hard time comprehending such a thing. He was still staring at the message and shaking his head when he dismissed his radioman and sent him back to his shack.

On August 9, a second atomic bomb was dropped on Nagasaki. It did all the convincing necessary for the Japanese to see the light.

Less than a week later, just before noon local time on August 15, *Batfish* received a message from ComSubPac: "The president has announced that Japan has accepted our conditions and that V-J Day will be proclaimed upon formal signing of the surrender terms by Japan." The traffic was followed by the old nautical term "Splice the main brace." That meant for them to break out the booze and celebrate the end of the war.

Stan Javorski let out another whoop when he copied that message.

Though the war had officially ended, it did not mean that *Batfish* was in safe waters. Indeed, an incident the next day proved to the crew that despite the end of hostilities, they could not let their guard down.

Early the next morning, a lookout reported what he swore were the wakes of two torpedoes, both headed their way. The boat zigged hard to avoid the fish, and then went deep. An hour later *Batfish* was back on the surface. There was never any sign of another vessel or any more torpedoes.

It could have been a Japanese vessel that had not gotten the word yet about the end of hostilities. Or maybe one that chose not to believe it. Or even one that simply wanted to strike one final blow against the victors.

Of course, it could have been the overactive imagination of a young lookout who had been warned, in no uncertain terms, to be on extra-sharp alert in this awkward time. Either way, everyone on board was aware of how ironic it would have been to lose the boat after the war was finished. Or how fitting it might have been to have Batfish's war experience end in a fit of déjà vu: by almost being sunk by a friendly aircraft and threatened by torpedoes from an enemy submarine, just the way the whole grand adventure had begun east of the Panama Canal.

Finally the war was over. Batfish's seventh war patrol ended almost exactly three years after she had been launched in Portsmouth, New Hampshire.

The various skippers and crew members of the 310 boat during World War II were certain that they had sunk thirteen ships during her seven patrols, approximately 37,000 tons. That's the count from the patrol reports of Captains Merrill, Fyfe, and Small. But the Joint Army-Navy Assessment Committee had a different count. For the official tally, the committee relied heavily on surviving Japanese records to determine what had been lost or damaged. Those records were incomplete and, to say the least, inaccurate. They often showed vessels in different parts of the world at the same time they were almost certainly being sunk somewhere else by Allied vessels or aircraft. Sometimes the Japanese didn't even have records of some warships having ever been built or launched. As some of the crew later noted, a lot of Japanese sailors died on ships and submarines that did not officially exist.

Batfish was officially credited with six and a half sinkings for 11,248 tons. Other official Navy sources would later modify that to be nine ships, 12,332 tons. That was something of which to be proud, certainly, but nowhere near what the men who fired the torpedoes maintain that they had accomplished.

They did get credit for the three submarines. It's just that nobody knows for certain which submarines they were! Naval historians still debate the question to this day.

The survivors of Batfish don't bother. They know what they did.

Batfish's service didn't end with the war. Neither did that of some of her officers and crewmen.

The boat became part of the inactive reserve fleet, housed at Mare Island, and designated to be used as a "training vessel." Crew members scattered far and wide. Some career sailors had thirty days' leave before reporting somewhere else to serve their country. The rest of them were mustered out of the Navy, often as abruptly as they had been taken in, and sent home to their waiting families to marry, go to school, earn a wage, become civilian citizens again. Many of them had left home before adulthood. Now they were coming back as world travelers, seasoned men who had seen far more than most people ever experience—some wonderful, some so awful the sights would never leave their nightmares as long as they lived.

When the Korean War heated up in the early 1950s, *Batfish* was once again called into service. In March of 1952, she left the Bay Area and headed for her new home in Key West, Florida. There she served in training ships in the increasingly important art of ASW—antisubmarine warfare.

She later spent some time in Charleston, then as a training vessel in New Orleans. But by this time, the fleet boat had long since outlasted its usefulness. Nuclear-powered submarines were patrolling the world's oceans, boats with the ability to stay down not for hours, but for *months*. It was a new kind of submarining, and though the old salts still felt that same sense of brotherhood for their "nuke boat" kin, to this day, some maintain that the guys who ride the nukes are candy-asses, and that the only real submariner is a "smoke boat" submariner.

The name *Batfish* was struck from the Navy's list of active vessels on the first day of November 1969, twenty-six and a half years after she was born. Many of her sisters had long since been scrapped or given to foreign navies. Others had been used for target practice, helping other subs and battleships hone their ASW skills by making the ultimate sacrifice. That was what happened to *Archerfish*, *Batfish*'s closest sister. *Archerfish* had sunk the massive Japanese aircraft carrier *Shinano* on the ship's maiden voyage out of Tokyo Bay. That's still the record holder for the largest vessel ever sunk by a submarine. Despite her own historical significance, *Archerfish* was torpedoed off San Diego about a year earlier by *Snook* (SSN 592).

Batfish's hatches were welded closed and she was relegated to a backwater storage berth, likely to rust away there if she couldn't be sold to an Allied country, or if the Navy didn't decide to cut her up for scrap or put torpedoes in her side the same way she had done to those three IJN boats down there near the Philippines.

Some of *Batfish*'s officers and other crew members would continue to serve with distinction, even if their old boat was a step away from the scrap heap.

John From, one of the officers aboard *Batfish* on war patrols three through six, went on to command nuclear subs. He also became commander of the submarine base that his old boat once proudly called home, Pearl Harbor. From passed away in March of 2004.

A *Batfish* torpedoman, Lynus J. "Dutch" Larch (war patrols one through six), was later in his career a crewman on the world's first nuclear-powered submarine, the USS *Nautilus* (SSN 571), when she accomplished a feat that made headlines around the world. In August of 1958, the submarine steamed beneath the geographic North Pole, becoming the first vessel to ever reach that spot on the globe.

Wayne Merrill retired from the Navy in 1949 as a lieutenant commander. He became an engineer in the civilian world, and then retired to his small Missouri hometown. Ever willing to command, he later became acting mayor of the town. Several of his former crew members paid him the ultimate sailor's compliment: "Great guy. At least he wasn't a horse's ass."

Captain Merrill passed away in Centralia, Missouri, on February 10, 1991, at the age of seventy-eight. He had retired in 1953 from Wilcox Company in Kansas City, where he worked as an electrical engineer, and was a member of the American Legion post at Brunswick, Missouri.

John Kerr Fyfe had a distinguished career in the U.S. Navy, eventually retiring as a rear admiral. He is buried at Arlington National Cemetery. Fyfe was an old man of thirty when he assumed command of *Batfish*. The average age of his crew on the 310 boat was nineteen and a half.

After his one patrol as *Batfish*'s skipper, Walter Small became Admiral Nimitz's personal aide and eventually commanded ComSubPac. He had accomplished his primary goal: to become an admiral. Small once listed on his résumé that he had, at one time in his career, "managed a ninety-man engineering organization including an annual budget of $80,000, two and a half years." That "organization" was USS *Batfish*. Admiral Small passed away in June 2004.

The USS *Batfish*'s name lived on in the form of SSN 681, a nuclear submarine commissioned in September of 1972. For the next quarter century, that incarnation would ply the seas of the world. Most of her duty remains classified. She was decommissioned on November 2, 1998.

TWENTY-THREE

Out to Pasture

March 1973

It rained hard in northeastern Oklahoma, so hard that the Arkansas River rose well beyond flood stage, spilling out into pastures and cornfields. The precipitation painted the rolling hills a brilliant green, giving the area its chamber-of-commerce nickname, Green Country.

But at the Port of Muskogee, the "abandoned USS *Batfish*" (as a nationally distributed United Press International dispatch described her) floated precariously in the swift water, straining at her moorings as if even she were tired of all the infighting and broken promises. As if she most wanted to break loose and steam on back down the river until she could find some salt water somewhere in which to drift.

The UPI article ran in papers all over the country the week of March 12, accompanied by a sad photo of the boat, listing thirty degrees to her port side as if kicked over by a giant boot, her decking and railing damaged by vandals. Along side the *Batfish* was a man in a small boat, staring woefully at the mess that had once been one of the country's most storied naval vessels.

"Proclaimed 'the state's No. 1 tourist attraction' less than a year ago, the state's Tourism and Recreation Commission unanimously voted to draft a letter disowning the ship and asking the Navy to take the sub back," the piece reported. It went on to say that the U.S. Navy wanted no part of the vessel, and especially of its growing price tag, which was now reaching $386,000.

"A lot of people want the *Batfish* but not the debt," Lieutenant Governor George Nigh was quoted as saying. There was the rumor, perpetuated by

Nigh, that Fort Smith, Arkansas, had her eye on the submarine and might consider bringing her back downriver for their city.

Other articles picked up by the nation's press ran under such headlines as "Oklahoma Tries to Disown Noted Sub," "Abandoned Sub, Once Tourist Lure, Now River Menace," and "Muskogee Attraction 'Batfish' Listing in River Flood."

The Army Corps of Engineers didn't care who was responsible for the thing or what kind of press it was getting. They just wanted somebody to secure her so she wouldn't break loose in the flood and damage the docks, or possibly even take out the brand-new bridge over the river that allowed travelers to take Highway 62 from the Muskogee Turnpike eastward toward Tahlequah, the capital of the Cherokee Nation.

Karl Wheland, identified as "a World War II submariner who helped with the three-year struggle to bring the *Batfish* to Oklahoma," was quoted as saying, "With a little farsightedness this situation would not have occurred." He said about fifty ex-submariners had spent many hours "doing up the brightwork" on *Batfish*, but that the problem of the boat's continued existence is "at the right level where there doesn't seem to be the incentive to finish it."

As the rains continued, it was a dreary outlook indeed for the *Batfish*.

There was a scathing article in the March 14 edition of the *Muskogee Daily Phoenix and Times-Democrat*, written by the paper's city editor, Rob Martindale, in which a local Muskogee naval history researcher laid all blame for the condition of *Batfish* on the lieutenant governor. "Nigh Accused of Using *Batfish* for Political Purposes," the headline screamed across the top of the paper's front page. The researcher was Reverend Bruce Brotherton, a young local student pastor. He charged that Nigh was "sitting on state funds and releasing false information to delay construction of a War Memorial Park at Muskogee for political reasons."

Brotherton was convinced that Nigh was deliberately stalling, allowing the project to founder, and then, as Nigh initiated his inevitable campaign for governor, he would charge in and rescue the submarine, grabbing all the positive press for cleaning up the mess.

The article also raised the old issue of *Batfish* being the "wrong" submarine, noting once again that the legislation creating the commission specifically proclaimed that they were to secure and bring the *Piranha* to Musko-gee. Brotherton called the charge "totally false."

"The name of the submarine was written into the legislation, Brotherton said, with the stipulation that the name could be substituted," the article reported. "He said that an inspection showed that renovation of *Piranha* would cost 'millions' and that this submarine 'did not have a very attractive war record.'"

Brotherton further charged that the lieutenant governor was wrong when he claimed that he had no knowledge of the Oklahoma Maritime Advisory Board's actions in bringing *Batfish* to Muskogee. He noted that Nigh loaned board members his private airplane to go to Orange, Texas, in order to make the final arrangements for the transfer of the sub. Further, a representative of the lieutenant governor's office attended all but one of the board's meetings, and minutes of every board meeting had been sent to Nigh as well as to Governor Hall. The young preacher accused Nigh of "sitting on his bonds," and not doing what was necessary to complete the War Memorial Park.

"They say the young people of America don't have any respect," Brotherton told the reporter. "But here [the park] is a permanent reminder of patriotism and we all get embroiled in politics with self-seeking individuals trying to cash in on it."

Bruce Brotherton was more than a naval historian. He had taken an interest in the project when he first heard about it, and became a volunteer tour guide, leading visitors through the boat when it was first tied up at the riverbank. He also volunteered many nights as a watchman after a shortwave radio and other equipment was stolen out of the crew's mess compartment.

CBS television, the national network, came out to Muskogee to do a story on the submarine, and coincidentally, Lieutenant Governor Nigh was in town as well. "Good men used bad judgment," he told the network cameras. He blamed the Maritime Advisory Board for all the troubles, reminding everyone that they had spent money—and lots of it—that they weren't authorized to spend. "I think this whole mess has done one good thing. It has proved the Arkansas River navigable," he said.

Finally Nigh told the nation that his commission had asked the Navy to take the submarine back.

"Do you think they will?" the CBS reporter asked.

"They can insist, but I don't think they will attack," Nigh said with a grin.

Of course, by then the Navy had informed Nigh that *Batfish* belonged to the state of Oklahoma, and the Navy fully expected the good folks of that state to live up to the terms of the contract that had been signed when the submarine was handed over. And even if they someday did allow the return of the vessel, it would be up to the citizens of Oklahoma to pay the cost of the transit of the submarine back to a designated naval boneyard, wherever it happened to be.

At about the same time, United States Senator Dewey Bartlett, a former Marine dive-bomber pilot in World War II and the former governor of Oklahoma who signed the original *Batfish* legislation, reentered the fray. He dropped a bomb in the form of a press release, stating his "personal concern" about what was going on out there in Muskogee. He mentioned how impressed he had been with the success of the USS *Drum* in Mobile, but that "I was more impressed with [*Batfish*'s] potential for changing Oklahoma's image in the eyes of the world—from that of a 'dust bowl' state to one of a luxuriant Green Country with commerce and navigation to the sea! Nothing could so well emphasize this contract as a U.S. Navy submarine with a brilliant war record crossing the Arkansas border into Oklahoma, bound for its home 'Port of Muskogee.'"

The senator ended his news release with a plea for everyone involved to do whatever was necessary to see that *Batfish* would soon have her new home and could begin fulfilling her mission.

> From this point on the fate of the submarine seems to be entirely in the hands of political decision makers—unless the Navy decides to sell it for scrap. What an end to contemplate for a project which held such bright promise for the future in tourism, educational values and memorial purposes. My commendation goes to all of those visionary and energetic Oklahomans who achieved the impossible as an engineering feat in bringing THE BATFISH to Green Country. I sincerely hope that by some fortuitous reconsideration their efforts will not have been in vain.

It should be noted that Senator Bartlett's release was distributed with a business card attached—the card of Albert C. Kelly, Chairman, Oklahoma Maritime Advisory Board, and former dollar-a-year employee of then-governor Bartlett. The old submariner was pulling in some political favors to try to get his boat out of the flood and up there in the park where she belonged.

It was also about this time that Ace Kelly and the sub vets executed yet another end run to get ahead of those who were taking potshots at their boat.

Only a week later, with the Arkansas River still swollen and swift from all the rains, the Oklahoma Submarine Veterans of World War II and several members of the Oklahoma Maritime Advisory Board sat down and hammered out an agreement. The sub vets organization would come up with enough money to reinstate the insurance on the boat. They would also arrange for the digging of a slip that would allow the boat to be towed onto the memorial park property. Then they would prepare her for public display and construct the fifteen thousand-square-foot building for the museum, create a parking lot, and do the necessary landscaping. Money from admissions would be used to repay the cost for accomplishing all this, as well as to maintain the sub, the grounds, and the museum. The Maritime Advisory Board would still be stuck with the nearly four-hundred-thousand-dollar debt already incurred. And they would agree to lease the submarine back to the sub vets group for a dollar a year. The whole thing would cost the taxpayers of Oklahoma and Muskogee not one red cent.

M. W. Fuller, the sub vets state commander; Ronald Banks, the group's secretary/treasurer; Albert Kelly, chairman of the advisory board; William Beane, the board's secretary/treasurer; and board member Nick Guagliardo all signed the contract. The board members did so as well, and the sub vets accepted their signatures without hesitation, despite the continuing claim that the advisory board had no power to sign anything, that they were merely in existence to "advise."

It seemed an elegant—if not quite legal—solution to an ugly problem. There was one little factor that gave the matter some urgency: They would have to hurry and dig the trench and move *Batfish* before the flooded river receded. As part of the deal, Admiral John Kirkpatrick, a former advisory board member, agreed to loan the submarine veterans group an amount "not to exceed $60,000" to get *Batfish* out of the river and into her permanent moat on the war memorial property. Such generosity was nothing new for Kirkpatrick. He had also been instrumental in getting funding for the National Cowboy Hall of Fame in Oklahoma City.

Under normal circumstances, that amount of money would have not been close to enough to do the job. But Mother Nature had smiled on the submariners, if not on riverside farmers and ranchers. With the river at flood stage, moving the submarine inland would be much easier to accomplish. If the contract and this monetary arrangement had ever been submitted to the state government for proper approval, and if it had wound around and around through the maze of state bureaucracy, it would have been too late to take advantage of this God-given opportunity. The rains would have stopped, the summer sun would have come out, the river would have retreated, and the sixty thousand dollars would not have touched the cost of moving the boat.

Kirkpatrick emphasized the importance of letting the flood work to their advantage in a memo to all Oklahoma submarine vets on the second of April: "Estimates received at this time would indicate my guaranty of $60,000 is adequate, provided work is started with absolutely no delay. Excessive delay could render this project practically impossible," he told the old submariners.

Lieutenant Governor Nigh was informed that the submarine veterans had agreed to take the boat off his hands, and that the vessel would be moved out of the river immediately. Before he could stop them or question the legal ramifications of what they were proposing to do, work began to drag the old boat out of the flooded river and into her new slip.

Or at least, it was supposed to. When bulldozers, earthmovers, winches, and a small army of workers showed up on April 4 to start the process of digging a small canal through the riverbank, they found that the local union had slapped up a picket line, protesting the lack of local construction workers on the crew. Kirkpatrick and the other sub vets took one look at the river, and at the clearing sky, and promptly mediated an agreement between the contractor and the union. Work soon began without the blockade of picketers.

As the digging continued, a small article in the Tulsa paper on April 11 noted that the state Tourism and Recreation Commission had voted unanimously to ask the legislature to give the *Batfish* to a Muskogee public trust, and to create the Muskogee War Memorial Park Authority to take control and move the vessel into the park. Ken Meyer, one of the bankers who had been unwavering in his support of the submarine project, was appointed chairman of the new entity.

The commission also voted unanimously to rescind its request to the U.S. Navy that they take back *Batfish*.

The commission was a bit late. Work was progressing. The sub vets couldn't risk losing the high water, so they had simply gone ahead and were getting it done. But the action of the commission at least gave some legitimacy to Admiral Kirkpatrick and Ace Kelly's bold arrangements.

In its April 19 editions, the *Tulsa Tribune* had an aerial photo of the gigantic scar that was being bulldozed out of the riverbank. The caption noted that the slip would be 450 feet long, and that when it was ready, bulldozers and a towboat would move the submarine into place.

Bright and early on the morning of Saturday, April 21, 1973, an assemblage of construction workers and submarine veterans showed up to help with the effort. State Deputy Commander of the World War II submarine veterans, Charlie Williams of Tulsa, had sent a note to each of the group's members, advising them to show up ready to work. He asked for each of them to bring a twelve-inch crescent wrench.

It wasn't even good daylight yet when the workers removed the last chunk of earth between the big ditch and the Arkansas River to allow the river water to flood their canal. Hearts fell. The rains had stopped and the river's level had receded noticeably in the last few days. There was not nearly enough water in the new slip to float the submarine.

Here, once again, came the Army Corps of Engineers, just as they had when *Batfish* proved too tall to slip beneath the bridge in Little Rock. And they had a similar solution to this latest knotty problem. The Corps had been kind enough to store plenty of water behind a dam upriver. When they got the word, they opened the floodgates and let loose enough H_2O to give them the necessary fourteen feet to fill up the muddy ditch.

While this was going on, workers pumped out the water in the submarine's ballast tanks that had helped stabilize her in all the months she had been sitting there, waiting in the river. They carefully floated her into alignment with the mouth of the slip; then four bulldozers began pulling her in stern first, using three-hundred-foot-long cables, while the tugboat *Apache* routed her along with her snout.

The weather was on-again, off-again, hot with brilliant sunshine, then cold with a thick overcast and spits of rain. Even so, over a hundred people lined the bank to watch the boat's progress. The Muskogee paper pointed out that the berthing was taking place just two weeks shy of the thirtieth-anniversary date of the submarine's launching at the naval yards in Portsmouth, and just short of a year since she had come wallowing up the Arkansas in that flotilla of barges, a tugboat, and streamer-strewn yachts.

As they eased her into her final resting place, Charlie Williams rang a ship's bell fifty-two times, commemorating the fifty-two boats lost in World War II. Everyone along the riverbank and slip cheered while *Apache* vigorously blew her whistle in celebration.

Over the next week, the "plug" was replaced at the river end of the slip to keep the Arkansas from entering again. Slowly, the workers used water to raise the submarine's elevation; then dirt was used to backfill around her. Her keel rested firmly in four feet of sand, and there was enough water in the indention around her to make it appear she was afloat, even if earthen banks effectively prevented her from ever drifting away.

By May 1, the boat was redirected so that her bow overlooked the river, now a striking distance away from where this water creature sat, and a good thirty-six feet lower in elevation.

As one writer put it, the submarine had been "put out to pasture." She was literally surrounded by dirt and green grass. Thanks to a take-charge retired admiral and a group of submarine veterans who refused to allow their dream to die, their boat was finally in place. Now, they could start getting her ready, hopefully by Memorial Day, to have her second opening to the public.

When the contractor's bill for moving *Batfish* showed up, it was for $60,246.50. That was within the contract with Madden Excavating, but $246.50 more than Admiral John Kirkpatrick had agreed to pay. He informed the submarine veterans that they might want to solicit donations to cover the overage. He also told them that they should be good stewards of any money they took in at the park, that they should not spend anything that they didn't have. And he reminded them pointedly that the sixty thousand dollars he had advanced as promised was a loan, not a gift.

Now the rush was on to open the sub to the public. Submarine veterans from all over the state pitched in to try to get her spick-and-span, but the sandblasting and painting that had been done the previous year had suffered in the winter weather and the spring floods. New paint helped spruce up her looks. The decking that had rotted was replaced. Her propeller guards, bent in the move, were straightened. Rusty parts below decks were cleaned up. Some of the submariners swore that if they leaned back and allowed themselves the time, they could imagine that they were at sea, about to run the Bungo Straits or stalk a tanker coming out of Tokyo Wan.

But they didn't have that luxury too often. There was too much work yet to be done to make the old girl presentable when the public came calling once again.

The opening on Memorial Day was almost anticlimactic, certainly not a full-blown dedication ceremony. It was a breezy day and, according to the newspaper, about fifty people showed up. Ace Kelly was once again the master of ceremonies of the informal event and, in a brief speech, he announced that the park would soon get a PT boat and a Sherman tank to put on display, and that more announcements would be coming soon.

Notably absent that day were the official owners of *Batfish*, the new Muskogee War Memorial Park Authority and its chairman, the banker Ken Meyer. Now that they had accomplished most of what they set out to do, and for which they had all worked so hard, there was a growing friction among the various entities who had rammed this project through to completion. The Maritime Advisory Board had been eliminated by the legislature two weeks earlier in Bill 67, and all rights to the sub were transferred to the Muskogee authority. Even so, Albert Kelly assumed that he still had authorization to run the boat, just as he had done since he had come up with the idea of securing her in the first place. John Kirkpatrick was concerned about Kelly not allowing the proper people to run the sub and memorial park, as well as the lack of accountability in financial matters, but he didn't want hurt feelings or a public showdown on such an important day in the life of the project. He admired Kelly for all that he had done, telling the sub vets that Kelly had devoted more time and energy to the project than anyone, but that didn't give him the right to confuse the management that was now in place. Kirkpatrick asked Meyer and the park authority members to pass up the Memorial Day event. They gracefully obliged.

Typically undaunted, Kelly convened the now nonexistent Oklahoma Maritime Advisory Board on the thirtieth of June and elected officers to serve for the upcoming year. Of course, Ace was reelected as chairman. He made the point in the meeting's minutes that the board had been created by the governor, his friend Dewey Bartlett, and if it ever was disbanded, it would take the governor of Oklahoma to do it.

The tenuous situation hit rough seas in June, only a few weeks after reopening. Ken Meyer and the authority had yet to receive any accounting of the proceeds and expenses since the boat had once again started accepting paid visitors across her brow. There were reports that Ace Kelly had been allowing people into the submarine free. Lots of people, the authority claimed. While it stated publicly that they didn't want to alienate any of the sub veterans, the authority went ahead and requested the assistance of the Muskogee Police Department in making certain that no one allowed nonpaying customers to tour the boat. They needed every penny of admissions revenue to keep the whole project on an even keel.

Kirkpatrick was worried that if the boat run aground on financial shoals one more time, the Navy would finally take her back and scrap her. Nobody wanted that. He simply had to do something to make sure the legally commissioned "skipper" of *Batfish* had complete control of his boat if this latest "patrol" was to be successful.

That "something" was canceling the insurance on the boat. Ace Kelly knew that his boat would suffer from that action, so he quietly left. The afternoon of July 13, Ken Meyer, accompanied by Muskogee police and a locksmith, came down and changed the locks on the museum building and the boat. They also asked Dick Fogle, the submarine veteran who had been working as the unsalaried project manager under the authority of the Maritime Advisory Board, to please pack up his personal tools and leave the premises.

With insurance reinstated, attendance increased, despite a few instances when visitors became ill from mild heatstroke in the hot interior of the submarine, now baking in the intense Oklahoma summer sun. Over a thousand visitors a week passed through the museum building, across the walkway, and into the submarine. The state paved the parking lot, settling a severe dust issue. The Memorial Park Authority hired a junior high school teacher, Bill Tobey, to run the operations until Labor Day, when school started up again. Dick Fogle had been allowed to return to the premises and worked trimming weeds and at other jobs to keep the area and the boat presentable. Ken Meyer told a reporter that the park had a $1,250 deficit when the park authority took over operations in mid-July but that, by the end of August, they had two thousand dollars in the bank.

The lawsuit by Midwest Dredging to try to recover the money owed them for transporting *Batfish* from New Orleans was eventually settled by Tulsa judge Robert G. Green in June of 1974. He determined that the Oklahoma Maritime Advisory Board did indeed owe the company thirteen thousand, but the men who had signed the contract for the board, Karl Wheland and Albert C. Kelly, could not be held personally responsible for the debt (other board members had been removed from the lawsuit back in December 1973). He said the advisory board would now be obligated to pay the money "if and when funds are available."

The judge did not mention in his ruling that the board no longer existed.

In the matter of the *Silvermain*, the freighter that had almost capsized *Batfish* in New Orleans and sent one of the barges to the bottom of the Mississippi, the results were not so good. The ship's insurance company settled for $133,000. Three thousand of that went to the owner of the barge that was lost. Attorneys in the matter claimed the rest. Not a penny of that long-anticipated money made its way to Muskogee.

Four years later, *Batfish* became an issue in the 1978 Oklahoma gubernatorial race. Republican candidate Ron Shotts accused Democrat George Nigh of bungling the project.

"George Nigh turned and abandoned ship when the going got tough," Shotts charged, using appropriate nautical imagery. "Does that mean the lieutenant governor will turn and run in the face of the many hard decisions which will have to be made by Oklahoma's next governor?"

The charges apparently didn't sway enough voters. George Nigh was elected Oklahoma's twenty-first governor on November 7, 1978.

The old boat continued to have her problems down through the years. An article in the *Tulsa World* in October 1979 talked about vandalism on the boat, as witnessed by its manager at the time, retired Marine diver Harold Hooper, a veteran of the ill-fated Bay of Pigs invasion in Cuba and recipient of seven Purple Hearts.

The article reads, "Like all old subs, this one still carries the smell of an old burned-out electrical motor. But sometimes there is another smell.

" 'I found two or three pounds of pot in here at one damn time,' Hooper says. 'And I've found cases and cases of beer. They sneak down here and have their parties, and there's a thousand damn places for them to hide in this sunofagun.' "

The wholesale vandalism of the ship continued. The article had a long list of items that had been carried out of the submarine, including nameplates, tubes from radios, gauges, and even a copy of the Geneva Convention that was glued to a desktop.

Hooper blamed it on the kids of Muskogee.

Commander Jake Fyfe donated to the park a copy of the *Batfish* episode of the NBC television drama *The Silent Service*. NBC informed the group that it was perfectly okay to show the film to park visitors so long as there was no admission charge to see it. But shortly after the film canister arrived, it, too, was stolen. Karl Wheland had donated a tape of submarine sound effects, including an especially effective dive klaxon. It, too, disappeared.

Still, the visitors continued to come to see her. One of them had a very unique interest in touring *Batfish*. The gentleman had traveled all the way from Japan to take a close look at the submarine that had shot his training ship out from under him during the war thirty years before. Many of his shipmates had died, and he was glad to be alive and able to come see her. Glad, too, that the old boat was still around and open to the public so he and others could visit regardless of their past relationship with the old girl.

Those who maintained *Batfish* were proud of their foreign guests but still sensitive to the criticism of the numbers of visitors who climbed aboard and walked her decks. An article in the *Tulsa World* in March of 1980 indicated that the count of paid admissions had dropped to about nineteen thousand the previous year. A member of the park authority went on the defensive, pointing out that the boat was self-sufficient and she was not costing the citizens of the town or the taxpayers of the state of Oklahoma a penny to operate.

Naturally, many of those who did come to see her were former crew members, grateful that they could spend time with her. That was especially true of those who had served aboard the boat during her seven World War II patrols. A May 1987 newspaper story mentioned that the annual *Batfish* reunion was to be held that weekend at the park. It made note of the fact that all three of her World War II skippers would be in attendance— Lieutenant Commander Wayne R. Merrill, Commander John K. Fyfe, and Commander Walter L. Small.

There was another newspaper article in May of 1993 that chronicled the ceremonies at the boat to document her fiftieth anniversary. A group representing the Oklahoma Submarine Veterans of World War II placed flags on each of the fifty-two plaques commemorating the boats lost in the war as the ship's bell tolled and each boat's name was called aloud.

About forty World War II *Batfish* crewmen were in the audience that day to hear Lieutenant David Houton, a naval officer from Tulsa, give a speech. Sitting just behind Houton on the stage set up next to *Batfish* in War Memorial Park was an aging but spry Jake Fyfe. After Houton's speech, the old skipper finally stood to talk and immediately showed that he had lost none of his aggressive spirit. He proceeded to take issue with a couple of things the young officer had said.

"First of all, Dave, we are called sub*mar*iners not sub*mar*iners." The old salts in the audience yelled and applauded, showing their approval.

By all accounts Houton took the corrections in good spirits. Of all people, J. K. Fyfe should know what he was talking about.

Fyfe concluded his brief speech that day by calling the group of World War II submariners to the front of the crowd. As he looked down from the stage at their lined faces and gray hair, as if he were surveying them from *Batfish*'s bridge as they stood around the boat's cigarette deck, he said, "The years have taken their toll. These boys were an average age of nineteen or so then. We're the *Batfish* family. I love these guys. Let's give a round of applause for these old warriors."

The crowd dutifully obliged.

Ace Kelly was not there that day. The fiercely determined man who was able to bring together a disparate group of sub sailors, the state government, the U.S. Navy, the Army Corps of Engineers, and many more to secure the "wrong" submarine and bring her over a thousand miles up an unproven navigable waterway to a spot almost five hundred feet above sea level—and do it all with no real authority, no operating capital, and in the face of a legion of doubters—got to see his vision in place for only a few years. Kelly was driving alone, crossing a railroad track in Depew, Oklahoma, on January 3, 1977, when a train struck his car broadside. He died instantly.

Some said his impatience to get moving, his reluctance in waiting for anything to get out of his way, got the best of him that day.

Today, the *Batfish* memorial is open from March 15 through October 15 every day but Tuesday. Volunteers are still welcome to come work at the boat on the annual Volunteer Day, though some show up at other times to do whatever they can to preserve the boat.

An effort was begun in the summer of 2004 to have the submarine listed in the National Registry of Historic Places. The *Batfish* Memorial Foundation was also formed in 2004 "to raise funds to provide for the maintenance and preservation of the USS *Batfish* (SS 310) memorial for future generations and remembrance of all those Oklahomans who have served in the military of the United States." The foundation announced two fund drives for the coming year with the specific goals of raising enough money to professionally sandblast and paint the hull and to replace the decking.

Despite plans to do so throughout her second lifetime in Muskogee, *Batfish* still, as of this writing, has not had a formal dedication ceremony. Thousands have still been able to visit her, to walk her decks, to squeeze through her compartments. And, if the submariners of Oklahoma and the men who rode the boat over her twenty-six years continue to have their way, you will always be able to stand in front of her bridge, to imagine how it must have been to hear the whine of an approaching torpedo or the click of a depth charge, to smell the fragrance of the diesel fuel, to gaze from her bow as it points eastward, toward Tahlequah and the heart of the Cherokee Nation over there across the Arkansas River.

You can stand on her deck as she points toward another people who lived with honor and who will never forget (or willingly allow the rest of us to forget) what happened to them.

She, as were they, was taken from her native element, plopped down in strange territory, but has now become a permanent and key part of the local landscape.

And now, you know her story.

Their story.

Reunion

"I can assure you that they went down fighting and that their brothers who survived them took a grim toll of our savage enemy to avenge their deaths."

—Vice Admiral C. A. Lockwood on the submariners
lost in World War II

May 2004

It's bumpy flying into Will Rogers Airport in Tulsa aboard the little Canadair regional jet from Dallas. Thunderheads mark the horizon, and, when I get in the rental car and tune the radio to KRMG, the news-talk station, I hear an odd, sonarlike pinging every few minutes. The announcer finally brings me up to speed. We're under a thunderstorm warning, and the sound effect is to let everyone know there's rough weather in the area without interrupting regular programming.

I'm a little apprehensive about crashing the party at the annual *Batfish* reunion in Muskogee. I'm not sure how the submariners will like an NQP like me hanging around with a tape recorder, interrupting their reminiscing, asking dumb questions, and prompting them to retell their stories one more time and a little louder for the microphone. I had met Billy Isbell (war patrols four through seven) and his wife, Flo, at my literary agent's place in Gulf Shores, Alabama, several months before, when I was contemplating doing this book. Isbell was gracious enough to promise to introduce me around at the reunion, to plot the course for me with his shipmates, if you will. And he assured me they wanted nothing more than to have their story told—provided it was told correctly.

But just before I leave home for the flight to Muskogee, I get word that Billy has suffered a serious heart attack while loading his car, getting ready for the drive up to Oklahoma. For the first time in years, he won't be making the reunion this time.

"Don't worry," Flo tells me, relaying Billy's message to me from the hospital. "If you listen, they'll talk."

I drive into the thunderstorms at Broken Arrow. Lightning dances amid a crop of radio towers alongside the Muskogee Turnpike, and it's raining so hard I can hardly see the road. I imagine it must have been something like this on *Batfish*'s first war patrol, when she got caught in that typhoon and tried to chase down a convoy in the deluge.

In addition to Billy Isbell, another loss casts a pall over this year's get-together. Harold "Bud" Mobbs (war patrols two through five), from down in San Antonio, the man who has spearheaded the *Batfish* reunion for years, died suddenly just a few weeks before. I wonder how that's going to affect the submariners' willingness to put up with a curious writer. Will anyone be in a mood to talk?

Without realizing it, I take the correct exit off the turnpike for War Memorial Park at Muskogee, but I have navigational problems and turn right at the intersection instead of left, toward the boat. Even though I've temporarily left the rain behind, I didn't even notice the faded sign directing visitors that way. I wind through neighborhoods and back roads and finally go to find the hotel, check in, and do a bit of reconnaissance before trying to locate the boat. But by the time I get to my room, the bottom of the sky has dropped out again, lightning unzipping the sky. I decide to save the visit to the boat for another day. I go instead to find the meeting room where the reunion is supposed to be going on.

The Bacone Inn is owned by Bacone College, a Baptist church–affiliated school that boasts of being the oldest college of continuing education in Oklahoma, "embracing a historic educational mission to American Indians." The hotel's big meeting room is a few steps down off the small lobby. Inside, knots of people, self-segregated by sex, sit together, laughing and talking. Men in blue vests thumb through open scrapbooks that lie all about, some pointing, some laughing, some squinting hard as they try to remember a name or a place or an event they see in the photos.

At the back of the room, tables are covered with snacks, Crock-Pots, a stunning variety of drinks (hard and soft), and a wheezing coffee urn that I soon learn never runs dry.

Before I can even find my way to the coffee, I am greeted by a couple of gentlemen who have obviously been stationed on lookout for me. Even from cardiac intensive care back in Alabama, Billy Isbell has made sure to alert them that I was coming. The men are Virgil "Blackie" Lawrence and Bob "Steamboat" Fulton.

I wasn't a total stranger to either man. I had interrupted their dinners with phone calls a couple of months before, and, once they were sure I wasn't trying to sell them something, both ex-*Batfish* sailors had spent a liberal amount of time speaking with me, supplying me with information and anecdotes I could never have gathered in the usual places.

Both men are surprisingly vigorous and clear-eyed and seem genuinely glad to welcome me to their fraternity party. But I know how important this time with their shipmates is to them, and I'm afraid they won't want to fool with the likes of me.

Not to worry. Billy Isbell is correct—they are more than willing to tell me their stories. In fact, nobody wants their experience preserved more than they do. Bob and Blackie become my de facto hosts for the duration, making sure my coffee cup is filled, that I sample this snack or that, and that every attending World War II crew member gets steered over to the corner where I sit with my recorder propped up, listening.

Most of the week, attendees wander in and out of the main meeting room at will, sitting in bunches and reliving their time on *Batfish*. Or they gather in groups loosely based on which patrols they were on or what their jobs were on the boat. They go eat at the Chinese buffet next door or the Mexican place down the street. There seems to be no formal agenda, only a couple of scheduled events.

The organization of it all—or the lack thereof—reminds me of the descriptions of the crew's mess on board a submarine. The mess was the gathering place for any sailor off watch, where most of the socializing on the boat occurred and where everyone had access to the galley to fix a sandwich or snack anytime he wanted to, so long as he cleaned up his crumbs and dishes after he finished eating, and before the cooks came back on duty at five in the morning.

At the reunion, the men spend most of the time telling their stories to each other, though they've surely heard them all plenty of times before. Sometimes they even tell them the same way two times in a row. More than one vet assured me that all sea stories begin with the words "Now this is no shit." The tales still get laughs, groans, and sad nods in all the same, well-marked places.

They'll argue half a day about the exact time and place they got the five-inch deck gun installed, or when they completed the overhaul on the engines in the aft room. Mare Island? No, Pearl! Couldn't have been Pearl. We weren't in Pearl until after the next patrol. Had to be Fremantle.

They'll also argue good-naturedly about who it was who ended up in the brig when they were in Perth, or Hawaii, or wherever, and whatever happened to the old son of a bitch anyway?

I have no doubt most of those stories have been told every single year. But it dawns on me that this is one of the ways they try to make sure that what happened to them is never forgotten, a sort of informal oral history, maintained over tortilla chips and dip and cold Budweiser out of the can. Even those veterans who seem to have trouble remembering if they've put sugar in their coffee or not, who lose their places when talking about the weather or the route they took to drive to Muskogee this year, suddenly have total recall of the tiniest detail of an incident that happened sixty years before. They can invariably spin the whole story, with near-literary embellishment, on cue and without hesitation.

Meanwhile their wives play bridge and pinochle and do needlepoint and compare photos of kids and grandkids and great-grandkids, probably thankful that, at least for one week every year, someone else can listen to those tales.

I'm Blackie and Bob's guest at the Friday-night banquet, a more formal affair with something that resembles an agenda. Most of the attendees are wearing suits and ties instead of their usual jeans, ball caps, and blue vests, festooned with all the patches. It was at a banquet a few years before that Captain Fyfe was called up to say a few words while the guest speaker prepared his slide presentation. Well, there was trouble with the projector and the skipper ended up telling jokes for a good half hour, many of them ribald enough to embarrass most any nonsailor. But nobody minded. He had the room laughing uproariously.

The big announcement at the meeting this year is that the World War II vets are officially passing the torch. From this point forward, the second commissioning crew will organize and run the reunion each year. It's a watershed decision. Most of those in the room nowadays are crew members who rode *Batfish* in the fifties and sixties. It makes sense to me that many of the men who served during that era are just now at retirement age, and are free and healthy enough to take over the reins and come out to Muskogee for a week each year.

I don't ever get a count, but there must be less than a dozen or so men there representing the first commission, the war years. About two hundred sailors served on *Batfish* during her seven war patrols.

After the meal, I'm introduced to one of the banquet speakers, Shirley Reiner, the current chairperson of the War Memorial Park board of trustees. She excitedly tells the group about plans to make more improvements to the park as well as to the boat. She and the town seem to genuinely appreciate the treasure they have sitting out there in that bean field and intend to make sure she gets proper treatment.

At last, it seems that the rough seas are finally calming for the old smoke boat.

The reunion always winds down on Saturday with a special event. The vets gather at what they almost always call in conversation "the boat" for a special ceremony, one that occurs at almost all sub reunions. It's the symbolic and deeply touching tolling of the bell.

This particular Saturday is cool, even though it's mid-May. The storms I sailed through earlier in the week have brought with them a cold front. Despite brilliant sunshine, a brisk wind whips downriver from the north, muting the clanging of the ship's bell and the recitation of the names of each of the fifty-two boats lost in the war. It is a humbling ceremony wherever one happens to experience it, but there, only a few feet away from one of the actual vessels, and surrounded by waist-high pedestals that pay homage to each lost boat, it packs an especially powerful punch. Except for a lot of luck and considerable skill, *Batfish* could just as easily have had her name spoken among the litany. *Grayling. Perch. Amberjack. Seawolf. Darter. Trigger.* They are all mentioned, from the first one to go down, *Sealion*, three days after the attack on Pearl Harbor, to the last one, *Bullhead*, lost on the same day the atomic bomb was dropped on Hiroshima and only a few days before peace was declared.

As the tolling and the recitation continue, you can see in the faces of the older *Batfish* crewmen gathered there that they are more than aware that their fate could just as well have been the same as that of those brother submariners.

The Cherokees say that if you retrace the route of the Trail of Tears you can feel the presence of those who died along the way. A mighty tactile awareness strong enough so it assures that the memory of those martyrs will never fade.

Standing there among the plaques commemorating the lost boats, listening to the sharp sound of the bell, it's easy to feel the presence of those submariners whose sacrifice the ceremony commemorates. Mostly youngsters, some hardly old enough to drive a car. Sons, brothers, fathers, husbands. Men who didn't hesitate to sign up and leave home and go to war in a machine most of them had never even seen in real life.

Reunions and ceremonies like the tolling of the bell make sure their memory doesn't fade with the passage of time, that their stories and experiences remain as real as the chill wind and the brilliant sunshine that bless the Green Country on the day of the ceremony.

After the event is completed, some of the old sailors stand in small knots, talking, laughing, sharing final stories. Others, though, wander off by themselves, strolling through the park, considering the boat, remembering their time aboard her, and leaning against her side as they gaze down toward where the Arkansas River flows, out of view just beyond the newly leaved trees. Their wives instinctively know to allow them this brief moment alone. They stand back and pretend to read the inscriptions on the plaques or sit on benches under the shade trees and wait patiently.

The bell ringing and the recitation of the names of the lost boats are clearly a sacred rite for these old warriors. A cleansing, like the Cherokee going to "long man," the river, for purification and strength before battle. They know what it is to go to war to restore harmony, to follow the "Blood Law" and avenge the wrongful death of a tribe member. And even after spending most of a week at this place, they are reluctant to leave this shrine to their sacrifice.

Four months after the *Batfish* reunion, I find myself in Saratoga Springs, New York, at the United States Submarine Veterans annual convention.

Thousands of submariners from all eras, including many still on active duty, attend this meeting each year. I have a novel I cowrote with former nuclear sub skipper George Wallace, and a book about *Archerfish*, written with the significant help of a former crew member on the boat, Ken Henry, and I'm spending most of the time behind a table full of books in the vendor area. On the convention's final day, I look up from signing a book and see Bob "Steamboat" Fulton coming my way.

"You still doing the book on *Batfish?*" he asks in his direct, upstate New York way.

I assure him that I am, that a major New York publishing house has picked it up and I'm working hard on it.

"Maybe this will help," he says, and hands me a heavy black vinyl bag. Inside is a cloth-covered spiral notebook, bulging with full plastic sleeves. The scrapbook contains an amazing assortment of photos, ribbons, souvenirs, liberty cards, scrip, newspaper clippings, and so much more. Not copies in many cases—the real original items. This book is clearly a lifetime collection, relics from a great adventure this man was fortunate enough to experience and blessed enough to survive. One he loves to tell about if anyone is willing to take the time to listen.

"Bob, I appreciate this so much, but I can't be responsible for this!" I tell him. I can only imagine how valuable this collection is to him. What if I lost the book on the plane going home? Or it got misdirected somehow when I tried to return it to him? I offer to leave my book signing, take it right that minute to the hotel's business center, and copy as much of the material as I think I can use.

"No. Don't worry about it. Take it and use what you can. I'll get it back from you someday. I want you to tell this story. And I want you to tell it right."

A few weeks later, I get the names of a few members of the former Oklahoma Maritime Advisory Board. One of them, Nick Guagliardo, is only too happy to talk to me and tell me anything I want to know. A few days after our telephone conversation, I'm at Keesler Air Force Base near Biloxi, Mississippi, doing a book signing at the base exchange, when I get a telephone message from Guagliardo.

"Look, I gathered up all the stuff I have on the *Batfish*," he tells my voice mail. "Maybe you can use some of it. I'm going down to Kinko's and copy it and have them bind it together and send it to you. You can pay me for the copying and shipping if you want to."

A few days later, I receive the massive book. It contains all the minutes of the board meetings, newspaper clippings, letters, personal handwritten notes, and even receipts for the new locks on the gates at the submarine when she was moved to her new berth.

"Maybe this will help you tell the story," Nick tells me. "And tell it right."

That had been my admonition. To tell the story. And tell it right.

Bob, Billy, Blackie, Nick, and all the rest—I hope I did.

I'm a novelist, not a historian. To be more precise, I'm a storyteller. I love the empty slate that fiction affords me, where I can allow my imagination to take me wherever the muse dictates and not necessarily be bound by unchangeable reality or the fixed personalities of characters who actually existed. At the same time, I faithfully ascribe to the notion that any writer, whether he pens fiction or nonfiction, must write "the truth."

So when I heard about these parallel stories of USS *Batfish*, and when I came to know these characters (many of them personally), I decided I wanted to write it all down for others to read. I was convinced that I would have had a difficult time ever making up the stories or the characters, even if my muse was particularly chatty. And I knew, too, that these stories needed to be told, and told in a way that would be accessible to more than just the men who lived them or die-hard submarine buffs and maritime historians.

That, I thought, required a novelist's touch. I hope I brought that to this book.

At the same time I felt that it was a requirement to color within the lines, I was obligated to follow the rules. I had to be sure I stuck to the facts, that I allowed the story to tell itself and the people who populate it to be themselves, without ornamentation for dramatic or literary effect. In order to do that, I relied on a number of people and sources to assist me with research and to tell me, in their words, what happened to them and their shipmates so that I could get it down right.

Most of the factual information came from actual deck logs, patrol logs, and patrol reports, which have been made available by the Naval Archives in Washington. Various former crew members arranged that copies of this information were made available to me so that I had a complete set from which to work. Some of the material is also reproduced on the *Batfish* Web site, www.ussbatfish.com. Bless the skippers for being so descriptive in many of their entries. It helped put color in the cheeks and a twinkle in the eyes of many of these men.

A number of other government historical sources and archival information were also used to piece together the boat's story, from launch to when her name was struck from the list of active vessels, including documents from the Naval History Division of the Office of the Chief of Naval Operations.

I am forever indebted to Bill Isbell, who provided the lists of former crew members, as well as contact information for them. Bill started me off on this voyage with reminiscences of his own adventures on *Batfish*. He also kindly agreed to read the manuscript and give his ideas about both its accuracy and its tone. So did my literary agent, Bob Robison, who is also an old smoke boat sailor and would never allow me to get away with moving port to starboard or aft to bow.

I owe so much to Virgil "Blackie" Lawrence, Robert "Steamboat" Fulton, and Jim Butterworth, who spent generous amounts of time on the telephone with me, also giving me material I could never have captured without their willingness to share it with a total stranger. Then, when I got to Muskogee for the annual reunion, Blackie and Bob took more time talking into my microphone and made certain I was able to interview as many of the World War II crewmen who were there as I could manage in three days.

In addition to Blackie and Bob, Jim Butterworth, Jim Callanan, Stan Javorski, and Dick "Hershey" Hosler helped fill hours of tape with their recollections. Thanks, too, to Leon Simpkins, Kelsey "Chainfall" Farrell, and others from the second commission who provided me with background on the boat.

I've also mentioned already Bob Fulton's providing me with his scrapbook of photos, memorabilia, and souvenirs. It was a treasure trove of information. I'm guarding it with my life, Bob!

Of tremendous assistance with information on *Batfish*'s "eighth patrol" to her final resting spot in Muskogee was Nick Guagliardo, a former member of the Oklahoma Maritime Advisory Board. Not only did he spend considerable time with me on the phone, but, as mentioned earlier, he also pulled together his truly amazing collection of documentation, put it into chronological order, had it duplicated and bound, and trusted me to reimburse him for his expenses.

I did, by the way.

I was often steered in the right direction in my research and had facts and anecdotes further confirmed by the now-out-of-print book *Batfish, The Champion "Submarine Killer" Submarine of World War II* by the late Hughston E. Lowder (sixth patrol) with Jack Scott. It was an exhaustive, step-by-step recounting of all the boat's World War II patrols. According to the authors' acknowledgment, Captains Wayne Merrill, Jake Fyfe, and Walter Small each reviewed the manuscript prior to publication and made corrections and additions to the details of each of their patrols. Having this backup account as reviewed by the skippers helped to verify patrol log narratives and anecdotal remembrances from other sources.

Wherever I have used material that appeared in various newspapers and other publications, I have directly credited those entities.

Thanks also to Linda Fletcher, the manager at War Memorial Park in Muskogee, for taking time to talk to me during my visit to the boat and for providing me with some names of folks to contact for more information about how *Batfish* came to rest out there in that grassy field.

Much of the information on the Cherokees and their culture came from publications and Web sites of the Cherokee Nation Cultural Resource Center and the Cherokee Nation of Oklahoma.

Finally, you will note that in this book I have used the novelist's convention of putting words in people's mouths and thoughts in their heads, even though sometimes it is impossible to know for certain what those words and thoughts actually were at the time they were uttered or considered. That's especially true with men who are no longer with us, or when I'm relying on recollections that are over half a century old.

Recognizing that, I still felt strongly that it was important to allow these characters to think and speak in order to more effectively tell the story and to allow the reader to get to know these men, to humanize them. In most cases, I was able to rely on remembrances of those who were actually there, or used notes, memos, patrol logs, or other sound evidence and corroboration to make an educated guess.

I hope I haven't misrepresented any facts or mischaracterized any person in the process. If I did, it was unintentional and done for all the right reasons.

Ultimately, we all have to offer thanks to the hundreds of men who served aboard *Batfish* during her long, productive life, including those on the second commission who get short shrift in this book. They did their duty, too.

And thanks to all those who made certain she didn't rust away at some pier somewhere when the course of her duty was done.

To each of you, then, a sincere "Satisfactory in all respects!"

APPENDIX

World War II Roster of USS *Batfish* (SS 310)

Submariners denoted with a "0" are those who served aboard the *Batfish* between war patrols.

Name	War Patrols
A. F. Abel	7
Joseph L. Adams Jr.	1, 2
Thomas F. Allen Jr.	1, 2, 3
Richard W. Anderson	0
Donald D. Athen	6, 7
Raymond O. Baldes	1, 2
Glenn A. Bearinger	7
George Beck	1, 2
George T. Becker	1, 2, 4, 5, 6, 7
Harold W. Belcher	1, 2, 3, 4, 5, 6
William G. Bell	1, 2, 4, 5
Fred Benfield Jr.	1, 2, 3, 6, 7
James A. Bennett	7
Gerson I. Berman	3, 4, 5, 6, 7
Raymond A. Birdsall	2, 3, 4, 5, 6, 7
John C. Bohreer	6

Name	War Patrols
Robert G. Black	1, 2, 3, 4
Joseph J. Breslin	4, 5, 6, 7
Randall S. Brockway	1, 2, 3
Glenn G. Burnett	5
Sherman E. Burns	1, 2
James T. Butterworth	4, 5, 6, 7
James B. Callanan	6, 7
William W. Campbell Jr.	6, 7
Charles W. Carter	2, 3, 4, 5, 6, 7
Charles L. Cartmill	1, 2, 3, 4, 5, 6, 7
John T. Cassidy	4, 5, 6
Armand W. Cavalli	1, 2, 3
John E. Cherowbrier Jr.	1, 2, 4, 5, 6
John B. Cleppe	1, 2
Harry L. Coker	3, 4, 5, 6, 7
Milton Coleman	3, 4, 5, 6, 7
Robert A. Collar	1, 2, 3, 6, 7
Kenneth E. Comfort	1, 2, 3, 6, 7
Wallace E. Comstock	5, 6, 7
Edward E. Cornwall	6
Juan E. Cosmijo	1, 2
Thomas E. Cousins	1, 2, 3
Clifford B. Cox	3, 4, 5, 6, 7
Joseph A. Cox	7
Robert T. Craig	6, 7
Edwin J. Cramer	3, 4, 5, 6, 7
William I. Crockett	1, 2, 3, 4, 5, 6, 7
Robert T. Cutshall	0
Wiley V. Davis	1, 2, 3, 4, 5, 6, 7
Henry C. DeGrotte Jr.	6, 7
Edward Delworth	5, 6
David L. Dennis	4, 5, 6, 7
John W. Ditwig	5, 6

Name	War Patrols
Edward J. Dougherty	1
Albert J. Drzewiecki	1, 2, 3
Edward W. Duefrene	4, 5, 6, 7
William L. Elliott	4, 5, 6, 7
Albert J. Evinger	4, 5, 6, 7
Joseph M. Farnsworth	1, 2, 3, 4, 5, 6
Pierce T. Fitzgerald	0
Ivan Fontenot	1, 2, 3, 4, 5
John L. From Jr.	3, 4, 5, 6
Robert E. Fulton	1, 2, 3, 4, 5, 6, 7
John K. Fyfe	3, 4, 5, 6
James L. Garnet	1, 2, 3, 4, 5, 6
Roy D. George	7
Manuel A. Gerhardt	6, 7
William M. Gibson	1, 2, 3, 4, 5, 6
John Glace	3, 4, 5, 6, 7
George R. Gnitka	4, 5
Adolph Goldfarb	1, 2, 3, 4, 5
Malcolm E. Goodman	4, 5
Wallace B. Grant	6, 7
William H. Gray	1, 2, 3
Homer E. Grimes	0
Glen C. Hall	0
Lewis T. Hammond	1, 2, 3, 4, 5, 6
Francis J. Hayes	5, 6, 7
Donald A. Henning	1, 2, 3, 6
Richard R. Hill	1, 2, 3, 7
James M. Hingson	1, 2, 3, 4, 5
Carl C. Hoffman	4, 5, 6
Richard F. Hosler	4, 5, 6, 7
Richard E. House	5, 6
Robert T. Hubbard	0
William B. Huey	6, 7

Name	War Patrols
Donald A. Hyde	1, 2, 3, 4, 5
William J. Isbell	4, 5, 6, 7
Stanley J. Javorski	3, 4, 5, 6, 7
Charles R. Johnson	1, 2, 3, 4, 5
Nathaniel L. Kelly	4, 5, 6
Fred R. Kerns	7
Joseph R. Kilrain	1, 2, 3, 6
Leroy E. Koetz	7
Michael Kost	6
Herman W. Kreis	3, 4, 5, 6, 7
Leon E. Labrecque	1, 2
Richard W. Lamb	0
Frederick A. Landbeck	1, 2, 3
Lynus J. Larch	1, 2, 3, 4, 5, 6
David W. Laughlin	1, 2, 3, 6, 7
Virgil W. Lawrence	3, 4, 5, 6, 7
Russell E. Leasure	3, 4, 5, 6, 7
Kermit L. Lechner	1, 2, 3, 4, 5
Dewey A. Lee	0
Edward O. Littell	1, 2, 3, 4, 5
Arthur F. Loader	1, 2, 3
E. H. Longfellow	7
Hughston E. Lowder	6
David W. MacEachron	7
Kenneth B. MacKay	7
James A. Madden	7
Richard J. Maxwell	3, 4
Francis J. Mayhew	1, 2, 3, 4, 5
Wayne L. McCann	1, 2, 3, 4, 5, 6
Joseph E. McDonald	3
Emmett N. McGill	1, 2, 3, 4
Everett G. McKinney	7
Howard R. McLarney	1, 2, 3, 4, 5

Name	War Patrols
Edward J. McNamara	1, 2, 3, 4, 5
Wayne R. Merrill	1, 2
Edgar V. Miller	3, 4
William J. Mitchell	3
Harold V. Mobbs	2, 3, 4, 5
Jacob Mohr	0
Peter G. Molteni	1, 2
Joseph R. Moore Jr.	5
O. A. Morgan	1, 2
Henry J. Morin	1, 2, 3
Peter V. Morreale	6, 7
Numeriano G. Morrill	1, 2
John H. Mossman	1, 2, 3, 4
Arthur C. Murphy	1, 2
Ralph W. Nelson	4, 5, 6, 7
David W. Newton	5, 6, 7
James R. Norris	4, 5
John P. O'Brien	4, 5
Eugene C. O'Donnell	7
Douglas H. Olson	3, 4, 5
Robert F. Oswald	1, 2, 3, 4, 5, 6, 7
Everett A. Palmer	4, 5, 6, 7
Domenic A. Paolo	1, 2
Henry B. Parzych	0
Reuben H. Pepper	1, 2, 3, 4, 5, 6
Donato Persico	7
Wesley P. Peterson	1, 2, 3, 4
Joseph F. Pope	3
William O. Powell	6, 7
William W. Randolph	0
Donald W. Record	1, 2, 3
Ray A. Ricketts	7
Charles J. Robare	1, 2, 3, 4, 5

Name	War Patrols
Leroy Robinson	3, 4, 5, 6, 7
Walter S. Rogers	1, 2
Daniel E. Rollison	0
J. L. Ruffin	6
William G. Rush	1, 2, 3, 4
John R. Ruthven	1, 2, 3, 4
Raymond L. Sanks	6, 7
Marcus M. Schlief	4, 5, 6, 7
Fred Schuldheisz	4
Charles B. Sheats	6
C. A. Sieck Jr.	7
Paul Simson	0
Vernon R. Slunaker	1, 2, 3, 4, 5, 6
Walter L. Small	7
George L. Smith	0
Lyford O. Smith	1, 2
Robert G. Snow	1, 2, 3
Ara A. Sogoian	6, 7
Wilbur G. Sprague	0
Clark K. Sprinkle	6, 7
Raymond M. Stoinski	1, 2, 3
William M. Strauss	7
Robert S. Sweet	1, 2
Felix Tamani	7
Lewis H. Teeter	1, 2, 3, 4, 5
J. E. Thibodeau	5, 6, 7
Charles R. Thomas	0
Thomas A. Thomas	4, 5, 6
Robert E. Thompson	1, 2, 3, 4, 5
George H. Trimble	7
Joseph R. Tuma	1, 2, 3, 4, 5, 6, 7
Franklin A. Van Leuven	1, 2, 3
Arthur F. Vicari	1, 2, 3

Name	War Patrols
Charles L. Wade	3
Richard H. Walker	Unknown
Emory A. Waller	5, 6
Hubert M. Warnick	7
Martin C. Warren	1, 2, 3, 6, 7
Alfred P. Wasleske Jr.	7
John W. Waterhouse	0
James L. Weiler	1, 2, 3, 4, 5
Adelbert F. Weis	2, 3, 4, 5, 6
Earl C. Wightman	7
Ernest R. Witte	1, 2, 3, 4, 5, 6, 7
Grover C. Wood	0
John J. Yankovich	3, 4, 5
Edward J. Zimmerman	0

USS *Batfish* World War II War Patrols

Patrol	Captain	Left from	Date	Duration	Vessels Destroyed*	Tonnage*
1	Merrill	Pearl Harbor	Dec 1943	50 days	2	15,700
2	Merrill	Pearl Harbor	Feb 1944	53 days	0	0
3	Fyfe	Pearl Harbor	May 1944	43 days	4	9,500
4	Fyfe	Pearl Harbor	Aug 1944	41 days	2	2,900
5	Fyfe	Fremantle, Australia	Oct 1944	53 days	2	5,000
6	Fyfe	Pearl Harbor	Jan 1945	61 days	3	4,500
7	Small	Pearl Harbor	June 1945	59 days	0	0

*As claimed in war patrol summaries

Members of Oklahoma Maritime Advisory Board

Ronald L. Banks
W. E. Battenfield
William P. Beane
Dr. Glen Berkenbile
Joseph E. Chambliss
B. Hayden Crawford
Allen Day
O. R. "Dick" Fogle
Geen Gilmour
Nicholas V. Guagliardo
Brooks Hall
E. E. Hendricks

Senator James Inhofe
Albert C. Kelly
Glade Kirkpatrick
John Kirkpatrick
Ned Lockwood
Horace E. Mitchell
E. E. Reardon
Elijah H. Simms
Roy E. Smallwood
Orlan A. Soli
Karl Wheland
Charles L. Williams

INDEX

Don Keith is an award-winning author, journalist and broadcast personality. He was twice named Personality of the Year by *Billboard* magazine. His first novel, *The Forever Season*, was named Fiction of the Year by the Alabama Library Association. *Gallant Lady*, his true story of the USS *Archerfish*, was a featured selection of the Military Book Club. Don lives in Indian Springs Village, Alabama, with his wife, Charlene. His Web site is www.donkeith.com.